D1209218

TWO LAMAISTIC PANTHEONS

EDITED WITH INTRODUCTION AND INDEXES

BY

WALTER EUGENE CLARK

Wales Professor of Sanskrit
in Harvard University

FROM MATERIALS COLLECTED BY THE LATE
BARON A. VON STAËL-HOLSTEIN

Text and Plates
(Two volumes bound in one)

PARAGON BOOK REPRINT CORP.
New York
1965

Originally published in 1937 by Harvard University Press
as volumes 3 and 4 of the Harvard-Yenching Institute
Monograph Series.

Reprinted 1965
by special arrangement with Harvard University Press
by Paragon Book Reprint Corp.
14 East 38th Street, New York, N. Y. 10016

An unabridged reprint in one volume
of the work originally published
in two volumes.

Library of Congress Catalog Card Number: 65-28578

Printed in the United States of America

CONTENTS

Volume I

Introduction . . . . vii–xxiv

Sanskrit Index 3–68

Tibetan Index 71–122

Chinese Index 125–169

INTRODUCTION

INTRODUCTION

In the year 1928 Baron A. von Staël-Holstein brought from Peiping to Cambridge and presented to the Harvard College Library materials for the study of four Lamaistic Pantheons. Only one of these Pantheons has ever been fully described and published in the West.

The first is a xylograph copy of a Pantheon of three hundred figures composed by the Chang Chia (Tibetan Lcaṅ-skya) Hutuktu Lalitavajra in the time of the emperor Ch'ien-lung (1736–96 A.D.). The Tibetan names are given underneath, and each figure is accompanied by a *dhāraṇī*. This Pantheon has been fully described by Eugen Pander in "Das Pantheon des Tschangtscha Hutuktu" (edited by Albert Grünwedel in *Veröffentlichungen aus dem kgl. Museum für Völkerkunde in Berlin*, I, 2/3, 1890) and in "Das lamaistische Pantheon" in *Zeitschrift für Ethnologie*, 1889, and was edited by Sergei Fedorovich Oldenburg at St. Petersburg in 1903 in the fifth volume of the *Bibliotheca Buddhica*. It has been the chief source used by western scholars in describing Lamaistic iconography. The original wood blocks are still preserved, and prints are still procurable in Peiping.

The second is a complete set of photographs from a copy of the so-called Five Hundred Gods of Narthang. This is unedited, but Grünwedel, in his descriptions of Lamaistic iconography, has made considerable use of a copy which is in Berlin. The main part of this work, in my copy, is named Rin-ẖbyuṅ (Ratnasambhava) and consists of 143 numbered folios, of which the last contains the colophon. It is preceded by a folio labelled *gcig-goṇ*, which I have numbered 0, containing the figures of rGyal-çhab-rje, rJe-rin-po-che, and mKhas-grub-rje. There are two folios numbered 70, the second of which I have numbered 070. There is also a duplicate of folio 117 placed after 110; this I have numbered 0110. This is followed by sNar-thaṅ, which consists of thirteen folios, the last of which contains the colophon. This is referred to as S. Then comes the rDor-phreṅ (or ẖphreṅ) (Vajramālā), which consists of twenty folios — the last three containing the colophon. This is referred to as R. Each of the 174 illustrated folios contains three pictures (which I have labelled a, b, and c) and three *dhāraṇīs*. The names of the figures are given underneath in Tibetan. Many of the pictures contain two or more figures, and in some cases I have had difficulty in dividing the

Tibetan, in knowing whether it contains one name or two. Several names which were indistinct or blurred in the photographic reproduction were cleared up by reference to an original in the possession of the late Berthold Laufer of the Field Museum in Chicago — an original which he kindly put at my disposal.

The third is a complete set of photographs of a unique manuscript which is entitled *Chu Fo P'u-sa Shêng Hsiang Tsan* (諸佛菩薩聖像贊) and is ascribed to an unnamed Chang Chia Hutuktu. Staël-Holstein believes that this Pantheon is to be ascribed to the same Lalitavajra who composed the Pantheon of three hundred figures mentioned above. This manuscript now belongs to the National Library of Peiping. When the photographs were made the volume was still owned by a Chinese bookseller of Peiping. It contains 360 figures accompanied by 360 eulogies in Chinese. The figures are classed into twenty-three divisions and the figures in each division are numbered.

I	(1–10)	般若祖師	XIII	(158–177)	觀世音菩薩化像
II	(11–18)	秘密祖師	XIV	(178–193)	毘盧佛壇場內菩薩
III	(19–28)	菩提道祖師	XV	(194–200)	諸樣菩薩
IV	(29–62)	大秘密佛	XVI	(201–205)	保護佛母
V	(63–76)	諸樣秘密佛	XVII	(206–227)	救度佛母
VI	(77–81)	五方佛	XVIII	(228–271)	諸樣佛母
VII	(82–116)	三十五佛	XIX	(272–289)	十八羅漢
VIII	(117–126)	十方佛	XX	(290–296)	諸樣羅漢
IX	(127–132)	六勇佛	XXI	(297–317)	勇保護法
X	(133–139)	藥師佛	XXII	(318–322)	財寶天王
XI	(140–144)	諸樣佛	XXIII	(323–360)	諸樣護法
XII	(145–157)	文殊化像菩薩			

The Tibetan and Chinese names of the divinities are given below and above; the Mongolian and Manchu names are given at the two sides.

The book seems to have been the original from which was made a certain type of Lamaistic plaque which is found in large numbers in Peiping and in western museums, and which was manufactured during the reign of Ch'ien-lung. Staël-Holstein has verified this fact by a comparison of a large number of such plaques with the figures in the book. He has also found in Peiping curio shops over a hundred of the bronze moulds which were used in making the plaques. This Pantheon was not made by adding sixty figures to the Pantheon of Three Hundred referred to above. Many of the figures among the three hundred are omitted and many new ones are added.

For a description and discussion of this manuscript see Staël-Holstein, "Remarks on the Chu Fo P'u Sa Shêng Hsiang Tsan," in the *Bulletin of the Metropolitan Library*, Vol. I (1928).

The fourth consists of a complete set of photographs of a unique Lamaistic Pantheon found in the Pao-hsiang Lou (寶相樓), a Lama temple situated in the garden of the Tz'ŭ-ning (慈寧) palace in the Forbidden City at Peiping. In July 1926 Staël-Holstein received permission from Mr. Chuang, President of the Palace Committee, to visit a number of Lama temples situated in the Forbidden City — temples which for many years seem to have been entirely neglected. In the upper storey of one of these temples, the Pao-hsiang Lou, he found a collection of bronze statuettes constituting a Lamaistic Pantheon which had consisted originally of 787 figures. But it had been visited by thieves, for some of the cabinets had been broken open and thirty-one of the statuettes had been removed. The fact that the pedestals of the images bore contemporary inscriptions (of the reign of Ch'ien-lung) giving the Chinese names of the divinities and personages represented constitutes a unique feature of the Pantheon and greatly enhances its value. Realizing the importance for Lamaistic iconography of this large collection of inscribed images, Staël-Holstein set about immediately to have the statuettes photographed. Money was furnished by Mrs. Mason Bross of Chicago, and the photographs were taken, or Chinese assistants supervised, by the late Mr. Benjamin March.

The work was done during December 1926 and January and February 1927. All the statuettes of the Pantheon in the upper storey of the temple had been photographed, and Staël-Holstein was just about to transfer operations to the ground-floor to make a complete record of the images there before proceeding to the other temples in the same garden when an official letter from the Palace authorities informed him that his photographers would not be allowed to continue their work.

The upper storey of the temple consists of seven chapels. The central chapel contains only a life-sized image of the great Tibetan reformer bÇoṅ-kha-pa. There are six side chapels, three on each side of the central chapel. Of these, number one is the northernmost and number six the southernmost. Each side chapel contains a central altar and two cabinets, one on each side of the altar. On each altar there are nine bronze images, and in each cabinet (except those which have been broken into by thieves) there are sixty-one bronze images. The boxes in the cabinets are arranged in five rows — each row containing from eleven to thirteen boxes. Originally, therefore, there must have been 787 statuettes (including the large statue of bÇoṅ-kha-pa). Thirty-one images had been stolen, but ten empty inscribed pedestals remained. So there are 756 images and 766 inscriptions. On the walls of the side chapels are inscriptions in Chinese, Tibetan, Mongolian, and Manchu, stating the parts of the Buddhist scriptures to which the divinities of each chapel belong and giving the names of some of the most important divinities in each chapel. Five of the chapels are devoted to Tantric divinities. Only one chapel, the first, is devoted to deities from other parts of the canon.

The following notes concerning the Pao-hsiang Lou have been given to me by Mr. James R. Ware of the Harvard-Yenching Institute.

The Pao-hsiang Lou 寶相樓 stands east of a building known as the Hsien-jo Kuan 咸若館, which is in the flower-garden of the Tz'ŭ-ning 慈寧 palace of the Forbidden City in Peiping. The construction of this palace was completed July 20, 1653.[1]

Some day there will probably be published from among the archives of the Ch'ing dynasty precise data concerning these statues. From the information now available it is possible to indicate only the following facts. A guide-book (without date) to the Forbidden City which has been prepared under the Chinese Republic, the *Ku Kung T'u Shuo*, "The Old Palaces Illustrated and Explained," 故宮圖說, pamphlet number two, page six, describes the location of the buildings as given above and tells us that the Pao-hsiang Lou contains a collection of Tibetan Buddhas, and that the Chi-yün Lou 吉雲樓 which stands to the west of the Hsien-jo Kuan is filled from top to bottom with Tibetan Buddhas.

On examining ch. 18 of the *Kuo Ch'ao Kung Shih* we learn why so many Buddhas are found here. This palace was inhabited by Ch'ien-lung's mother, who seems to have been very religious.[2] Her sixtieth birthday, in 1751, was an occasion for great rejoicing and presents were showered upon her by her son. Among the gifts was one set of nine Buddhas, and a complete set of Amitāyur Buddhas.[3] We are not told the number of the Buddhas in this last set. Ten years later, on her seventieth birthday, she was presented with more Buddhas: nine sets of Amitāyur Buddhas totaling 900 statues, nine sets of the same totaling 9000 statues, nine Buddhas, nine Amitāyur Buddhas, nine Buddhas,

[1] For location of buildings, cf. *Ta Ch'ing Hui Tien Shih Li* 大清會典事例 ch. 862, *Kuo Ch'ao Kung Shih* 國朝宮史 ch. 13.19b–20b, and the latter's *Hsü Pien* 續編 ch. 58.1–2; for date, *Tung-hua Lu* 東華錄, Wang Hsien-ch'ien's edition, Shun-chih 順治 tenth year, 1653, and *Ch'ing Shih Kao* 清史稿, *pên chi* ch. 5.8a.

[2] Cf. *Ch'ing Shih Kao*, biographies, ch. 1.11a–b; *Kuo Ch'ao Kung Shih* 4.4b.

[3] Cf. *Kuo Ch'ao Kung Shih* 18.2a, 2b, 10a, 12b.

nine Amitāyur Buddhas, nine Bodhisattvas, nine *fo-mu*, eighteen *lo-han*, and nine Buddhas.[1]

This is a summary of all the information that, to my knowledge, has been published. It is impossible to identify any of the statues just mentioned as our collection. Unfortunately, the *Kuo Ch'ao Kung Shih Hsü Pien* does not list the presents which Ch'ien-lung must have given his mother in 1771 on her eightieth birthday. Our set may have been made at that time.

The present publication gives a complete reproduction of the 360 figures of the *Chu Fo P'u-sa Shêng Hsiang Tsan* and of the 766 preserved images or inscribed pedestals (omitting the large central image of bÇoṅ-kha-pa) of the Pao-hsiang Lou Pantheon.

The Chinese index gives the Chinese names of the figures in these two Pantheons. Some of the names of the Pao-hsiang Lou Pantheon are difficult to read on the photographs and still more difficult on the collotype plates. To facilitate reference the entries in the Chinese index have been numbered, and a number referring to the entry number of the index has been placed under each figure on the plates. The transliteration is that of Wade-Giles.

The Tibetan index, in addition to the Tibetan names of the *Chu Fo P'u-sa Shêng Hsiang Tsan*, includes the names of the figures in the Five Hundred Gods of Narthang (which is unedited) and in the Pantheon of Three Hundred, edited by Oldenburg in *Bibliotheca Buddhica*, Vol. V. The Tibetan transliteration follows that adopted by A. von Staël-Holstein in *Bibliotheca Buddhica*, XV, xi, except that I have used ś for ç.

The Sanskrit index gives a Sanskrit reconstruction of the names of all the figures in these four Pantheons in so far as I have been able to make them out on the basis of Chinese and Tibetan.

A refers to the Pao-hsiang Lou Pantheon. The six side chapels (from north to south) are numbered 1 to 6. The statuettes on the central altar are referred to as M1–9. The boxes in the cabinets to the left (north) and right (south) of the central altar are numbered A1–61 and B1–61.

B refers to the *Chu Fo P'u-sa Shêng Hsiang Tsan.*

C refers to the Five Hundred Gods of Narthang.

D refers to the Pantheon of Three Hundred edited by Oldenburg.

[1] Cf. *ibid.* 18.12b–15a.

The Sanskrit names given to the figures of the *Chu Fo P'u-sa Shêng Hsiang Tsan* are based on the Tibetan. The Chinese names, when they differ markedly from the Tibetan, have occasionally been referred to in the index.

I have queried many of my reconstructions. The names with question marks are given merely as plausible suggestions. A few of the names given without query may turn out to be incorrect. Some of the names which are given in Chinese transcription without an attempt at reconstruction could be turned into some sort of Sanskrit, but the Sanskrit forms would be so hypothetical that I have preferred to leave the Chinese names as they are. My own knowledge of Chinese is almost negligible. Those who have a good knowledge of Chinese and Japanese and who have access to the proper Tantric ritualistic texts will doubtless be able to complete the reconstructions and to emend the faulty ones.

The exact Sanskrit forms of the names of many of the Tārās are doubtful. The Chinese form of Akṣobhya and Acala is the same; I am not sure that I have always been right in deciding which name to use. The Chinese Wên-shu 文殊 may apply both to Mañjusrī and Mañjughoṣa. I have used both Saṁvara and Śaṁvara, the former for the Tibetan *sdom-pa,* the latter for the Tibetan *bde-mchogs* and the Chinese *shang-lo* 上樂.

General Remarks

Weller's *Tausend Buddhanamen des Bhadrakalpa* is especially helpful for the Buddhas of Chapel 1.

1A5–8, 1A14–17, 1A18–21, 1A26–29, and 1B6–9 occur in Weller's book in the same grouping. This fact has helped in the reconstruction of the Sanskrit of several doubtful names.

B82–116 and A1A13, 22–25, 30–34, 37–61, the Thirty-five Buddhas of Confession, correspond almost exactly to the list given in a formula of confession preserved from the *Upālipariprcchā Sūtra* by the *Śikṣāsamuccaya,* p. 169. According to Nanjio, *A Catalogue of the Chinese Translation of the Buddhist Tripiṭaka,* no. 1109, the *Upālipariprcchā* was translated into Chinese by Guṇavarman in 431 A.D.

The chief differences are the following:

1. Vajragarbhapramardin (B83) and Vajrābhedya (A1A33 and Chinese of B83) take the place of Vajrapramardin.
2. Ratnāgni (B88 and A1A47) takes the place of Ratnaśrī.

3. Padmajyotirvikrīḍitābhijña (B106 and A1A38) takes the place of Nirmala and is placed before Brahmajyotirvikrīḍitābhijña.
4. Suparikīrtitanāmaśrī (B109 and A1A24) takes the place of Suparikīrtitanāmagheyaśrī.
5. Yuddhajaya (B112 and A1A52) takes the place of Vicitrasaṁkrama.
6. The Chinese of B113 and A1A51 have Suvikrāntagāmin and the Tibetan of B113 has Vikrāntagāmiśrī for Vikrāntagāmin.
7. The Tibetan of B116 has Śailendrarāja and the Chinese of A1A13 has Sumeruparvatarāja (= Śailendrarāja) for Ratnapadmasupratiṣṭhita-Śailendrarāja. The Chinese of B116 gives the full form.

The Thirty-five Buddhas of Confession (*ltuṇ-bśags-kyi-saṅs-rgyas*) are referred to by Wassiljew, *Der Buddhismus*, pp. 170, 186, from the *Ratnakūṭa* (presumably the *Upālipariprcchā Sūtra*) and from an *Ākāśagarbha Sūtra*. An altogether different list is given by E. Schlagintweit, *Buddhism in Tibet*, pp. 96, 122 ff., from a Tibetan text entitled *sDig-pa thams-cad bśags-par gter-chos*. See also T. Oda, *Bukkyō Daijiten*, 織田得能, 佛教大辭典 p. 631.

An interesting problem is the relation between certain figures in our two Pantheons and the Nepalese *Kriyāsaṁgraha*, a Balinese text which has been published and discussed by Bosch, and the central portion of the Kongōkai-mandara 金剛界曼荼羅 of the Japanese Shingon sect.

For the *Kriyāsaṁgraha* see B. H. Hodgson, *Essays on the Languages, Literature, and Religion of Nepal and Tibet*, p. 34, and Hara Prasad Shāstri, *A Descriptive Catalogue of Sanscrit Manuscripts in the Government Collection under the Care of the Asiatic Society of Bengal*, Vol. I, "Buddhist Manuscripts," pp. 122–123.

For the Balinese text see F. D. K. Bosch, "Buddhistische Gegevens uit Balische Handschriften" in *Mededeelingen der koninklijke Akademie van Wetenschappen te Amsterdam*, Afdeeling Letterkunde, Deel 68, Serie B, no. 3 (1929).

For the sixteen *vajra*-Bodhisattvas see also Sylvain Lévi, *Sanskrit Texts from Bali*, pp. xxii–xxvi (Gaekwad's Oriental Series, Vol. LXVII).

For the Shingon Mandara see Bunyiu Nanjio, *A Short History of the Twelve Japanese Buddhist Sects*, pp. 92–94; H. Smidt, "Eine populäre Darstellung der Shingon-Lehre" in *Ostasiatische Zeitschrift*, Vol. VI (especially pages 184–190); Bosch, *op. cit.* (especially plate II); S. Toganoo, *Mandara no kenkyū* 栂尾祥雲, 曼荼羅の研究, pp. 512–14; *Taishō daizōkyō* 大正大藏經, Iconographical section, IV, 350.

For substantially the same thirty-seven figures in the *maṇḍala* of Sarvavid-Vairocana, except for differences in the first two groups, see Tucci, *Indo-Tibetica*, III, pp. 32–36, 40–42.

The central portion of the Kongōkai-mandara consists of thirty-seven figures:

I. Five Buddhas.

1. Vairocana
2. Akṣobhya
3. Ratnasambhava
4. Amitābha
5. Amoghasiddhi

II. Four female *vajrī*-divinities.

6. Sattvavajrī
7. Ratnavajrī
8. Dharmavajrī
9. Karmavajrī

III. Sixteen *vajra*-Bodhisattvas.

10. Vajradhara
11. Vajrarāja
12. Vajrarāga
13. Vajrasādhu
14. Vajraratna
15. Vajratejas
16. Vajraketu
17. Vajrahāsa
18. Vajradharma
19. Vajratīkṣṇa
20. Vajrahetu
21. Vajrabhāṣa
22. Vajrakarma
23. Vajrarakṣa
24. Vajrayakṣa
25. Vajrasandhi

IV. Twelve Tārās in three groups of four each.

a.

26. Lāsyā
27. Mālyā
28. Gītā
29. Nṛtyā

b.

30. Gandhā
31. Puṣpā
32. Dīpā
33. Dhūpā

c.

34. Ankuśī
35. Pāśī
36. Sphoṭā
37. Ghaṇṭā

Numbers 1–5 are B77–81 and numbers 2–5 are A4A11, 51 and A4B41, 50. The Vairocana belonging to the group is probably Vajradhātu Vairocana A4A25.

Numbers 6–9 are B263–266 and A4A22–24, 52.

Numbers 10–25 are B178–193 and A4A9–10, 12, 13, 49, 50 and A4B39–40, 42–43, 44, 49, 51–54.

Numbers 26–37 do not occur in B. Numbers 26–29 are A4B45, 55–57 (names ending in *fo-mu* 佛母). The names occur also in A2B6, A3A48, 50; A3B27 (names ending in *fo-mu*) and in A2B7–9 (names ending in *mu* 母). Numbers 30–33 are A2B22–25 (names ending in *mu*) and A3A30, 40, 53 (names ending in *fo-mu*). Numbers 34–37, with prefixed *vajra*, are A2B10–13 (names ending in *mu*), and without *vajra*, A3A10, 54, 56 (names ending in *fo-mu*) — Ghaṇṭā being omitted.

The *Sādhanamālā* (Gaekwad's Oriental Series, Vols. XXVI, XLI), pages 157, 312, 324, gives the first two sub-groups in connection with Mañjuśrī (Dharmaśaṅkhasamādhi) and with Prajñāpāramitā; and pages 179–180, 197–198, 228–229 give the second sub-group as Tārās and the third sub-group (either with or without a prefixed *vajra*) as attendants of Vajratāra. See also Bhattacharyya, *Indian Buddhist Iconography*, pp. 123–125; Foucher, *Etude sur l'iconographie bouddhique de l'Inde*, II, p. 69; Hara Prasad Shāstri, *op. cit.*, p. 43, in connection with the Sarvadurgatipariśodhana. Bhattacharyya, pp. 38–39, gives the second and third sub-groups as attendants of Lokanātha (Avalokiteśvara).

Note also *Sādhanamālā*, p. 191, Sphoṭatārāṁ nigaḍahastāṁ; and Hara Prasad Shāstri, *op. cit.*, p. 123, Vajrasphoṭasya śṛṅkhalā for sphoṭa in the sense of "chain."

The sixteen Bodhisattvas (A4B1–5, 14–17, 46–48, 58–61),

Jālinīprabha	Gaganagañja
Vajragarbha	Maitreya
Akṣayamati	Amoghadar´in
Prajñākūṭa	Apāyajaha
Samantabhadra	Jñānaketu
Śokanirghātanamati	Amitābha
Gandhahastin	Candraprabha
Śūraṅgama	Bhadrapāla

occur in a group after the figures of the Kongōkai-mandara in the *Kriyāsaṅgraha* (cf. Hara Prasad Shāstri, *op. cit.*, p. 123) and in S. Toganoo, *Mandara no kenkyū*, pp. 515–516, with the exception that the two lists have Pratibhānakūṭa for Prajñākūṭa.

Very puzzling are the groups of figures whose names end in *ting fo* 頂佛, A4A42–46, 53–61, or *ting p'u-sa* 菩薩, A5A24, 53–54, or which have simply *p'u-sa* without *ting*, A5A37–40, but clearly belong to the Uṣṇīṣarājas. Concerning these see *Hôbôgirin*, pp. 148–150, under the word Bucchô 佛頂; Przyluski, "Les Vidyārāja," in *Bulletin de l'École Française d'Extrême-Orient*, XXIII (1923), pp. 301–318 (based on the Mañjuśrīmūlakalpa); S. Toganoo, *Mandara no kenkyū*, pp. 496–497; Hodgson, *op. cit.*, p. 34, who gives from the *Kriyāsaṅgraha* the names of eight *uṣṇīṣas* who are attached to Vairocana — Mahoṣṇīṣa, Sitātapatroṣṇīṣa, Tejorāśi, Vijayoṣṇīṣa, Vikiraṇoṣṇīṣa, Udgatoṣṇīṣa, Mahodgatoṣṇīṣa, and Vijayoṣṇīṣa.

It is doubtful whether the *ting* of A4A42–46 is to be translated as *uṣṇīṣa*. The figures may belong to an entirely different ritualistic group. *Ting* might be *kūṭa*, *śikhin*, *ketu*, etc.; and 4A45 seems to be Ratnaśikhin since the figure corresponds exactly to B144. Tentatively I have given Tejauṣṇīṣa (cf. 4A58), Kamaloṣṇīṣa (cf. *Hôbôgirin*, p. 149), and Vajroṣṇīṣa. *Chu-p'in* 諸品 is uncertain. In 6A54 (cf. B238) I have translated it as Viśvā, and in 5B59 as Citrā.

Of the *rāśis* or signs of the zodiac, six are certain — 3A3, 17, 27, and 3B21, 23, 34. 3A19 is pretty certainly Kumbha. Some of the others are probably present, but I have not been able to make them out.

For Keśinī, Upakeśinī, Citrā, Vasumatī, and Ākarṣaṇī, A5B17, A5B58–61, see S. Toganoo, *Mandara no kenkyū*, p. 499. The names of the last four are not in their normal Chinese forms. The identifications are hypothetical.

For Gaurī, Caurī, Vetālī, Ghasmarī, Pukkasī, Śabarī, Caṇḍālī, and Ḍombī at A2B44; A3A41–45, 59–61; A3B15–17, 39, 59 see *Sādhanamālā*, pp. 445–46, 479, and Finot, "Manuscrits sanskrits de Sādhanas retrouvés en Chine," *Journal Asiatique*, 1934, II, 11, 29, 45. See also Tucci, *Indo-Tibetica*, III, 125–6, 131–2.

For Mahābala, Nīladaṇḍa, and Takkirāja, A2A11–13, as grouped with Siddhaikavīra (Mañjughoṣa) and with Uṣṇīṣavijayā, see *Sādhanamālā*, pp. 137, 418, 420.

For A2A5–8 and A2B49–52, Bhairavavajra with *khaḍga*, *padma*, *daṇḍa*, *ghaṇṭā*, and *mudgara*, see Cordier, *Catalogue du fonds tibétain de la Bibliothèque Nationale*, I, 165 and Hara Prasad Shāstri's quotation, *op. cit.*, p. 145, from the *Kṛṣṇayamāri Tantra*.

For A2A26–29 and A2B37–40, Bhairavavajra with *īrṣyā*, *rāga*, *moha*, and *mātsarya*(?), see Hara Prasad Shāstri's quotation, *op. cit.*, p. 145, from the *Kṛṣṇayamāri Tantra*.

Of the Mahāyakṣasenāpatis (or the 12 generals of Bhaiṣajyaguru), A6A1–4 and A6B18–21, 33–36, the only ones of which I feel sure are Kumbhīra and Indra. The other names seem to have become much corrupted before they reached their final Japanese forms.

T. Oda, *Bukkyō daijiten*, p. 934, gives:

1. Kumbhīra	7. Indro
2. Vajra	8. Pajra
3. Mihira	9. Mahoraga
4. Aṇḍīra	10. ?
5. Anila	11. Catura
6. Śaṇḍila	12. Vikarāla

Ting Fu-pao, *Fo-hsüeh Ta-tz'ŭ-tien* (丁福保, 佛學大辭典), II, pp. 188–89, gives 10 as Kinnara.

See also *Hôbôgirin*, p. 34 for Anteira or Andara or Annara, p. 56 for Basharadaishô (= Vajra), p. 70 for Bikara, — they will be treated in full under Yakushi; Petrucchi, in Stein, *Serindia*, p. 1409, who gives a list of the Chinese names taken from the *Butsuzō-zuï* 佛像圖彙, IV. 1. See also Sylvain Lévi, "Le Catalogue géographique des Yakṣa dans la Mahāmāyūrī" in *Journal Asiatique*, 1915, I, 19 ff., Ernst Waldschmidt, *Bruchstücke buddhistischer Sūtras aus dem zentralasiatischen Sanskritkanon*, pp. 172–175, 201–202 (in *Kleinere Sanskrit-Texte*, Vol. IV, of the *Königlich Preussische Turfan-Expeditionen*), and Noël Peri, "Hārītī, La Mère-de-Démons," in *Bulletin de l'École Française d'Extrême-Orient*, XVII, Part III, p. 25, who gives Indra and Kumbhīra and the names of five others (all of which end in *lo* 羅), but I have found no Sanskrit text which throws light on the names.

Of the planets, in addition to Sun and Moon, A5A2 is Rāhu, A3B9 is Ketu, A2B20 is Aṅgāraka, and A3A4 and 3B10 seem to be Budha and Sita. I have not been able to make out the others although I suspect that A2B18, 19 may represent planets.

For the seven medical Buddhas (A1B37–43, B133–139, C13–15) and their attendants Candravairocana and Sūryavairocana, A6A21, 27 and C13a, c, see Pelliot, "Le Bhaiṣajyaguru," in *Bulletin de l'École Française d'Extrême-Orient*, III, 35–36.

The names of the Buddhas of the Ten Quarters are given at B117–126. The first eight are given at A1B44, 49–55 in the same form, but the last two are different. This list does not correspond at all to lists of Buddhas of the Ten Quarters given in other texts. Cf. T. Oda, *Bukkyō Daijiten*, p. 948.

For the Mahāsiddhas see Grünwedel's "Die Geschichten der Vierundachtzig Zauberer" in *Baessler Archiv*, V. 4/5 (1916), and "Der Weg nach Śambhala" in *Abhandlungen der Bayerischer Akademie*, XXIX, 3. 93–4; Bhattacharyya, *Sādhanamālā*, Vol. II, pp. xl ff.; *Journal Asiatique*, 1934, II, 218–230. I have given the names in the Sanskrit form given by P. Cordier, *Catalogue du fonds tibétain de la Bibliothèque Nationale.*

A2A54–57 are four female figures (*fo-mu*) of *vajra* plus *rasa, gandha, śabda,* and *rūpa* (see also A3B5). Cf. Tucci, *Indo-Tibetica*, III, 156, and *Guhyasamāja* (Gaekwad's Oriental Series, Vol. LIII), pp. 1–3. A2A18–21 are four female figures (*mu* 母) of *vajra* plus earth, air, fire, and water. Cf. *Guhyasamāja*, p. 1. For the latter I am uncertain what Sanskrit words to choose. In both groups of names it would probably be better to put *vajrī* at the end of the compound.

Note the five Tithis (A3A5–8, 18), the twelve Pāramitās (A4A1–4, 14–17 and A4B, 33–36), the ten Bhūmis (A4A5–8, 18–20, 26–28), the ten Vaśitās (A4B6–9, 18–23), and the four Pratisamvits (A4B10–13).

I have not been able to trace the groups ending in hsi-mu 西母 or ma-hsi-mu 嘛 (A6B10–12, 23–24).

A Tibetan xylograph of 18 folios entitled Dam-can-chos-kyi-rgyal-poḫi-mṅon-rtogs-bskaṅ-bstod-zod-las-gser-skyems-dra-ga-bskul-rnams-bzhugs-ste, which was sent to me from Peiping by Staël-Holstein in September 1935, helps to solve several difficulties. The importance of the xylograph and its bearing on certain groups of figures in the Palace Pantheon was pointed out by two of his assistants, Mr. B. I. Pankratoff and Lama Thabs-ldan-śes-rab.

After describing Chos-kyi-rgyal-po and Ça-muṇḍi, folio 3b1–6 has yab-yum-gñis-kyi-ḫkhor-du-gśin-rje-ya-ba-ti-be-con-ḫẓin-pa-phya-bsaṅ-ḫkhor-lo-ḫẓin-pa-rmig-pa-gsal-śiṅ-ḫẓin-pa-ral-pa-çhar-dgu-can-mduṅ-ḫẓin-pa-rnams-rgyal-poḫi-çhul-daṅ-blon-poḫi-çhul-daṅ-sde-dpon-gyi-çhul-daṅ-pho-ñaḫi-çhul-du-gnas-pa. gzhan-yaṅ-gśin-rje-mig-dmar-daṅ-tel-pa-daṅ-glaṅ-mgo-can-la-sogs-pa-lag-na-gsal-śiṅ-daṅ-ḫkhor-lo-daṅ-mduṅ-la-sogs-paḫi-mçhon-cha-sna-çhogs-pa-thogs-pa. . . . . gśin-rjeḫi-pho-ña-mo-nag-mo-lcags-kyu-thogs-pa-dus-kyi-zhags-pa-mo-nag-mo-zhags-pa-thogs-pa-gśiṅ-rje-dam-sri-ma-nag-mo-be-con-thogs-pa-gśiṅ-rje-sreg-ma-nag-mo-mche-ba-ḫbar-ba-thogs-pa. gzhan-yaṅ-dus-mçhan-ma-daṅ-gsod-ma-daṅ-nag-mo-daṅ-nam-gru-daṅ śa-ka-li-daṅ-gśin-rje-ḫbebs-ma-daṅ-gśin-rjeḫi-mçhan-mo-nag-mo-la-sogs-pa. Compare with this folio 16b2 gśin-rje-chos-kyi-rgyal-po-yum-mchog-çamuṇḍi-ya-ba-ti-la-sogs-paḫi-pho-brgyad-pho-ña-mo-la-sogs-paḫi-mo-brgyad and folio 17b3 to folio 18a5 ya-ma-du-tiḫi-zhes-bya-ba-lag-na-lcags-kyu-nag-po-thogs. . . . . kā-la-pā-śa-zhes-bya-ba-lag-na-dus-kyi-zhags-pa-thogs. . . . . ya-ma-daṇḍi-zhes-bya-ba-lag-na-be-con-nag-po-thogs. . . . . ya-ma-daṁṣṭri-zhes-bya-ba-za-byed-mche-ba-ḫbar-ba-can. . . . . . . kā-la-ra-ti-la-sogs-pa-gsod-pa-mo-daṅ-nag-mo-daṅ-nam-gru-śa-ka-li-la-sogs. . . . . gzhan-yaṅ-naṅ-gi-dkyil-ḫkhor-na-ya-ba-ti-daṅ-phya-bsaṅ-daṅ-rmig-pa-ral-pa-çhar-dgu-sogs-la-la-rgyal-poḫi-çhul-du-gnas-la-la-blon-poḫi-çhul-du-gnas-kha-cig-dag-ni-sde-dpon-çhul-la-la-pho-ñaḫi-çhul-du-gnas-lag-na-be-con-ḫkhor-lo-daṅ-gsal-śiṅ-mduṅ-sogs-mçhon-cha-thogs.

A, 2A1 Daṇḍadharā (yo-mu) is ya-ma-daṇḍi (lag-na-be-con-nag-po-thogs) or gśin-rje-dam-sri-ma-nag-mo-be-con-thogs-pa.

A, 2A2 Daṁṣṭrādharā (yo-mu) is ya-ma-daṁṣṭri (za-byed-mche-ba-ḫbar-ba-can) or gśin-rje-sreg-ma-nag-mo-mche-ba-ḫbar-ba-thogs-pa.

A, 2A3 Dūtī(?) or Cetī(?) (yo-mu) is ya-ma-du-ti (lag-na-lcags-kyu-nag-po-thogs) or gśin-rjeḫi-pho-ña-mo-nag-mo-lcags-kyu-thogs-pa.

A, 2A4 Kāladhvajā(?) or Kālaketu(?) (yo-mu) seems to correspond to dus-mçhan-ma. Perhaps Kālalakṣanā would be better. Is kā-la-ra-ti the same as dus-mçhan-ma?

A, 2A14 Chiang-lin (yo-mu) seems to correspond to gśin-rje-ḫbebs-ma.

A, 2A15 Sphoṭadharā (yo-mu) must belong to this group, but I am unable to identify her.

A, 2A16 Pāśadharā (yo-mu) is kā-la-pā-śa (lag-na-dus-kyi-zhags-pa-thogs) or dus-kyi-zhags-pa-mo-nag-mo-zhags-pa-thogs.

A, 2A17 Aṅkuśadharā (yo-mu) is gśin-rje-pho-ña-mo-nag-mo-lcags-kyu-thogs-pa or ya-ma-du-ti (lag-na-lcags-kyu-nag-po-thogs).

A, 2B18 Mi-k'o-pa is a transliteration of Tibetan rmig-pa.

A, 2B19 Ch'a-sang is a transliteration of Tibetan phya-bsaṅ. Tibetan *phya* is pronounced *cha*.

A, 2B20 Aṅgāraka (graha) may represent gśin-rje-mig-dmar. According to *Mahāvyutpatti* 3179, mig-dmar (red-eye) is a name for Aṅgāraka (Mars). Note that one of the names of Śanaiścara (Saturn) is gśin-rje-bdag-po.

A, 2B21 Fa-chiu-ku (yo-chu) seems to correspond to Tibetan ral-pa-ḉhar-dgu-can.

A, 2B33 Ya-wa-ti corresponds to Tibetan ya-ba-ti.

A, 2B34 Dharmarāja is chos-kyi-rgyal-po.

A, 2B35 Ti-la-pa corresponds to Tibetan tel-pa.

A, 2B36 A-wa-niu-t'ou (yo-chu) seems to correspond to glaṅ-mgo-can.

BIBLIOGRAPHY

In addition to the works referred to in the Introduction the following books and articles have proved most useful.

Bhattacharyya, B., *An Introduction to Buddhist Esoterism*, Oxford, 1932.

Bhattasali, N. K., *Iconography of Buddhist and Brahmanical Sculptures in the Dacca Museum*, Dacca, 1929.

Comparative Analytical Catalogue of the Kanjur Division of the Tibetan Tripitaka, published by the Otani Daigaku Library, Kyōto, 1930–32.

Csoma, Alexandre, and Feer, Léon, "Analyse du Kandjour et du Tandjour," *Annales du Musée Guimet*, II, Paris, 1881.

De Visser, M. W., "The Bodhisattva Ti-tsang in China and Japan," *Ostasiatische Zeitschrift*, II, III.

De Visser, M. W., "The Bodhisattva Ākāśagarbha in China and Japan," *Verhandelingen Amsterdam Akademie*, XXX, 1.

De Visser, M. W., "The Arhats in China and Japan," *Ostasiatische Zeitschrift*, VII, 87, 221; IX, 116; X, 60.

Eitel, Ernest J., *Hand-book of Chinese Buddhism*, London, 1870, Tōkyō, 1904.

Getty, Alice, *The Gods of Northern Buddhism*, Oxford, 1928.

Grünwedel, Albert, *Mythologie des Buddhismus in Tibet und der Mongolei*, Leipzig, 1900.

Mythologie du Buddhisme au Tibet et en Mongolie, Leipzig, 1900.

Grünwedel, Albert, "Description of a Collection of Lamaistic Objects," *Bibliotheca Buddhica*, VI, St. Petersburg, 1905.

Hackin, J., *Guide-Catalogue du Musée Guimet, Les collections bouddhiques*, Paris, 1923.

Hôbôgirin; Dictionnaire encyclopédique du bouddhisme d'après les sources chinoises et japonaises, I, 1929; II, 1930; Fascicule Annexe, 1931, Tōkyō.

Kern, H., and Nanjio, Bunyiu, "Saddharmapuṇḍarīka," *Bibliotheca Buddhica*, X, St. Petersburg, 1912.

Lalou, Marcelle, *Iconographie des étoffes peintes dans le Mañjuśrīmūlakalpa*, Paris, 1930.

Lévi, Sylvain, and Chavannes, Éd., "Les seize Arhat protecteurs de la loi," *Journal Asiatique*, 1916, II, 5–20, 189–304.

Mahāvyutpatti edited by Sakaki, Tōkyō, 1926.

"Mañjuśrīmūlakalpa," *Trivandrum Sanskrit Series*, Vols. LXX, LXXVI, LXXXIV (1920–25).

Petrucci, Raphael, and Binyon, Laurence, "Essays on the Buddhist Paintings from the Caves of the Thousand Buddhas, Tun-Huang," in Aurel Stein's *Serindia*, Vol. III, pp. 1392–1431.

Rajendralala Mitra, *The Sanskrit Buddhist Literature of Nepal*, Calcutta, 1882.

Rockhill, W. W., *The Life of the Buddha*, London, 1884.

Roerich, George, *Tibetan Paintings*, Paris, 1925.

Rosenberg, O., *Introduction to the Study of Buddhism*, Part I: "Vocabulary," Petrograd and Tōkyō, 1916.

Schiefner, Anton, *Tāranātha's Geschichte des Buddhismus in Indien*, St. Petersburg, 1869.

Schulemann, Günther, *Die Geschichte der Dalailamas*, Heidelberg, 1911.

"Shrīcchakrasambhāra Tantra" in *Tantrik Texts* edited by Arthur Avalon, Vol. VII, Calcutta, 1919.

von Siebold, Philipp Franz, *Nippon*, Berlin, 1930–31 (Würzburg und Leipzig, 1897).

"Śiksāsamuccaya of Śāntideva" edited by C. Bendall, *Bibliotheca Buddhica*, I, St. Petersburg, 1897–1902; translated by C. Bendall and W. H. D. Rouse, London, 1922.

Thomas, F. W., "Deux collections sanscrites et tibétaines de sādhanas," *Muséon*, IV, 1903, pp. 1–42.

Van Gulick, R. H., "Hayagrīva," *Internationales Archiv für Ethnographie*, Supplement to Vol. XXXIII, Leiden, 1935.

Waddell, L. A., *The Buddhism of Tibet, or Lamaism*, London, 1895 (2nd ed., Cambridge, 1934).

Waddell, L. A., "The 'Dhāraṇī' Cult in Buddhism," *Ostasiatische Zeitschrift*, I, 155, Berlin, 1913.

Waddell, L. A., "Evolution of the Buddhist Cult," *Asiatic Quarterly Review*, XXXIII (1912), 105.

Waddell, L. A., "The Indian Buddhist Cult of Avalokita and his consort Tārā," *Journal of the Royal Asiatic Society*, 1894, 51, London, 1894.

Waddell, L. A., "Tibetan Manuscripts and Books, etc., collected during the Younghusband Mission to Lhasa," *Asiatic Quarterly Review*, XXXIV (1912), 80–113.

Waley, Arthur, *A Catalogue of Paintings Recovered from Tun-huang by Sir Aurel Stein . . . in the Museum of Central Asian Antiquities, Delhi*, London, 1931.

Wentz, W. Y. Evans, *The Tibetan Book of the Dead*, London, 1927.

SANSKRIT INDEX

SANSKRIT INDEX

Akṣayamati (Bodhisattva). A, 4B3
Akṣobhya. Ch. adds Buddha. A, 4A40; A, 4A51; A, 4B26; B, 78; C, R10c; C, S8b
  guhyasamāja. C, R1c
  yab-yum. D, 57
Akṣobhyavajra. A, 2A49; A, 5A61
    Cf. Vajrākṣobhya.
  guhyasamāja. Ch. adds Buddha. A, 2M5; B, 32
Agni (deva). A, 3A21; A, 5A50; D, 286
Agnibhayatrāṇa. C, 40b
Agra(?)matirājatathāgata (Buddha). A, 1B43
  Cf. Abhijñārāja. C, 14b; D, 141
    Dharmasāgarāgra(?)mativikrīḍitābhijñārāja. B, 138
Aṅkuśadharā (or Aṅkuśī).
    Cf. Vajrāṅkuśī.
    Cf. Sādhana, pp. 198, 228.
  fo-mu. A, 3A54
  yo-mu. A, 2A17
Aṅgaja. A, 1B46; B, 272; C, 5b; D, 193
  Ch. Ang-chi-ta and Yin-chieh-t'o.
    Cf. JA 1916, 2, 292, 295–97.
Aṅgāraka (graha). A, 2B20
  Tib. mig-dmar.
Aṅgirodeva (Bodhisattva). A, 5A9
Acala. Ch. Acalavajra.
  avaninihitajānu (nīla). C, 61b
  aṣṭakapi. B, 348; C, 63a
  krodha. D, 174; D, 219
  caturbhuja. A, 6A50; B, 350; C, 62b
  catuṣpada. C, 62c
  nīla. A, 4B29; B, 338; C, S5a
    avaninihitajānu. C, 61b
    bkaḥ-gdams-lugs. C, 61c
  rakta. C, 91b
  sita. A, 6A30; B, 340; C, 62a; C, S4c

Acalā [bhūmi] (fo-mu). A, 4A8
Ajapālipāda(?) (mahāsiddha). D, 19
Tib. ẓa-wa-ri-pa. Cf. Cordier 1, 199–201.
Ajita. A, 1B47; B, 273; C, 5c; D, 194
Atīśa.
ārya. B, 19
mahāryaśrī. D, 29
Anaṅgavajra (Bodhisattva). A, 6B56
Anantasvaraghoṣa (Bodhisattva). A, 5A40
Cf. Hôbôgirin, pp. 148–150.
Anantaujas. Ch. adds Buddha. A, 1A56; B, 100
Jina. D, 115
Anuttaravajrapāṇi (bhūtaḍāmara). C, S11c
Anucārin(?) (Buddha). A, 1B44; B, 117
antarasādhana.
Dharmarāja. D, 239
Mañjughoṣa. A, 2A46; B, 31
Zhaṅ-blon-rdo-rje (mārajit). C, 113a
Aparājita.
Cf. Krodhāparājita.
Aparājita (yakṣa). C, 113c
Cf. Cordier 2, 91.
Aparājitā. Ch. to B, 261 fo-mu. A, 6B7; B, 261
krodha (devī). A, 5B57
Tārā. Ch. adds fo-mu. B, 213
pīta (fo-mu). A, 6A25
Aparimitāyus.
Cf. Amitāyus.
Apalāla (nāgarāja). C, 115a
Apāyajaha (Bodhisattva). A, 4B48
Cf. Sarvāpāyajaha.
Abhayaṁdada (Bodhisattva). A, 5B3
Abhijñārāja. C, 14b; D, 141
Cf. Agra(?)matirājatathāgata (Buddha).
A, 1B43
Dharmasāgarāgra(?)mativikrīḍitābhijñārāja.
B, 138
sic dhāraṇī to C, 14b.

Abhimukha.
Bodhisattva. A, 5A58
rakta. D, 285
Abhimukhī [bhūmi] (fo-mu). A, 4A19
abhisambodhi.
Cf. Vairocana (abhisambodhi).
Abheda. A, 1B5; B, 287; C, 10b; D, 208
Abhyudgatarāja (Buddha). A, 1B49; B, 118
Abhyudgatoṣṇīṣa(?) (Bodhisattva). A, 5A53
Cf. Hôbôgirin, p. 148.
Amaravajra (devī). C, 65a
Cf. Cordier 2, 109.
Amitābha. Ch. adds Buddha. A, 1B31; A, 2A42; A, 4B41; B, 80; C, 84c; C, R10b
Jina. D, 132
Bodhisattva. A, 4B59
yab-yum. D, 59
Amitāyus (or Aparimitāyus). Ch. adds Buddha. A, 6M5; A, 6B38; B, 64
Jina. D, 85
caturbhuja. Ch. adds yin-yang. B, 63
caryātantra. D, 82
nirmāṇakāya. C, 63b
sita. C, 64a
mi-traḫi-lugs. C, 64b
ba-ri-lugs. C, 63c
Amṛtakuṇḍalin. Ch. adds vajra. A, 2B56; B, 346; C, R12b
Cf. Cordier 1, 138; 2, 224, 547; Hôbôgirin, p. 30.
krodha. D, 215
Amṛtabinduvajra. Tib. bdud-rçi-thig-pa. A, 2A47
Cf. Cordier 1, 199.
amoghatrāṇa(?) (Vajrapāṇi). A, 2B4
Amoghadarśin. Ch. adds Buddha. A, 1A45; B, 90
Cf. Weller 60.
Jina. D, 105
Bodhisattva. A, 4B47
Amoghapāśa. Ch. adds Avalokiteśvara. B, 171
anucara (rakta). C, 35a
ārya. D, 96

īśvara (= Lokeśvara) Avalokiteśvara (Bodhisattva). A, 6B54
pañcadeva (ba-ri-lugs). C, 34c
pīta. C, 35b
rakta (anucara). C, 35a
kha-che-paṇ-chen-lugs (= Kāśmīramahāpaṇḍitakrama). C, 36b
amoghapūjāmaṇi (Avalokiteśvara). C, 88b
Amoghavikrāmin (Bodhisattva). A, 6A7
Amoghasiddhi. Ch. adds Buddha.
A, 1B32; A, 2A41; A, 4M3; A, 4A38; A, 4A48; A, 4B28; A, 4B50; B, 81; C, R11a
yab-yum. D, 60
amoghāṅkuśa (Avalokiteśvara). C, 88a
arapacana.
Mañjughoṣa. C, S3a
raktapīta (sa-lugs). C, 65c
Arthadarśin (Buddha). A, 1B6
Cf. Weller 30.
Arthapratisaṁvit. A, 4B12
arthasādhana (Vārāhī). C, 26b
ardhacaturthākṣara (Avalokiteśvara). C, 69c
avaninihitajānu (Acala, nīla). C, 61b
Cf. Bhattacharyya, p. 60.
Avalokiteśvara. Ch. usually adds Bodhisattva.
A, 1M3; A, 1A11; A, 5A34; A, 6A20; C, 93c; D, 147
Cf. Lokeśvara.
anucara. C, 16c
amoghapāśa (īśvara = Lokeśvara). A, 6B54
Cf. Amoghapāśa.
amoghapūjāmaṇi. C, 88b
amoghāṅkuśa. C, 88a
ardhacaturthākṣara. C, 69c
aṣṭabhayatrāṇa. C, 86c
īśvara (= Lokeśvara). A, 6A46
ekādaśamukha. A, 6M4; A, 6A36
Cf. Ekādaśamukha.
dpal-mo-lugs. C, 34b
kṛṣṇa (pañcamukhadvādaśabhuja). A, 6B53

khasarpaṇa. A, 6A45; B, 160; C, 37b
Cf. Khasarpaṇa.
gaganarāja. C, 39b
Cf. Gaganarāja.
guhya (īśvara = Lokeśvara). A, 2A48
guhyasādhana. D, 75
caturbhuja. A, 6M6; A, 6A35; B, 158; C, S5c: D, 89
rakta. A, 6B51
cittaviśrāmaṇa. Ch. cintāmaṇi. B, 175; C, 38a; C, 38c
cintāmaṇi. B, 176
pañcadeva. C, 38b
cintāmaṇicakra. C, 39c
jinasāgara. A, 3B41; B, 34; C, 43c
Buddha. A, 3M9
trailokyavaśaṁkara. A, 6B50; B, 167
nīlakaṇṭha (īśvara = Lokeśvara). A, 6B52
pañcadeva (cintāmaṇi). C, 38b
pañcamukhadvādaśabhuja (kṛṣṇa). A, 6B53
padmanarteśvara. A, 6A9
Cf. Padmanarteśvara.
dvibhuja. B, 164
padmapāṇi. C, 87b
padmavikāsana. B, 159
mahābhūmika. A, 6A11
rakta. Tib. bhu-kham-dmar-po. B, 172
māyājālakrama. B, 170
rakta.
caturbhuja. A, 6B51
mahābhūmika. Tib. bhu-kham-dmar-po. B, 172
vajragarbha. C, 43a
vajragarbhapramardin. Ch. vajrābhedya. B, 177
vajradharma. B, 163
viśveśa. C, 87a
ṣaḍakṣara (jo-bo-lugs). C, 33b
ṣoḍaśabhuja. A, 6B40
siṁhanāda. A, 6A34; B, 161; D, 94
sukhāvatī. C, 87c
bkaḥ-gdams-lha-bzhiḥi-naṅ-gi. C, 34a

mounted on a wolf(?) Figure does not correspond.
A, 6A10
īśvara (= Lokeśvara). A, 6B49
In both cases change hou (roar) to hou (wolf?)?
Then they correspond to the Chinese of B, 162 and B, 166
Hālāhala and Harihariivāhana Lokeśvara.
Avaivartikaśrīcakra. Ch. adds Buddha. A, 1B53; B, 122
Tib. of B, 122 Avaivartikacakrasambhavaśrī(?).
Aśoka (Buddha). A, 1B36
Cf. Weller 25.
Aśokatathāgata (Buddha). A, 1B41
Aśokaśrī. Ch. adds Buddha. A, 1A54; B, 102
Jina. D, 117
Aśokottama. Dhāraṇī adds śrī. C, 14c
Aśokottamaśrī. Ch. adds tathāgata. B, 136; D, 139
Aśvajit. A, 1B10
aṣṭakapi (Acala). B, 348; C, 63a
aṣṭadaśasthaviraparivāra (Muni). C, S1a–c
Cf. Grünwedel, p. 7.
aṣṭadeva (gur-mgon = Pañjaranātha = Mahākāla).
C, 122a
aṣṭanāgaparivāra (Vaiśravaṇa, raudra). C, 105a–c
aṣṭabhayatrāṇa.
Avalokiteśvara. C, 86c
Ekādaśamukha. C, 40a
Asaṅga. B, 2
bhaṭṭāraka. D, 6
Ākarṣaṇī(?) (devī). A, 5B61
Ākāśagarbha (or Khagarbha). Ch. adds Bodhisattva.
A, 1M8; A, 1A1; A, 2A38;
B, 196; C, 85c; D, 150
Ākāśadhvaja (Lho-brag). D, 39
Ākāśanetra (Bodhisattva). A, 5A35
ācārya(?) (Vajrapāṇi). Ch. hsien-hsing. B, 74; C, 54c
Cf. Grünwedel, p. 160.
ājñāvinivarta (Gaṇapati). C, 114a
Cf. Cordier 2, 88.
Ānanda. A, 1B12; B, 291
Ānandadhvaja (Sa-skya-paṇḍi-ta = Pāṇḍubhūmipaṇḍita).
D, 38

Ābhāsaraśmi(?) Buddha. A, 1B34
Cf. Weller 647.
Ābhāsvara(?)tathāgata (Buddha). A, 1B39
Cf. Ratnacandra. C, 15a
Ratnacandrapadmapratimaṇḍitapaṇḍita(?)tejaḥsvaraghoṣarāja. B, 134
Svaraghoṣarāja. D, 137
āyuḥsādhana (Śaṁvara, sita). C, 22c
āyurdhara (Vaiśravaṇa, sita). C, 106b
āyurvardhana.
Caturmukha (sita). C, 132a
Vaiśravaṇa (sita). B, 318; D, 264
Āyurvaśitā. A, 4B18
Āyurvaśī(?) (devī). Dhāraṇī gives ayuḥwāśi dewi. D, 300
Tib. Çhe-ḥgugs-lha-mo.
Cf. jagadvaśī(?) (Tārā). B, 216
āyuṣpati.
Mahākāla. B, 316; D, 231
Cf. Cordier 2, 172.
śyāma. C, 118b
Āryacundātārā. C, 54b
Āryajāṅgulī (fo-mu). B, 236
Āryatārā (śyāma). C, 94b
Āryadeva. B, 3
bhaṭṭāraka. D, 4
Āryamañjuśrī. C, 93b
Āryamahāratna. C, 0b; D, 41
Cf. bÇoṅ-kha-pa. A, 1A36; B, 21
Āryasitātapatrā (fo-mu). B, 248; D, 162
Āryātīśa. B, 19
Āryāmoghapāśa. D, 96
Indra.
Cf. Śakra, Śatakratu.
Indra (mahāyakṣasenāpati). A, 6B35
Indraketudhvaja (Jina). D, 125
Indraketudhvajarāja. Ch. adds Buddha. A, 1A23; B, 110
Indraḍākinī. C, 26a
īrṣyā (Bhairavavajra). A, 2A26; A, 2B40
Īśvara (deva). A, 5A23

Uḍḍiyānatārā (pīthīśvarī). C, 45b
Uttamaśrī (Buddha). Tib. dPal-mchog-daṅ-po.
A, 4M2; A, 4B31
Upakeśinī(?) (devī). A, 5B58
upadeśakrama (Garuḍa, śabala). C, 79b
Upagupta. B, 293
Upananda (nāgarāja). D, 291
Upapattivaśitā. A, 4B6
Upāyakauśalyapāramitā. A, 4A2
upāsaka.
Dharma. C, 10c
Dharmatala. B, 288
Cf. Dharmatala. D, 209
Hva-śaṅ. B, 289
Cf. Hva-śaṅ. C, 11a; D, 210
Umā. A, 5B36
devī. A, 5B54
Ulkādharā (fo-mu). A, 3A23
Uṣṇīṣacakravartin. A, 2B61
Cf. Cordier 2, 259.
Cf. Krodhoṣṇīṣacakravartin. D, 217
Vajroṣṇīṣacakravartirāja. A, 2A10
Uṣṇīṣajvāla. D, 192
Uṣṇīṣatārā. Ch. Uṣṇīṣavijayatārā (fo-mu). B, 210
Uṣṇīṣavijayā. Ch. Vijayā (fo-mu).
A, 6M3; A, 6B26; B, 247; C, 64c; D, 164
Tārā. C, 95c
dvibhuja. C, 90a
navadeva. C, S2b
Uṣṇīṣasitātapatrā. C, 75a; C, S2a
Ūrṇā(?) (fo-mu). A, 5A55
ūrdhvapāda (Vārāhī). Tib. gnam-zhabs-ma. C, 27c
Cf. Sādhana, p. 439.
Ṛkṣavaktraḍākinī. D, 189
Ṛddhivaśitā. A, 4B7
Ekajaṭā. C, 98a
anucarā. C, 35c; C, 53b
devī. Ch. fo-mu and adds dvibhuja. B, 239; C, 136c
caturviṁśatibhuja. Ch. fo-mu. B, 237
dvibhuja (fo-mu). A, 6B59

ekamātṛ.
Śrīdevī. D, 236
Lab-sgron. D, 35
ekavīra.
Bhairava. Ch. adds vajra. B, 46
Bhairavavajra. A, 2B29
Mahākāla (kartarīdhara). C, 125b
sādhanavinirgata Jambhala (bahudeva). C, 108a
Hayagrīva (sahaja, jo-boḥi-lugs). C, 58a
Ekādaśa (deva). A, 3B11
Ekādaśamukha. Ch. adds mahākāruṇika (Avalokiteśvara). B, 173
Avalokiteśvara. A, 6M4; A, 6A36
dpal-mo-lugs. C, 34b
aṣṭabhayatrāṇa. C, 40a
mahākāruṇika. C, S5b; D, 95
ekānta (gur = Mahākāla, rṅog-lugs). C, 123a
ekāntanāyaka (Jambhala, pīta). C, 107b
Cf. Cordier 2, 207, 267, 268.
Oṣadhi (Buddha). A, 1A6
Cf. Weller 16.
Kanakabharadvāja. A, 1B58; B, 279; C, 7c; D, 200
Kanakamuni (Buddha). B, 131; C, 83b
Kanakavatsa. A, 1B17; B, 278; C, 7b; D, 199
kanakavarṇa (Tārā). Ch. Mahāprajñākanakatārā (fo-mu). B, 209; C, 95b
Kanyā (deva). A, 3B23
Kapālatārā (bhaṭṭārikā). C, 54a
kapāladhara (Hevajra). A, 3M6
Kamaloṣṇīṣa(?) (Buddha). A, 4A44
Cf. Hôbôgirin, p. 149.
Karkaṭadeva(?) (Bodhisattva). A, 5A11
kartarīdhara. Cf. Mahākāla (kartarīdhara).
Cf. Cordier 2, 208, 269.
karmakarī (anucarā).
Nāgī°. C, 59c
Yakṣa°. C, 60a
Yama°. C, 59b
Vajra°. C, 59a

Karmaḍākinī. C, 141c; D, 226
  anucarā. C, 71a; C, 118c
  uttara. C, 30c
Karmanātha (kākāsya). Ch. Kākāsyamahākāla.
  B, 304; C, 121b
Karmayama.
  Cf. Cordier 1, 182–183.
  Dharmarāja (nīla). C, 137b
  rakta.
    rudhiravarṇa. C, 138a
    ma-ru-rçe-bzhis-bskor-pa. C, 137c
karmayoganātha (Caturmukha). C, 131c
Karmavajrī. A, 4A52; B, 264
  Ch. Chin-kang-yeh fo-mu and Chih-hsing-chin-kang fo-mu.
Karmavaśitā(?). A, 4B21
Kalaśī [maṅgala]. D, 297
Kalpabhadrasamudra (Dalai Lama). B, 28
  Tib. skal-bzaṅ-rgyal-mçho.
    Cf. Sumatikalpabhadrasamudra (Jinendra).
      D, 50
kākāsya (Karmanātha). Ch. Kākāsyamahākāla.
  B, 304; C, 121b
  Cf. Cordier 1, 127, 129–130; 2, 213.
Kātyāyana. A, 1B24
Kāmarāja. Cf. Ṭakkirāja.
    Cf. Cordier 2, 266, 268.
  krodha. D, 214
  rakta. C, 3b
  vajra. A, 2A13
kāmadhātvīśvarī (Pārvatī). D, 248
Kāyahevajra. C, R3b; C, R6b
  Cf. Cordier 2, 155.
Kārttikeya(?) (deva). A, 5A14
Kāla. B, 295
  Cf. Rockhill, Life, p. 170.
Kālacakra. Ch. adds rāja (Buddha). B, 35; C, R14b
    Cf. Cakradhararāja (Buddha).
  krama Jambhala (śyāma). C, 109c
  Garuḍa (śabala, tantrakrama). C, 79a

Śrī. D, 65
sahaja. C, 23c
Kāladhvajā(?) or Kālaketu(?).
devī. A, 5B28
yo-mu. A, 2A4
Kālāgni (deva). A, 3B7
Kālika. A, 1B14; B, 275; C, 6b; D, 196
Kāśyapa. A, 1B25
Cf. Mahākāśyapa.
Kāśyapa (Buddha). Tib. of B, 132 om. Buddha.
B, 132; C, 83c
Kāśyapadeva (Bodhisattva). A, 5A49
kīlapāda (gur-mgon = Pañjaranātha = Mahākāla).
C, 122b
Kuñcikādharā (fo-mu). A, 3B54
Kuṇḍalī (khol-po° = dāsa). Mantra has piśāci kundhali.
C, 115c
Cf. Cordier 2, 174.
Kubera (Vaiśravaṇa, gsuṅ-mchog). C, 104b
kumārabhūta (Mañjuśrī). B, 146; D, 93
Kumbha(?) (deva). A, 3A19
Reading ku for yu?
Kumbhīra (mahāyakṣasenāpati). A, 6A4
Kurukullā. Ch. adds fo-mu. A, 3B40; B, 60; C, 3a; C, R4c
Ch. of B, 60 Chih-hsing fo-mu (=Tib. rig-byed).
Cf. Cordier 2, 51.
guhyasādhana. C, 70c
Kusuma (Buddha). A, 1A26
Cf. Weller 9.
Kusuma (Buddha) the second. A, 1A21
Cf. Weller 10.
Kusumaśrī. Ch. adds Buddha. A, 1A40; B, 104
Jina. D, 119
kūṭāgāra (Vajrapāṇi). C, 57a
kūrmapādī (Vārāhī). C, 28a
Cf. Cordier 1, 57; 2, 267.
Kṛṣṇacārin (or Kṛṣṇācārya or Kṛṣṇapāda or Kānhapāda).
B, 14
mahāsiddha. D, 15

Kṛṣṇāri (= Kṛṣṇ[ayam]āri). Ch. adds Bhairavavajra.
B, 43
Yamāri. C, R2a; D, 71
vajra (Buddha). A, 2M1
Bhairavavajra. A, 2B31
Ketugraha (deva). A, 3B9
Keśinī (devī). A, 5B17
Kaumārī(?) (devī). A, 5B29
Krakucchanda (Buddha). Tib. of B, 130 om. Buddha.
B, 130; C, 83a
Kruddhatārā (kālī). Ch. bhṛkuṭī for kālī. B, 219
Kruddhavārāhī (kālī). C, 29b
krodha.
sMe-ba-brçegs-pa. D, 172
sMe-brçegs (B reads me). B, 356; C, S9c
dhūmavarṇa. C, 77b
śyāma. C, 77c
feminine. A, 6B29; B, 351; C, 78a; D, 180
Ch. has wei-chi for sme-brçegs.
Cf. AQR 34, 105. Tibetan dhāraṇīs have ucchuṣmamahākrodha.
Krodhakāmarāja. D, 214
Cf. Cordier 2, 268.
Krodhaguhyapati. C, 89a
Krodhacandravajra. A, 5A42
Krodhanīladaṇḍa. D, 216
Cf. Cordier 2, 268.
krodhabhayanāśana (Śaṁvara). C, 78b
Cf. Cordier 2, 225–226.
Krodhamahābala. Ch. Mahābalavajra. B, 342; D, 218
Krodhayamāri. D, 212
Krodhavajrapāṇi. A, 2B3
Krodhavajrapātāla. D, 221
Cf. Cordier 2, 259, 267.
Krodhavighnāntaka. C, 74a
Krodhahayagrīva. D, 213
Cf. Cordier 2, 547.
Krodhahūṁkāra. C, R9a
Krodhācala. D, 174; D, 219
Cf. Cordier 2, 193.

Krodhāparājita. C, 90c; D, 211
  vajra. A, 5B56
Krodhāparājitā (devī). A, 5B57
Krodhāmṛtakuṇḍalin. D, 215
  Cf. Cordier 2, 224, 547.
Krodhoṣṇīṣacakravartin. D, 217
  Cf. Uṣṇīṣacakravartin. A, 2B61
    Vajroṣṇīṣacakravartirāja. A, 2A10
Kṣāntipāramitā. A, 4A14
Kṣitigarbha. A, 1M7; A, 1A4; A, 2A40; B, 197; C, 86a; D, 148
  Ch. (except A, 1A4 om. rāja) adds rāja (Bodhisattva).
Kṣetrapāla. B, 315; C, 116a; D, 233
Khagarbha.
  Cf. Ākāśagarbha.
khaḍgadhara (Bhairavavajra). A, 2A5; A, 2B52
  Cf. Cordier 1, 165.
khadiravaṇī (Tārā). Ch. "destroys all evils."
  B, 206; C, 97c; D, 161
    In B, 206 change ḫbye to kyi.
  Cf. A, 6B32 "purple veṇuvana Tārā."
Khasarpaṇa. C, S6a
  Avalokiteśvara. A, 6A45; B, 160; C, 37b
    Cf. Waley, Tun-huang Catalogue, p. xxxv, for the
      Chinese shui-yüeh.
Gaganagañja (Bodhisattva). A, 4B17
Gaganarāja. Ch. adds Bodhisattva. B, 174
  Avalokiteśvara. C, 39b
Gaṇapati (deva). A, 5A4
    Cf. A, 3A16. Lung-yü t'ien.
  ājñāvinivarta. C, 114a
  caturbhuja.
    rakta. C, 114c
    sita (jo-boḫi-lugs). C, 114b
  nātha (= Mahākāla), siṁhāsana. C, 128a
  pīta. C, 93a
  mahārakta. B, 360; C, 3c
    Ch. Raktagaṇapatirājavajra.
  rakta (caturbhuja). C, 114c
  siṁhāsana (nātha = Mahākāla). C, 128a
  sita (caturbhuja, jo-boḫi-lugs). C, 114b

gadādhara (Vaiśravaṇa, śyāmapīta). C, 103b
Gandhatārā. C, 49a
Cf. Sādhana, pp. 179, 184, 191, 197, 219, 228.
Gandhā. A, 2B25
Cf. Sādhana, pp. 157, 312, 324.
Gandhahastin (Bodhisattva). A, 4B15
Garuḍa.
Cf. Vajragaruḍa.
upadeśakrama (śabala). C, 79b
Kālacakra (śabala, tantrakrama). C, 79a
kṛṣṇa. A, 3B43; D, 184
tantrakrama (Kālacakra, śabala). C, 79a
pīta (bkaḥ-gdams-lugs). C, 79c
puṣpa. A, 3B42
yuta (Vajrapāṇi). A, 2B2
Cf. Cordier 1, 206; 2, 541.
Śaṁvara. Ch. adds rāja (Buddha). A, 3A46; B, 40
śabala. D, 185
upadeśakrama. C, 79b
Kālacakra (tantrakrama). C, 79a
gser-mig-ḥkhyil-ba. D, 186
Grünwedel, p. 191 ser-mig-ḥkhyil-ba.
garuḍapakṣavant (Hayagrīva, jo-boḥi-lugs). C, 58b
garbhasuvarṇasūtra (Śrī). C, 71b
Garbha(?) hevajra. B, 48; C, R2b
Tib. sÑiṅ-po-kyai-rdor; Ch. Hsi-hsin-chin-kang.
Gavāmpati. A, 1B11
Gītā. A, 2B8
Cf. Sādhana, pp. 157, 312, 324.
fo-mu. A, 3A50; A, 4B57
Guṇaprabha. B, 7
Cf. Tāranātha, p. 128.
Buddha. A, 1B21
Cf. Weller 29.
Guhyajñāna. C, 72c
Guhyapati.
krodha. C, 89a
sahaja (śānta). C, 88c
guhyasamāja. Ch. guhya.
Akṣobhya. C, R1c

Akṣobhyavajra. Ch. adds Buddha. A, 2M5; B, 32
Īśvara (= Lokeśvara) Avalokiteśvara. A, 2A48
Mañjuvajra. Ch. of B, 30 adds Buddha.
A, 2A32; B, 30; C, 17a; C, R1a; D, 68
Buddha. A, 2M4
Mañjuśrī (Buddha). A, 2M3; A, 4M8; A, 4A32
Lokeśvara. Ch. Avalokiteśvaraguhyabuddha.
B, 33
Vajrākṣobhya (Buddha). A, 2A35
vinirgata Jambhala (pīta). C, 107c
Cf. Cordier 2, 267.
Śrī. D, 62
sahaja. C, 17b
guhyasādhana.
Avalokiteśvara. D, 75
Kurukullā. C, 70c
Dharmarāja. D, 240
Mañjughoṣa. B, 148
Mañjuśrī. A, 2A30
Bodhisattva. A, 2M6
Mahākāla (trakṣad, ḍākamukha). C, 130c
Lokeśvara. C, 39a
Hayagrīva. Ch. adds vajra. B, 61; D, 167
Zhaṅ-blon-rdo-rje (mārajit). C, 113b
Gopaka. A, 1B4; B, 286; C, 10a; D, 207
gopāla (Vasudhārā). C, 112a
Gautamadeva (Bodhisattva). A, 5A13
Gaurī (fo-mu). A, 2B44; A, 3A45; A, 3B39
Cf. Sādhana, pp. 310, 445, 446, 479.
candrakānti(?) (Tārā). C, 95a
ñi-zla-lcam-dral (= sun moon brother sister). C, 139b
Grahamātṛkā. B, 269
mahāvidyā. C, R17a
vidyārājñī. C, 77a
Ghaṇṭā. C, 50b
Cf. Sādhana, p. 198.
ghaṇṭādhara (Bhairavajra). A, 2A8
Ghaṇṭāpāda. A, 3A36; B, 13
mahāsiddha. D, 14

Ghasmarī (fo-mu). A, 3A42; A, 3B15
Cf. Sādhana, pp. 446, 479.
Cakradhararāja (Buddha). A, 3M8
Cf. Kālacakra.
Cakrasaṁvara.
pīta. C, R7c
Śrī. Ch. Śaṁvararāja (Buddha). B, 36; D, 63
Cakrā [maṅgala]. D, 299
Caṇḍa.
trimukhaṣaḍbhuja. Ch. adds Vajrapāṇi. B, 75
Vajrapāṇi.
khra-thogs. C, 56a
chuṅ. Cf. Vajrapāṇi (hsiao) A, 2B5. B, 73; D, 169
rakta. C, 56b
caṇḍamahāroṣaṇa (Vajrapāṇi) bsruṅ-baḥi-mkhar-ras-chuṅ-lugs.
Tib. gtum-chen. Cf. Cordier 2, 13, 35. C, 55c
caṇḍamukha(?) (Caturmukha). Tib. gdoṅ-gñan-can.
C, 133b
Caṇḍālī (fo-mu). A, 3A60; A, 3B59
Cf. Sādhana, pp. 310, 443, 445, 479.
Caṇḍikā.
Cf. Cordier 2, 268; Sādhana, pp. 441, 498.
devī. B, 330; D, 244
caturbhujamahākālānucarā. C, 121a
go-chaḥi. C, 22a
caturḍākinīparivāra (Hayagrīva, jo-bo-lugs). C, 58c
Caturmukha.
Cf. Cordier 2, 200.
karmayoganātha. C, 131c
caṇḍamukha(?). C, 133b
nīla (ñams-sgrol). C, 133a
pīta (dhanavardhana). C, 132b
rakta (vaśaṁkara). C, 132c
śrīnātha (sādhanakālasambaddha). C, 131b
śrīnātha (sevākālasambaddha). C, 131a
sita (āyurvardhana). C, 132a
Candanaśrī. Ch. adds Buddha. A, 1A57; B, 99
Jina. D, 114

Candra (deva). A, 3A28; A, 5B55
candrakānti(?).
Gaurī (Tārā). C, 95a
Tārā. Ch. "great good autumn moon." B, 208
Candrakīrti. B, 9
bhaṭṭāraka. D, 22
Candraketu (or Śaśiketu) (Buddha). A, 1B33
Cf. Weller 78, 254.
Candraprabha (Bodhisattva). A, 4B60
Candraprabhā. A, 6B22
Candravairocana. Ch. adds Bodhisattva. A, 6A21; C, 13a
Cf. BEFEO 3, 35.
Carcikā (fo-mu). A, 2B41
Cf. Vajracarcikā.
caryātantra (Amitāyus). D, 82
Cf. Cordier, 2, 544.
caryābhūmi (Cittotpāda°). A, 4A29
Cāmuṇḍā (devī). A, 5B32
Cf. Cordier 2, 265, 268.
Citipati. B, 337; C, 138b; D, 253
Cittavaśitā. A, 4B19
cittaviśrāmaṇa (Avalokiteśvara). Ch. cintāmaṇi.
B, 175; C, 38a; C, 38c
Cf. Cordier 1, 195, 307.
Cittahevajra. C, R2c; C, R5c
Cf. Cordier 2, 155.
Cittotpāda (= adhimukti?) caryābhūmi (fo-mu). A, 4A29
Cittotpāda (= adhimukti?) vaśitā. A, 4B8
Citrā(?) (devī). A, 5B59
cintāmaṇi.
Avalokiteśvara. B, 176
pañcadeva. C, 38b
Tārā. C, 45c
Cf. Cordier 2, 73.
Mahākāla.
rakta. Cf. Cordier 2, 204. C, 0110c; C, 117c
sita. B, 317; C, 0110a; C, 117a; D, 229

cintāmaṇicakra.
  Avalokiteśvara. C, 39c
  Tārā.
    caturbhuja. A, 6B15
    sita. B, 230
Cintā[maṇi]rājñī (caturbhuja). B, 231
  Ch. adds Tārā (fo-mu).
Cīnakramatārā (fo-mu). B, 229
Cīnatārā (fo-mu). A, 6B48
Cundā. D, 159
  ārya (Tārā). C, 54b
  devī. Ch. fo-mu.
    caturbhuja. A, 6B60; B, 240
    bahubhuja. B, 241
    sita. C, 90b
Cūḍapanthaka. A, 1B61; B, 282; C, 8c; D, 203
Corabhayatrāṇa. C, 42c
Caurī (fo-mu). A, 3A44
  Cf. Sādhana, pp. 446, 479.
Chattrā [maṅgala]. D, 293
Chinnamuṇḍā. C, 26c
  Cf. Cordier 1, 56–57; 2, 117, 269.
jagaddama (Vajrapāṇi). A, 5A5
jagadvaśī(?) (Tārā). B, 216
  Tib. ḫgro-ba-ḫgugs-paḫi; Ch. shê-fu-shih-chien.
    Cf. Āyurvaśī(?) (devī). D, 300
Jambhala. Ch. adds vajra. C, S10c
  ekavīrasādhanavinirgata (bahudeva). C, 108a
  ekāntanāyaka (pīta). C, 107b
  kṛṣṇa. A, 6A22; B, 344; C, 108b; D, 267
  kālacakrakrama (śyāma). C, 109c
  guhyasamājavinirgata (pīta). C, 107c
  trimukhaṣaḍbhuja. D, 270
  nāgavāhana (sita). B, 355
  pañcadeva (sita, jo-boḫi-lugs). C, 108c
  pīta. A, 6A49; A, 6B30; B, 339; C, 51a; D, 265
    ekāntanāyaka. C, 107b
    guhyasamājavinirgata. C, 107c
  prāṇasādhana (rakta). D, 268
  bahudeva (ekavīrasādhanavinirgata). C, 108a

rakta.
prāṇasādhana. D, 268
grva-ba-mṅon-śes-lugs-kyi. C, 109b
sa-lugs. C, 109a
śyāma (kālacakrakrama). C, 109c
ṣaḍbhuja. A, 6A52; B, 341
sita. D, 266
nāgavāhana. B, 355
pañcadeva (jo-boḫi-lugs). C, 108c
Jayadā (fo-mu). A, 6B17
Jayā (devī). A, 5B41
jayākara (ḫBrom-ston). D, 28
Cf. Cordier 1, 128, 305.
Jayoṣṇīṣa (Buddha). A, 4A53
Cf. Hôbôgirin, pp. 148–149.
Jalabhayatrāṇa. C, 40c
Jāṅgulī. Ch. fo-mu. A, 6A53; A, 6B41; D, 181
ārya. B, 236
Tārā. B, 227
Jālinīdharā(?) (fo-mu). A, 3A55
Jālinīprabha (Bodhisattva). A, 4B1
Jālinīprabhākumāra. A, 5B14
Jinamitra. B, 314; C, 116a; D, 234
jinarṣabha (Vaiśravaṇa). C, 110c
jinavara (Ratna[pāṇi]). D, 79
jinasāgara (Avalokiteśvara). A, 3B41; B, 34; C, 43c
Buddha A, 3M9
jinendra.
Mahāpañcama. D, 46
Sumatikalpabhadrasamudra. D, 50
Jñānaketu (Bodhisattva). A, 4B58
Jñānaguru. D, 153
Cf. Waddell, p. 358.
Jñānaḍākinī (fo-mu). B, 52; C, R14a
Cf. Cordier 1, 100.
Jñānapāramitā. A, 4A17
Jñānavaśitā. A, 4B22
Jñānākara (Bodhisattva). A, 6A8
Cf. Weller 99, 436.

Jyotiṣprabha(?) (Buddha). A, 1B19
Cf. Weller 707.
Jvālānala(?) Ch. adds vajra. Tib. me-ltar-ḫbar-ba.
B, 349
Is it Vajrajvālānalārka? Cf. Cordier 1, 395; 2, 62.
Cf. Bhattacharyya, pp. 145–146; Sādhana, p. 512.
Jvālānala(?) (Buddha). A, 4B32
Tibetan description gives me-ltar-ḫbar-ba.
Jvālānaloṣṇīṣa(?) (Buddha). A, 4A56
Ṭakkirāja. Cf. Kāmarāja. B, 313; C, 116c; D, 235
Cf. Cordier 2, 260, 268; Sādhana, pp. 137, 418, 420.
Ṭakṣad (= raudrāntaka). Ch. Mahākāla.
Cf. Trakṣad and Mahākāla (Ṭakṣad, Trakṣad).
kṛṣṇa. B, 308
siṁhavāhana. B, 299
ḍāka.
Buddha° (Buddha). A, 3A58
Ratna°. A, 3A37
Vajra°. C, R3c
Viśva(?)° (Buddha). A, 3B52
Ḍāka (or Ḍākinī)bhayatrāṇa. C, 42b
ḍākamukha (Mahākāla, trakṣad, guhyasādhana). C, 130c
Ḍākinī. Ch. fo-mu. A, 3B3; B, 55
Indra. C, 26a
Ṛkṣavaktra. D, 189
Karma. C, 141c; D, 226
anucarā. C, 71a; C, 118c
uttara. C, 30c
Jñāna. B, 52; C, R14a
Nā-ro (= Nāḍī). A, 3A49; C, 25b; C, 28c
Padma. A, 3A13; C, 141c; D, 227
anucarā. C, 070c; C, 118c
paścima. C, 30b
Buddha. C, 141b; D, 223
anucarā. C, 118a
Maitrī. C, 25c
Ratna. C, 141a; D, 225
anucarā. C, 070b; C, 118a
dakṣiṇa. C, 30a
Loka. C, 32a

Vajra. A, 3A47; C, 29c; C, 141a; D, 224
anucarā. C, 070a
Viśva. C, 31b; D, 228
Vyāghravaktra. D, 187
Samaya. C, 31a
Sarva. C, 31c
Siṁhavaktra. D, 188
Cf. Siṁhavaktrā.
Ḍombī or Ḍombinī (fo-mu). A, 3A59
Cf. Sādhana, pp. 443, 445–446, 479.
Ḍombīpāda. B, 16
mahāsiddha. D, 20
Tathātā(?). A, 4B24
tantrakrama (Kālacakragaruḍa, śabala). C, 79a
Tamodghātamati(?) (Bodhisattva). A, 6A5
Tārā. Cf. Vajratārā. A, 5B10; C, 52a
fo-mu. A, 2A58; A, 3B47
anucarā. C, 36a; C, 37a
aparājita. B, 213
aṣṭabhuja. C, 53c
ārya (śyāma). C, 94b
āryacundā. C, 54b
uḍḍiyāna (pīthīśvarī). C, 45b
uṣṇīṣa. Ch. uṣṇīṣavijaya. B, 210
uṣṇīṣavijaya. C, 95c
kanakavarṇa. Ch. mahāprajñākanaka. B, 209; C, 95b
kapāla (bhaṭṭārikā). C, 54a
kruddha (kālī). Ch. bhṛkuṭī for kālī. B, 219
khadiravaṇī. Ch. "destroys all evils." B, 206; C, 97c; D, 161
In B, 206 change ḥbye to kyi.
Cf. A, 6B32 "purple veṇuvana Tārā."
gandha. C, 49a
gaurī (candrakānti?). C, 95a
candrakānti(?) Ch. "great good autumn moon." B, 208
gaurī. C, 95a
cintāmaṇi. C, 45c
cintāmaṇicakra.
caturbhuja. A, 6B15
sita. B, 230

cīna. A, 6B48
cīnakrama. Ch. cīna. B, 229
cundā (ārya). C, 54b
jagadvaśī(?). B, 216
Tib. ḫgro-ba-ḫgugs-pahi; Ch. shê-fu-shih-chien.
Cf. Āyurvaśī(?) (devī).
jāṅgulī. B, 227
Cf. Jāṅgulī.
trimukhaṣaḍbhuja (sita). A, 6B16
trailokyavijaya. C, 96b
divāśāntarātrikruddha. C, 45a
dīpa. C, 48c
duḥkhadahana. B, 224; C, 101c
durgottāriṇī. A, 6B58; B, 234
dhanadā. B, 233; C, 46b
dhūpa. C, 48b
nīla. A, 5M2; A, 5A33
padma. C, 47b
paripācaka. C, 99c
paripūraṇa. C, 102b
paripūrṇa or pariniṣpanna. B, 226
Ch. maṅgalaparipūrṇa.
pācaka. B, 218
pīta. C, 46c
pīthīśvarī (uḍḍiyāna). C, 45b
puṣpa. C, 48a
praphulla or saṁkusumita. C, 101b
pravīra(?). A, 6B31; B, 207; C, 94c
buddha. C, 47c
bhaṭṭārikā (kapāla). C, 54a
bhṛkuṭī. C, 100a
Cf. Bhṛkuṭī.
maṅgalāloka. C, 99b
maṅgalotpādana. B, 217
mahāśānti. B, 220; C, 100b
mārasūdana. B, 214
rakta (sa-lugs). C, 46a
ratna. C, 47a
rāganisūdana. Ch. hūṁkāramantra. B, 221; C, 100c
vanaratnakrama (sita). C, 2a

varada. C, 98b
vaśitottamada(?). C, 97a
vādipramardaka. C, 96c
vijaya. Ch. trailokyavijaya. B, 212
 sita. Ch. trailokyavijaya. B, 223
vipannirbarhaṇa(?). C, 99a
śokavinodana. Ch. nieh-p'an-chi-mieh. B, 215; C, 98c
śyāma. A, 6M8; C, S7a
 ārya. C, 94b
 kha-che-paṇ-chen-lugs. C, 44b
ṣaḍaṅga (gñan). C, 2c
ṣaḍbhuja (sita). Ch. pāṇḍaravāsinī. B, 232
sarvārthasādhana. A, 6A56; B, 235
 sic Ch. to B, 225.
sita. A, 6M2; A, 6B37; C, S6c; D, 160
 cintāmaṇicakra. B, 230
 trimukhaṣaḍbhuja. A, 6B16
 vanaratnakrama. C, 2a
 vijaya. Ch. trailokyavijaya. B, 223
 ṣaḍbhuja. Ch. pāṇḍaravāsinī. B, 232
 kha-che-paṇ-chen-lugs. C, 44c
 jo-lugs. C, 1a
 gñan-lugs. C, 1c
 ba-riḥi-lugs. C, 1b
siddhida. Ch. sarvārthasādhana. B, 225
siddhisambhava. C, 102a
sukhada. Ch. tu-t'o-shuai-pai. B, 222
sukhasādhana. C, 101a
svapnadeśaka. C, 51c
hūṁsvaranādinī. Ch. ākāśahūṁsvara. B, 211; C, 96a
bKaḥ-gdams-lha-bzhiḥi-naṅ-gi. C, 44a
 Cf. Cintā[maṇi]rājñī (caturbhuja). Ch. adds Tārā. B, 231
 Śrī (garbhasuvarṇasūtra). Has the Tārā mantra. C, 71b
Tithi.
 aṣṭamī. A, 3A7
 daśamī. A, 3A6
 navamī. A, 3A5
 ṣaṣṭhī. A, 3A18
 saptamī. A, 3A8
tīkṣṇa (Mañjuśrī). A, 6A42; B, 157

Tīkṣṇoṣṇīṣa(?) (Buddha). A, 4A61
Tula (deva). A, 3B21
Tejauṣṇīṣa(?) (Buddha). A, 4A42; A, 4A58
Tejorāśyuṣṇīṣa (Bodhisattva). A, 5A24
Cf. Hôbôgirin, pp. 148–149.
Tejo(?)vajra. A, 2B54
Tailikapāda. B, 17
mahāsiddha. D, 17
Trakṣad (= raudrāntaka). C, 116c
Cf. Cordier 2, 208.
Cf. Ṭakṣad and Mahākāla (Ṭakṣad, Trakṣad).
kṛṣṇa. D, 237
Cf. Drag-śad-mgon-po. D, 261
Trayodaśa (deva). A, 3B35
Trisamayavyūha (muni). C, 4c; C, 70b; D, 86
Cf. Cordier 1, 298; 2, 268.
Trailokyarāja. Ch. Trailokyavijayavajra. B, 343
trailokyavaśaṁkara (Avalokiteśvara). A, 6B50; B, 167
trailokyavaśyādhikāra (Mañjughoṣa). B, 154
Trailokyavijaya. D, 222
Buddha. A, 4B30
Bodhisattva. A, 5A60
vajra. A, 4M7
trailokyavijaya (Tārā). C, 96b
Cf. Vijayā.
daṁṣṭrādharā (yo-mu). A, 2A2
daṇḍadhara = beṅ and pang.
yo-mu. A, 2A1
Cf. Bhairava°.
Cf. Cordier 1, 165.
Mahākāla (beṅ).
Daṇḍabhayatrāṇa. C, 41c
Dalai Lama. A, 1B26
Kalpabhadrasamudra. B, 28
Daśākāro vaśī. C, S12a
Cf. Anthropos 22, 964; Abhandlungen der Bayerischen Akademie XXIX, 3, p. 97.
Dānapāramitā. A, 4A16
Digambarā (devī). C, 137a

Diṅnāga. B, 5
bhaṭṭāraka. D, 8
divāśāntarātrikruddha (Tārā). C, 45a
Dīpaṅkara (Buddha). A, 1B29
Dīpatārā. C, 48c
Cf. Sādhana, p. 219.
Dīpā. A, 2B24
Cf. Sādhana, pp. 157, 312, 324.
fo-mu. A, 3A30
Dīpayugmadharā (fo-mu). A, 3A24
dīrghāyus (Maṅgala°). Ch. adds devī. B, 335; C, 142b; D, 272
duḥkhadahana (Tārā). B, 224; C, 101c
Dundubhisvara (Bodhisattva). A, 6A15
Durgatiśodhanarāja. D, 78
Cf. Cordier 1, 283–286.
durgottāriṇī (Tārā). A, 6B58; B, 234
Cf. Sādhana, p. 237.
Durdāntadamaka (Bodhisattva). A, 5A59
Durdharṣa (nīla). D, 283
dūtī(?) or (ceṭī?) (yo-mu). A, 2A3
Dūraṅgamā [bhūmi] (fo-mu). A, 4A18
dṛḍhā (Pṛthivī, devī). B, 323
Cf. Mitra, Sanskrit Buddhist Literature, p. 245.
Devī. C, 116b; D, 232
ti-nu. C, 72a
Probably for Chinese ti-mu = Pṛthivī.
Dyuti(?) (Buddha). A, 4A21
Dvādaśa (deva). A, 3B12
Dvāradharā (fo-mu). A, 3B55
Dvāratālakadharā (fo-mu). A, 3B53
Dhanadā (fo-mu). B, 268
Tārā. B, 233; C, 46b
dhanavardhana (Caturmukha, pīta). C, 132b
Dhanaśrī. Ch. adds Buddha. A, 1A37; B, 107
Jina. D, 122
Dhanus (deva). A, 3A3
Dharmakīrti. B, 6
bhaṭṭāraka. D, 9
Dharmakīrtisāgara. Dhāraṇī adds ghoṣa. C, 14a

Dharmakīrtisāgaraghoṣa. Ch. adds tathāgata.
B, 137; D, 140
Dharmaghoṣatathāgata (Buddha). A, 1B42
Dharmatala. D, 209
upāsaka. B, 288; C, 10c
Dharmadhātu (fo-mu). A, 3A11
Dharmadhātuvāgīśvara. Ch. adds Buddha.
A, 4M1; A, 4A31; B, 67; C, R15b
dvibhuja. A, 6B57
Dharmadhātuvāgīśvara (Mañjughoṣa).
aṣṭabhuja. B, 151
Dharmapratisaṁvit. A, 4B10
Dharmameghā [bhūmi] (fo-mu). A, 4A6
Dharmarāja. A, 2B34; B, 312
Cf. Yama.
antarasādhana. D, 239
karmayama (nīla). C, 137b
kṛṣṇa. A, 5B26
guhyasādhana. D, 240
bāhyasādhana. D, 238
Dharmavajrī (fo-mu). A, 4A22; B, 263
Dharmavaśitā. A, 4B23
Dharmasāgarāgra(?) matavikrīḍitābhijñārāja. B, 138
Ch. tathāgata for rāja; Tib. mchog-gi-blos for agra(?)mati
Cf. Agra(?) matirājatathāgata (Buddha). A, 1B43
Abhijñārāja. C, 14b; D, 141
dhāraṇīvinirgata.
Mārīcī. C, 69a
Vasudhārā (devī). C, 111b
Dhītika. B, 294
Cf. Rockhill, Life, p. 170.
Dhūpatārā. C, 48b
Cf. Sādhana, p. 219.
Dhūpā. A, 2B23
Cf. Sādhana, pp. 157, 312, 324.
fo-mu. A, 3A40
Dhūmāvatī (devī). B, 310; C, 134a; D, 245
Ch. "able to burn up all enemies."
Cf. Cordier 1, 130–131; 2, 200.
Dhṛtarāṣṭra. B, 327; C, 11b; C, 140a; D, 284

Dhyānapāramitā. A, 4A3
Dhyānābhyudgatarāja (Buddha). A, 1B56
Dhvajā [maṅgala]. D, 296
Dhvajāgra(?) (Buddha). A, 4A41; A, 6A41
Dhvajāgrakeyūrā. B, 260 (Tib.); C, 92a; D, 191
fo-mu. A, 6A38; B, 260 (Ch.)
Nakṣatrarāja (Buddha). A, 1B18
Cf. Weller 15.
Nakṣatrarājavikrīḍita (Buddha). A, 1A7
Cf. Saddharma, p. 424.
nagna (Mahākāla, zaṅs-gri-can). C, 127c
Nanda (nāgarāja). D, 289
Nandīśvara(?) (deva). A, 3B36; A, 5A1
nartakavara.
Vaiśravaṇa. B, 324; C, 110b
rakta. C, 103c
navadeva.
Uṣṇīṣavijayā. C, 82b
Vaiśravaṇa (mahāpīta). C, 102c
Navaśikhin(?) (Buddha). Tib. gçug-dgu. A, 4M9
nāgaparivāra (aṣṭa, Vaiśravaṇa, raudra). C, 105a–c
Nāgabhayatrāṇa. C, 42a
nāgarakṣa (Mañjuśrī). C, 81b
nāgarāja.
Apalāla. C, 115a
Upananda. D, 291
Nanda. D, 289
Varuṇa. D, 290
sita. A, 5B46
nāgavāhana (Jambhala, sita). B, 355
Nāgasena. A, 1B3; B, 285; C, 9c; D, 206
Nāgārjuna. B, 1
śrīnātha. D, 5
Nāgārjunakrama.
Mahākāla (caturbhuja). C, 119b
Gur(= Mahākāla)-yum-can. C, 122c
Nāgī.
sita. A, 5B47
re-ma-ti. C, 135c
Nāgīkarmakarī (anucarā). C, 59c

Nāgeśvararāja. Ch. adds Buddha. A, 1A31; B, 85; C, 16b
Cf. Cordier 2, 66.
Jina. D, 100; D, 134
Nāḍapāda. B, 18
Cf. Cordier 1, 29, 87, 233; 2, 203, 228.
mahāsiddha. D, 16
Nāḍīḍākinī.
Cf. Nā-ro (ḍākinī).
Cf. Cordier 2, 269.
Nātha(= mGon-po).
Cf. Mahākāla.
nāmasaṁgīti (Mañjughoṣa, caturbhuja). B, 155
nāmasaṁgīti (Mañjuśrī, Bodhisattva). A, 6B47
Nārāyaṇa. Ch. adds Buddha. A, 1A53; B, 103
Cf. Weller 97, 251.
Jina. D, 118
Nārāyaṇa (deva). A, 5B50
Nārāyaṇī (devī). A, 5B30
Nā-ro (= Nāḍī) (ḍākinī). A, 3A49; C, 25b; C, 28c
nidhi (Mahākāla, beṅ). C, 124a
Tib. gter-ma.
Niruktipratisaṁvit. A, 4B11
Nirbhayavigatatamorāja(?) Ch. adds Buddha. B, 125
nirmāṇakāya (Amitāyus). C, 63b
nīlakaṇṭha (Lokeśvara). B, 169
īśvara (= Lokeśvara) Avalokiteśvara (Bodhisattva).
A, 6B52
nīladaṇḍa.
Cf. Cordier 2, 260.
krodha. D, 216
vajra. A, 2A12
nīlāmbaradhara.
Vajrapāṇi. B, 72; C, 55a; D, 170
Cf. Cordier 1, 198–199.
ḫgro-bzaṅ-lugs. C, 56c
Cf. Vajrapāṇi (Buddha, shan-hsing). A, 5M6
Tib. ḫgro-ba-bzaṅ-po.
nīlāśva (Vaiśravaṇa).
kṛṣṇa. C, 106a
raktaśūla. C, 103a

Nṛtyā. A, 2B9
Cf. Sādhana, pp. 157, 312, 324.
fo-mu. A, 3A48; A, 4B45
Nairātmā. Ch. fo-mu. A, 2A60; B, 53
Cf. Vajranairātmā.
pañcadeva.
Amoghapāśa (ba-ri-lugs). C, 34c
Avalokiteśvara (cintāmaṇi). C, 38b
Jambhala (sita, jo-boḥi-lugs). C, 108c
Pratisarā. C, S3c
pañcabuddha (Śaṁvararājabuddha). A, 3A33
pañjaranātha (= Gur-mgon). Cf. Mahākāla (gur).
Cf. Cordier 2, 193, 538.
paṇḍaka(?) (Mahākāla, trakṣad). C, 130a
Tib. ma-niṅ-ma.
Paṇḍitasiddhasvāmin. B, 23; C, 0c; D, 42
Tib. mKhas-grub-rje.
Padmacaryāpāramitā. A, 4B36
Padmajyotis (Jina). D, 121
Padmajyotirvikrīḍitābhijña. Ch. adds Buddha.
A, 1A38; B, 106
Padmaḍākinī (fo-mu). A, 3A13; C, 141c; D, 227
anucarā. C, 070c; C, 118c
paścima. C, 30b
Padmatārā. C, 47b
Cf. Sādhana, p. 219.
padmadhara (Bhairavajra). A, 2A6; A, 2B51
Cf. Cordier 1, 165.
Padmadharā (fo-mu). A, 3A12
Padmanarteśvara.
Avalokiteśvara.
dvibhuja. B, 164
Bodhisattva. A, 6A9
aṣṭadaśabhuja. Ch. adds Avalokiteśvara. B, 165
Hayagrīva. Ch. adds vajra. B, 62
go-chaḥi. C, 19a
padmapāṇi (Avalokiteśvara). C, 87b
padmavikāsana (Avalokiteśvara). B, 159
Cf. Cordier 1, 313; Bhattacharyya, p. 51.
Padmā [maṅgala]. D, 298

Panthaka. A, 1B2; B, 284; C, 9b; D, 205
Paramapitṛ. Tib. Pha-dam-pa. D, 34
Cf. Cordier 2, 175.
Paramāśva (go-chaḫi). C, 20a
Parikīrtitanāmaśrī (Jina). D, 124
Cf. Suparikīrtitanāmaśrī.
paripācaka (Tārā). C, 99c
paripūraṇa (Tārā). C, 102b
paripūrṇa or pariniṣpanna (Tārā). Ch. maṅgalaparipūrṇa. B, 226
Cf. Niṣpannatārā, Sādhana, p. 352.
Pariṣkāravaśitā(?). A, 4B20
Parṇaśabarī. C, S7c; D, 165
kṛṣṇa. C, 76b
caturbhuja. Ch. correctly dvibhuja. B, 250
nīla. C, 76a
pīta. C, 75b
rakta. C, 75c
śyāma. C, 76c
ṣaḍbhuja (fo-mu). A, 6B3; B, 249
Parvatadhararāja (Buddha). A, 1B27
pācaka (Tārā). B, 218
Pāṇḍaravāsinī.
devī. C, 89c
fo-mu. A, 2A59; A, 3B46; A, 5M8; A, 5A48
Cf. Ch. to B, 232.
Pāṇḍubhūmipaṇḍita = Sa-skya-paṇḍi-ta (Ānandadhvaja). D, 38
pāramitā.
Upāyakauśalya. A, 4A2
Kṣānti. A, 4A14
Jñāna. A, 4A17
Dāna. A, 4A16
Dhyāna. A, 4A3
Padmacaryā. A, 4B36
Prajñā. A, 4B34
Praṇidhāna. A, 4A1
Bala. A, 4B33
Vajracaryā. A, 4B35
Vīrya. A, 4A4
Śīla. A, 4A15

Pārvatī(= dmag-zor-ma).
Cf. Cordier 1, 128–129.
kāmadhātvīśvarī. D, 248
śrīmatī (rājñī). C, 134b
Pāśadharā (= Pāśī, Pāśinī).
Cf. Sādhana, pp. 198, 229.
fo-mu. A, 3A56
yo-mu. A, 2A16
Piṇḍolabharadvāja. A, 1B1; B, 283; C, 9a; D, 204
Piśāca (śṛgālamukha). C, 133c
pīthīśvarī (Uḍḍiyānatārā). C, 45b
Cf. Cordier 1, 117; 2, 268.
Pukkasī (fo-mu). A, 3A41; A, 3B16
Cf. Sādhana, pp. 310, 445–446, 479, 596.
Puṇyeśvarī(?). A, 5B21
Puṣpagaruḍa. A, 3B42
Puṣpatārā. C, 48a
Cf. Sādhana, p. 219.
Puṣpā. A, 2B22
Cf. Sādhana, pp. 157, 312, 324.
fo-mu. A, 3A53
Pūrṇabhadra (yakṣa). B, 354
pūrṇamatistotrasādhanakīrtita (Mañjughoṣa). C, 66a
Pṛthivī (devī). A, 5B44; D, 279
Cf. A, 5B45 T'u-ti and C, 72a Devī (ti-nu = ti-mu?).
dṛḍhā. B, 323
Prajñākūṭa (Bodhisattva) A, 4B4
Prajñākhaḍga. C, S12c
prajñācakra.
Mañjughoṣa.
sita. C, 66c
daṅ-po. B, 156
Prajñāntakavajra. A, 2A52
Cf. Sādhana, p. 137.
Prajñāpāramitā. A, 4B34
Prajñāpāramitā (fo-mu). A, 6A61; C, S11b; D, 158
caturbhuja. B, 252
dvibhuja. B, 251
pīta. C, 67b
sita. C, 67a

prajñālokakṛtya (Vārāhī, sita). C, 32b; C, 32c
Cf. Cordier 1, 60; 2, 118.
Cf. B, 270. Tib. has pad-dkar for phag-dkar; Ch. Vajravārāhī.
Prajñāsiṁha.
Cf. Svāmiprajñāsiṁha.
Praṇidhānapāramitā. A, 4A1
Praṇidhānamati. D, 155
Cf. Waddell, p. 358.
Praṇidhānavaśitā. A, 4B9
Pratibhānapratisaṁvit. A, 4B13
pratisaṁvit.
Artha. A, 4B12
Dharma. A, 4B10
Nirukti. A, 4B11
Pratibhāna. A, 4B13
Pratisarā (fo-mu). A, 6M9; A, 6B39; B, 205; C, 52b; C, R16b; D, 176
dvibhuja. B, 258
pañcadeva. C, S3c
rdo-rje-bur-nas-gsuṅs-paḫi. C, 74c
Pratyaṅgirā. D, 190
Cf. Mahāpratyaṅgirā.
pratyālīḍha (Bhairavavajra). A, 2B32
Prathamacittotpādasaṁśayacchedika(?). B, 126
Ch. first compassion cuts doubts.
Pradīpa (Buddha). A, 1B7
Cf. Weller 31.
Pradyota (Buddha). A, 1A28
Cf. Weller 7.
praphulla or saṁkusumita (Tārā). C, 101b
Tib. rab-rgyas.
Prabhākarī [bhūmi] (fo-mu). A, 4A26
Prabhāketu. D, 154
Cf. Waddell, p. 358.
Prabhāmati or Prajñāloka (Bodhisattva). A, 6A17
Prabhāsaśrī. Ch. adds Buddha. A, 1A55; B, 101
Jina. D, 116
Prabhūta (Buddha). A, 1B8
Cf. Weller 32. Tib. mthu-ldan.
Pramuditā [bhūmi] (fo-mu). A, 4A28

pravīra (?) (Tārā). A, 6B31; B, 207; C, 94c
prāṇasādhana (Jambhala, rakta). D, 268
Prāṇasādhanalohakīlasvayambhūrājñī (devī).
C, 134c
Bakula. A, 1B59; B, 280; C, 8a; D, 201
Balapāramitā. A, 4B33
bahudeva (Jambhala, ekavīrasādhanavinirgata).
C, 108a
bāhyasādhana.
Dharmarāja. D, 238
Zhaṅ-blon-rdo-rje (mārajit). C, 112c
Birbapa.
Cf. Virūpa.
Buddhakapāla. Ch. of B, 51 adds vajra.
A, 3B31; B, 51; C, R12c; C, R13a; D, 69
Buddha. A, 3M2
Cf. Cordier 2, 538.
Buddhaḍāka (Buddha). A, 3A58
Buddhaḍākinī. C, 141b; D, 223
anucarā. C, 118a
Buddhatārā. C, 47c
Cf. Sādhana, p. 219.
Buddhapālita (bhaṭṭāraka). D, 23
Cf. Tāranātha, p. 135.
Buddhabodhi. A, 4B25
Buddhalocanā (fo-mu). A, 2A61; A, 3B57; A, 5M9; C, 70a
Buddhoṣṇīṣa (Bodhisattva). A, 5A38
Budha (deva). A, 3A4
Bu-ston (sarvajña). D, 37
Bekçe or Begçe. Ch. Mahāraktamahākāla.
B, 336; D, 254
Bodhivajrasattva. sic Tib. B, 193
Ch. Vajrasattva (Bodhisattva).
bodhisattvaveṣa (Vajrapāṇi). D, 90
Brahmajyotis (Jina). D, 120
Brahmajyotirvikrīḍitābhijña. Ch. adds Buddha.
A, 1A39; B, 105
Brahmadatta. Ch. adds Buddha. A, 1A61; B, 95
Jina. D, 110

Brahman. B, 329; D, 278
deva. A, 3B13; A, 5A15; A, 5B43
Brahman. Ch. adds Buddha. A, 1A41; B, 94
Jina. D, 109
brāhmaṇarūpadhara (Mahākāla). D, 241
Cf. B, 307 Zhal-bram-gzugs. Ch. Brāhmaṇamahākāla.
brāhmaṇaśrīdharakrama (Vajravārāhī). C, 28b
ḫBrom-ston. B, 20
jayākara. D, 28
bhagavant (= bcom-ldan and legs-ldan).
bhayanāśana. Ch. vajra for bhagavant. B, 358
Mahākāla. B, 302; D, 256–258
Cf. Cordier 2, 92.
bhrātṛtraya. C, 124b
bhaginītraya (dByug-gum or gu-ma). C, 115b
bhaṭṭārikā.
Kapālatārā. C, 54a
Thod-pa-rgyan. C, 72b
Bhadra. A, 1B16; B, 277; C, 7a; D, 198
Bhadrapāla (Bodhisattva). A, 4B61
Bhadraśrī. Ch. adds Buddha. A, 1A58; B, 98
Jina. D, 113
bhadrasvareśvararāja(?) (Mañjughoṣa). B, 152
Ch. om. rāja.
Bhadrākarā(?) hsi-mu. A, 6B12
bhayatrāṇa.
Cf. IA 22, 9–10.
Agni°. C, 40b
Cora°. C, 42c
Jala°. C, 40c
Ḍāka° or Ḍākinī°. C, 42b
Daṇḍa°. C, 41c
Nāga°. C, 42a
Siṁha°. C, 41a
Hasti°. C, 41b
Bhayadavajra. A, 2B60
bhayanāśana.
Cf. Cordier 2, 225–226.
bhagavant. Ch. vajra for bhagavant. B, 358
Cf. Krodhabhayanāśana (Śaṁvara).

Bhinnakleśa(?) (Buddha). A, 1B57
  Cf. Sakaki 419.
  Cf. Apagatakleśa. Weller 267.
Bhūtaḍāmara. C, R15c; D, 84
  Vajrapāni. B, 71; C, 57b
   anuttara. C, S11c
   Buddha. A, 5M7
   gsar-ma. C, 57c
[bhūmi].
  Acalā. A, 4A8
  Abhimukhī. A, 4A19
  Dūraṅgamā. A, 4A18
  Dharmameghā. A, 4A6
  Prabhākarī. A, 4A26
  Pramuditā. A, 4A28
  Vimalā. A, 4A27
  Samantaprabhā. A, 4A5
  Sādhumatī. A, 4A7
  Sudurjayā. A, 4A20
Bhṛkuṭī. Cf. Sakaki 9316. A, 5B12; C, S9a
  Cf. Vajrabhṛkuṭī.
  anucarā. C, 35c; C, 36c; C, 37c
  Tārā. C, 100a
  fo-mu. Tib. of B, 256 devī. A, 5A32; B, 256
   Cf. Ch. of B, 219.
Bhairava (= Yamāri, Yamāntaka). Ch. adds vajra.
  A, 2B27; B, 42
   Cf. Vajrabhairava.
   Buddha. A, 2M7
  īrṣyā. A, 2A26; A, 2B40
  ekavīra. A, 2B29; B, 46
  kṛṣṇāri. A, 2B31
   Cf. Kṛṣṇāri. Ch. adds Bhairavavajra. B, 43
    Kṛṣṇārivajrabuddha. A, 2M1
  khaḍgadhara. A, 2A5; A, 2B52
  ghaṇṭādhara. A, 2A8
  daṇḍadhara Tib. beṅ. A, 2A7; A, 2B50
  padmadhara. A, 2A6; A, 2B51
  pratyālīḍha. A, 2B32
  mātsarya(?). A, 2A28; A, 2B38

mudgaradhara. A, 2B49
moha. A, 2A29; A, 2B37
rakta (Buddha). A, 2M8
Cf. Raktāri (= Rakt[ayam]āri).
rāga. A, 2A27; A, 2B39
vairocana. A, 2B28
ṣaṇmukha. A, 2B30
Buddha. A, 2M2
Cf. Ṣaṇmukha. Ch. adds Bhairavavajra. B, 44
Cf. Cordier 2, 540.
saṁkṣipta. C, 24c
Bhaiṣajyaguru. C, 13b
Dhāraṇī adds vaiḍūryaprabhārāja.
Bhaiṣajyagurutathāgata (Buddha). A, 1B37
Bhaiṣajyaguruvaiḍūryaprabhārāja. Ch. adds tathāgata.
B, 139; D, 142
Bhaiṣajyadevī. D, 276
bhramarasvara(?) (Mañjuśrībodhisattva). A, 6B46
bhrātṛtraya (Mahākāla, bhagavant). C, 124b
Makara (deva). A, 3A17
[Maṅgala]kalaśī. D, 297
[Maṅgala]cakrā. D, 299
[Maṅgala]cchattrā. D, 293
Maṅgaladīrghāyus. Ch. adds devī. B, 335; C, 142b; D, 272
[Maṅgala]dhvajā. D, 296
[Maṅgala]padmā. D, 298
[Maṅgala]śaṅkhā. D, 294
[Maṅgala]śrīvatsā. D, 295
[Maṅgala]survarṇamatsyā. D, 292
maṅgalāloka (Tārā). C, 99b
maṅgalotpādana (Tārā). B, 217
Mañjughoṣa. D, 145
antarasādhana. A, 2A46; B, 31
arapacana. C, S3a
raktapīta (sa-lugs). C, 65c
kṛṣṇa. C, 80a
guhyasādhana. B, 148
trailokyavaśyādhikāra. B, 154
dharmadhātuvāgīśvara (aṣṭabhuja). B, 151

nāmasaṁgīti (caturbhuja). B, 155
Cf. Mañjuśrībodhisattva (nāmasaṁgīti). A, 6B47
pūrṇamatistotrasādhanakīrtita. C, 66a
prajñācakra.
sita. C, 66c
daṅ-po. B, 156
bhadrasvareśvararāja(?). B, 152
raktapīta. D, 88
arapacana (sa-lugs). C, 65c
vādirāṭ. B, 150
vādisiṁha. C, 66b; C, S3b; D, 92
siṁhanāda. B, 149
sita. B, 145; C, S2c; D, 91
prajñācakra. C, 66c
kha-che-paṇ-chen-lugs. C, 65b
sthiracakra. B, 147
Mañjughoṣa (bhaṭṭāraka). D, 3
Mañjuvajra.
guhyasamāja. A, 2A32; B, 30; C, 17a; C, R1a; D, 68
Buddha. A, 2M4
vairocana. A, 2A31; C, R1b
Mañjuśrī (Bodhisattva). A, 1M4; A, 1A12; A, 2A25; A, 6A29; A, 6A33
anucara. C, 16c
ārya. C, 93b
kumārabhūta. B, 146; D, 93
guhya [samāja] (Buddha). A, 2M3; A, 4M8; A, 4A32
guhyasādhana. A, 2M6; A, 2A30
tīkṣṇa. A, 6A42; B, 157
nāgarakṣa. C, 81b
nāmasaṁgīti. A, 6B47
bhramarasvara(?). A, 6B46
rājalīlā. A, 6B45; B, 153
siṁhavāhana. A, 6A32
sita. A, 6B42
Mañjuśrīmitra. D, 21
Cf. Cordier 1, 268–269.
Maṇidhārin. C, 33a
Buddha. A, 1B20
Maṇibhadra (yakṣa). C, 110a

mativardhana (Mahākāla, pīta). C, 0110b; C, 117b
manohara (Vasudhārā). C, 112b
Tib. yid-ḥphrog.
Mantrānudhāraṇī (fo-mu). A, 6A58; B, 204
Sādhana, pp. 402, 408 has Mahāmantrānusāriṇī.
Cf. Mahāmantrā.
Mar-pa (bhaṭṭāraka). D, 32
Markaṭadeva(?) (Bodhisattva). A, 5A12
mahākāruṇika (Ekādaśamukha). C, S5b; D, 95
Mahākāla (deva). A, 3B18
Mahākāla (= mGon-po).
Cf. Karmanātha, Caturmukha, Kāmarāja.
āyuṣpati. B, 316; D, 231
śyāma. C, 118b
ekavīra (kartarīdhara). C, 125b
kartarīdhara. C, S12b
ekavīra. C, 125b
rakta (dakṣiṇapaścima). C, 125c
kha-che-paṇ-chen-lugs. C, 126b
trakṣad (sbrags-sgrub-ma). C, 129b
ẓñā-na-lugs. C, 127a
kṛṣṇa (beṅ, zaṅs-gri-can). C, 127b
Cf. Ṭakṣad (kṛṣṇa). B, 308
Trakṣad (kṛṣṇa). D, 237
gaṇapati (siṁhāsana). C, 128a
guhyasādhana (trakṣad, ḍākamukha). C, 130c
caturbhuja. B, 306; D, 243
anucarā Devīcaṇḍikā. C, 121a
nāgārjunakrama. C, 119b
mahāsiddhaśāntiguptakrama. C, 119a
rgva-loḥi-lugs. C, 119c
ḥçhal-lugs-kyi. C, 120a
lugs-gñis-gcig-tu-sgril-baḥi. C, 120b
cintāmaṇi.
rakta. C, 0110c; C, 117c
sita B, 317; C, 0110a; C, 117a; D, 229
nagna (zaṅs-gri-can). C, 127c
Nāgārjunakrama (caturbhuja) C, 119b
pañjara (= mGon-po-gur = Pañjaranātha).
Cf. gur below.

paṇḍaka(?) (trakṣad). C, 130a
pīta (mativardhana). C, 0110b; C, 117b
brāhmaṇarūpadhara. D, 241
Cf. Zhal-bram-gzugs. Ch. Brāhmaṇamahākāla. B, 307
bhagavant. B, 302; D, 256–258
bhrātṛtraya. C, 124b
mativardhana (pīta). C, 0110b; C, 117b
mahādevaśrījvāla (jo-boḫi-lugs). C, 125a
mahāsiddhaśāntiguptakrama (caturbhuja). C, 119a
rakta.
kartarīdhara (dakṣiṇapaścima). C, 125c
cintāmaṇi. C, 0110c; C, 117c
rkaṅ-gliṅ-can (= with thigh-bone trumpet). C, 120c
raudrāntaka.
Cf. ṭakṣad, trakṣad, drag-śad below.
vyāghravāhana. B, 301; C, 123b; D, 259
ṣaḍbhuja. B, 297; D, 230
śyāma.
āyuṣpati. C, 118b
zaṅs-gri-can-gyi. C, 126c
sarvāntarāyasaṁgrasana (or sarvavighnavināyaka). C, 116b
siṁhāsana (gaṇapati). C, 128a
siṁhavāhana.
trakṣad (jo-boḫi-lugs). C, 129a
Cf. Ṭakṣad (siṁhavāhana). B, 299
sita (cintāmaṇi). B, 317; C, 0110a; C, 117a; D, 229
gur (= pañjara). B, 305
Cf. Cordier 2, 193, 538.
Cf. Gur (ekānta, rṅog-lugs). C, 123a
Gur-gyi-mgon-po. D, 242
Gur-mgon (aṣṭadeva). C, 122a
Gur-mgon (kīlapāda). C, 122b
Gur-mgon-lcam-dral (= brother sister) C, 121c
Gur-yum-can (nāgārjunakrama). C, 122c
ṭakṣad-? (= raudrāntaka). B, 300
Cf. Ṭakṣad.

trakṣad (= raudrāntaka).
  Cf. Trakṣad.
  kartarīdhara (sbrags-sgrub-ma). C, 129b
  guhyasādhana (ḍākamukha). C, 130c
  paṇḍaka(?). C, 130a
  siṁhavāhana (jo-boḫi-lugs). C, 129a
  rkaṅ-thaṅ-ma (= on foot). C, 129c

  gños-lugs. C, 128b
  dvags-poḫi-lugs. C, 128c
  ḫbroṅ-zhal-can (= with head of wild yak). C, 130b
    Cf. ḫBroṅ-zhal-can. Ch. adds Mahākāla. B, 298
drag-śad (= raudrāntaka). D, 261
  Equivalent to ṭakṣad and trakṣad above.
beṅ (= daṇḍa). B, 303; D, 255
  dKaḫ-ma. For dKaḫ-bzlog-ma (= Gaurī, Umā, Pārvatī)? C, 123c
  gTer-ma (= nidhi). C, 124a
  zaṅs-gri-can (kṛṣṇa). C, 127b
bzhi-sbrags. C, 126a
zaṅs-gri-can-gyi (= with copper knife).
  nagna. C, 127c
  śyāma. C, 126c
  beṅ (kṛṣṅa). C, 127b
aṅ-gho-ra. C, 124c
  Cf. Śailadevanātha. D, 260
    Bekçe. D, 254
    Begçe. Ch. Mahāraktamahākāla. B, 336
Mahākālavajra. A, 2B59
Mahākāśyapa. B, 290
Mahākrodha. C, 84a
mahācakra.
  Vajrapāṇi. A, 2A33; B, 59
    Buddha. A, 2M9
  Śrī. D, 64
Mahājina or Mahājaya (Bodhisattva). A, 5A27
mahādevaśrījvāla (Mahākāla, jo-boḫi-lugs). C, 125a
  Tib. lha-chen-dpal-ḫbar.

mahāpañcama (Jinendra). D, 46
Cf. Vāgīśvarasumatisāgara. B, 26
mahāpīta (Vaiśravaṇa). B, 322
navadeva. C, 102c
Mahāpratyaṅgirā (fo-mu). A, 6A39; B, 259; D, 220
Mahāprabha (Buddha). A, 1A17
Cf. Weller 18.
Mahābala. C, S9b
Cf. Sādhana, p. 507.
krodha. Ch. Mahābalavajra. B, 342; D, 218
Cf. Cordier 2, 64.
Buddha. A, 1A8
Cf. Weller 14.
vajra. A, 2A11; A, 6B43
Mahābāhu (Buddha). A, 1A18
Cf. Weller 13.
mahābhūmika (Avalokiteśvara). A, 6A11
Cf. Avalokiteśvara (bhu-kham-dmar-po). B, 172
Mahāmati (Bodhisattva). A, 6A19
Mahāmantrā. D, 177
Cf. Mantrānudhāraṇī.
Mahāmāyā. Ch. adds vajra. B, 50; C, 17c; C, R13b; D, 67
vajra (Buddha). A, 3M7
Mahāmāyūrī (fo-mu). A, 6A60; B, 202; D, 178
mahāyakṣasenāpati.
Ê-ni-lo. A, 6A1
Chên-ta-lo. A, 6B19
Chu-tu-lo. A, 6B20
Kung-p'i-lu (= Kumbhīra). A, 6A4
Cf. JA 1915, 1, 57.
Mi-ch'i-lo. A, 6A2
Mo-ni-lo. A, 6B33
P'i-chieh-lo. A, 6B21
Cf. Hôbôgirin, p. 70.
Po-ch'ai-lo. A, 6A3
Cf. Hôbôgirin, p. 56.
Po-hu-lo. A, 6B18
P'o-i-lo. A, 6B36
So-ni-lo. A, 6B34

Yin-t'o-lo (= Indra). A, 6B35
Cf. JA 1915, 1, 38.
mahārakta (Gaṇapati). B, 360; C, 3c
Ch. Raktagaṇapatirājavajra.
Cf. Cordier 2, 87.
mahārāja (Vaiśravaṇa). Ch. devarāja. B, 320
Mahārājavarā(?) hsi-mu. A, 6B11
mahāryaśrī (Atīśa). D, 29
Mahālakṣmī (devī). C, 111a
Mahāvajradhara. A, 2A36
mahāvidyā (Grahamātṛkā). C, R17a
mahāśānti (Tārā). B, 220; C, 100b
Mahāśītavatī. D, 179
Mahāsāhasrapramardanī (fo-mu). B, 201; D, 175
mahāsiddha.
Ajapālipāda(?) D, 19
Kṛṣṇacārin (or Kṛṣṇācārya or Kṛṣṇapāda or Kānhapāda). D, 15
Cf. B, 14.
Ghaṇṭāpāda. D, 14
Cf. A, 3A36; B, 13.
Ḍombīpāda. D, 20
Cf. B, 16.
Tailikapāda. D, 17
Cf. B, 17.
Nāḍapāda. D, 16
Cf. B, 18.
Maitrīpāda. D, 18
Lalitavajra. D, 13
Cf. B, 15.
Lūhipāda. D, 12
Cf. B, 12.
Śāntiguptakrama (Mahākāla, caturbhuja). C, 119a
Śābaripāda. D, 10
Cf. A, 2B26
Sarahapāda. D, 11
Cf. B, 11.
Cf. siddheśvara (Hūṁkāra). D, 27
Mahāsukha (Buddha). A, 4B37
mahāsuvarṇa (Vaiśravaṇa). D, 263

Mahāsthāmaprāpta (Bodhisattva). A, 5A31
Maheśvara (deva). A, 5A17
Mahodgatoṣṇīṣa(?) (Bodhisattva). A, 5A54
Cf. Hodgson, p. 34.
Mahoṣṭhavajra. A, 5A26
Mahoṣṇīṣa (Buddha). A, 4A54; A, 4A59
Cf. Hôbôgirin, pp. 148–149.
mātsarya(?) (Bhairavavajra). A, 2A28; A, 2B38
Māmakī. Ch. fo-mu; Tib. devī. A, 3B45; A, 5M1; A, 5A45; C, 89b
māyājālakrama (Avalokiteśvara). B, 170
mārajit (Zhaṅ-blon-rdo-rje). B, 353
antarasādhana. C, 113a
guhyasādhana. C, 113b
bāhyasādhana. C, 112c
mārasūdana (Tārā). B, 214
Mārī(?) (re-ma-ti). Tib. bdud-mo. C, 135b
Dhāraṇī gives Mahākāli re-ma-tī.
Mārīcī (fo-mu). A, 6M1; A, 6A43; C, 52c; C, 97b; C, R16a; C, S4a; D, 163
aṣṭabhuja. B, 243
daśabhuja. B, 242; A, 6B61
dvādaśabhuja. A, 6B2
dvibhuja. B, 244
dhāraṇīvinirgata. C, 69a
pīta. A, 6A40
śyāmāśva. C, 91c
vajradhātvīśvarī. B, 246
sūcisūtradhara. C, 68c
bdud-rçuḥi-ma. A, 6B1; B, 245
Ch. pi-tsu "with jade girdle."
Mālyā. A, 2B7
Cf. Sādhana, pp. 157, 312, 324.
fo-mu. A, 3B27; A, 4B56
Milaraspa. A, 1A35
bhaṭṭāraka. D, 31
Mīna (deva). A, 3A27
Mukundadharā (fo-mu). A, 3B50
Muktiskandha (Buddha). A, 1A16
Cf. Weller 19.

mudgaradhara (Bhairavavajra). A, 2B49
  Cf. Cordier 1, 165.
Muni.
  aṣṭadaśasthaviraparivāra. C, S1a–c
  Trisamayavyūha. C, 4c; C, 70b; D, 86
  Buddha. A, 1A27
    Cf. Weller 8.
  Meruśikhara. C, 69b
    Dhāraṇī adds kūṭaprabhūrāja.
  vajrāsana (gço-ḫkhor-gsum). C, 4b
Munīndra. C, 5a
Meruśikhara (muni). C, 69b
  Dhāraṇī adds kūṭaprabhūrāja.
Maitrīḍākinī. C, 25c
Maitrīpāda (mahāsiddha). D, 18
Maitreya (Buddha). A, 1B28
    Cf. Weller 5.
  standing statue. A, 6A48
Maitreya. Ch. usually adds Bodhisattva.
  A, 1M1; A, 1A2; A, 2A53; A, 4B46; A, 6A18; C, 67c; C, 85a; D, 151
  anucara. C, 16a
  caturbhuja. B, 194
  trimukhacaturbhuja. A, 6A13
  dvibhuja. B, 195
Maitreya (bhaṭṭāraka). C, S4b; D, 1
moha (Bhairavavajra). A, 2A29; A, 2B37
Mohinī (go-chaḫi). C, 21a
  Cf. Sādhana, p. 498.
Maudgalyāyana. A, 1B23
yakṣa.
  Aparājita. C, 113c
  Pūrṇabhadra. B, 354
  Maṇibhadra. C, 110a
  Re-ma-ti. C, 136a
Yakṣakarmakarī (anucarā). C, 60a
Yakṣadeva. A, 3B22
Yakṣāḥ (aṣṭa, anucarāḥ). C, 104a
yakṣinī (Hārītī). C, 92c
Yakṣiṇyaḥ (aṣṭa, anucarāḥ). C, 104c

Yama.
Cf. Dharmarāja, Karmayama.
Cf. Bran-bdud-gśin-rje-nag-po. C, 139a
Yamakarmakarī (anucarā). C, 59b
Yamāntakavajra. A, 2A22; A, 2B45
Cf. Sādhana, p. 137.
Yamāri or Yamāntaka (= Bhairavavajra).
kṛṣṇāri. C, R2a; D, 71
Cf. Kṛṣṇāri.
krodha. D, 212
rakta. Ch. Raktabhairavavajra. B, 45; D, 72
Cf. Raktāri.
Yaśaḥketu or Yaśodhvaja (Buddha). A, 1A5
Cf. Weller 17, 186.
Yaśodharā(?). A, 5B9
Yāminī or Yāmī (go-chaḫi). C, 20c
Cf. Sādhana, p. 498.
Yuddhajaya. Ch. adds Buddha. A, 1A52; B, 112
Jina. D, 127
Yuvarājasvāmin. B, 22; C, 0a; D, 40
Tib. rGyal-çhab-rje.
Yogāmbara. Ch. adds Buddha. A, 3M1; A, 3B32;
B, 58; C, R13c
Cf. Cordier 1, 100.
Raktapa (= Heruka). C, R12a
Cf. Cordier 1, 32.
raktaśūla (Vaiśravaṇa). B, 321; D, 262
nīlāśva. C, 103a
Raktāri (= Raktayamāri). C, 24b
Cf. Yamāri (rakta).
Ratnacandra. C, 15a
Dhāraṇī completes name to correspond to B, 134.
Cf. Ābhāsvara(?)tathāgata (Buddha). A, 1B39
Ratnacandrapadmapratimaṇḍitapaṇḍita(?)tejaḥsvaraghoṣarāja.
B, 134
Svaraghoṣarāja. D, 137
Ratnacandra. Ch. adds Buddha. A, 1A44; B, 91
Cf. Weller 273.
Jina. D, 106

Ratnacandrapadmapratimaṇḍitapaṇḍita(?)tejaḥsvaraghoṣarāja (Buddha). Tib. to B, 134
Ch. has Ratnacandrajñānapratimaṇḍitābhāsvareśvararājatathāgata.
Cf. Ābhāsvara(?) tathāgata (Buddha). A, 1B39
Ratnacandra. C, 15a
Svaraghoṣarāja. D, 137
Ratnacandraprabha. Ch. adds Buddha. A, 1A46; B, 89
Jina. D, 104
Ratnacchattrodgata (Buddha). B, 123
Ratnacchattrodgataprabha (Buddha). A, 1B54
Ratnaḍāka. A, 3A37
Ratnaḍākinī. C, 141a; D, 225
anucarā. C, 070b; C, 118a
dakṣiṇa. C, 30a
Ratnatārā. C, 47a
Cf. Sādhana, p. 219.
Ratnapadma (Jina). D, 131
Ratnapadmasupratiṣṭhitasumeruparvata(= śailendra)rāja (Buddha). B, 116 (Ch.)
Tib. has Śailendrarāja q.v.
Cf. Śikṣ., p. 169.
Ratnapadmavikrāmin. Ch. adds Buddha. A, 1A49; B, 115
Ratna[pāṇi] (Jinavara). D, 79
Ratnamukuṭa (Bodhisattva). A, 5B15
Ratnavajrī. Ch. to B, 266 fo-mu. A, 6B9; B, 266
fo-mu. A, 4A23
Ratnavijayā. A, 5B18
Ratnaśikhin(?) Ch. adds Buddha. A, 4A45; B, 144; D, 144
Ratnasambhava. Ch. adds Buddha.
A, 1B30; A, 2A43; A, 4A11; A, 4A39; B, 79; C, R10a
yab-yum. D, 58
Ratnāgni. Ch. adds Buddha. A, 1A47; B, 88
Cf. Weller 392.
Śikṣ., p. 169 gives Ratnaśrī.
Jina. D, 103
Ratnāṅgavyūhadyuti (Buddha). A, 1B51; B, 120
Ch. om. vyūha.
Ratnārcis. Ch. adds Buddha. A, 1A32; B, 84
Cf. Weller 392.
Jina. D, 99

Ratneśvarī(?). A, 5B23
Raśmisamudgataśrīkūṭarāja. B, 142
Ch. Chi-kuang-chi-hsiang-wang fo.
rāga (Bhairavavajra). A, 2A27; A, 2B39
Rākṣasa. A, 5B37
= Nirṛti. Cf. von Siebold, Nippon, II, 114.
rāganisūdana (Tārā). Ch. hūṁkāramantra.
B, 221; C, 100c
rājalīlā (Mañjuśrī). A, 6B45; B, 153
rājñī.
Cintā[maṇi] (caturbhuja). Ch. adds Tārā. B, 231
Pārvatī (śrīmatī). C, 134b
Prāṇasādhanalohakīlasvayambhū (devī). C, 134c
Varṣā. D, 249
Vasanta. D, 247
Śarad. D, 250
Hemanta. D, 252
Rāhu (deva). A, 5A2
Rāhula. A, 1B13; A, 1B60; B, 281; C, 8b; D, 202
rudhiravarṇa (Karmayama, rakta). C, 138a
raudra.
Vajrapāṇi (gsum-sgril). D, 171
Vaiśravaṇa.
aṣṭanāgaparivāra. C, 105a–c
kṛṣṇa. B, 319
raudrāntaka.
Cf. Ṭakṣad, Trakṣad, Mahākāla (ṭakṣad, trakṣad, drag-śad).
Lalitavajra. B, 15
mahāsiddha. D, 13
rJe-lcaṅ-skya. D, 53
Lāsyā (fo-mu). A, 2B6; A, 4B55
Cf. Sādhana, pp. 157, 312, 324.
Lūhipāda. B, 12
mahāsiddha. D, 12
Lokaḍākinī. C, 32a
Lokeśvara.
Cf. Avalokiteśvara.
guhyasamāja. Ch. Avalokiteśvaraguhyabuddha. B, 33
Cf. Avalokiteśvara (guhya) īśvara (= Lokeśvara).
A, 2A48

guhyasādhana. C, 39a
nīlakaṇṭha. Ch. īśvara (= Lokeśvara) Avalokiteśvara.
A, 6B52; B, 169
rakta (caturbhuja). B, 168
saptākṣara. C, 23a
hariharivāhana. B, 166
Ch. mounted on a wolf(?) īśvara (= Lokeśvara) Avalokiteśvara.
Cf. A, 6B49.
hālāhala. B, 162
Ch. mounted on a wolf (?) Avalokiteśvara.
Cf. A, 6A10.
Locanaprabha (Bodhisattva). A, 5A56
lohakhaḍga (Hayagrīva). B, 76; C, 61a; D, 166
lohanāḍī(?) (Vajrapāṇi). A, 2A45
Ch. t'ieh-kuan.
Vajrakarma. Ch. adds Bodhisattva. A, 4B51; B, 181
Vajrakarmakarī (anucarā). C, 59a
Vajrakāla. A, 2B58
Vajrakuṇḍalin. A, 2B16
Vajraketu. Ch. adds Bodhisattva. A, 4B39; B, 187
Vajragandhā (fo-mu). A, 2A55
Vajragaruḍa.
Cf. Cordier 1, 207.
śabala. Ch. Garuḍavajra (Buddha). B, 41
Śaṁvara. C, 78c
Vajragarbha (Avalokiteśvara). C, 43a
Vajragarbha (Jina). D, 98
Vajragarbha (Bodhisattva). A, 4B2
Vajragarbhapramardin(?) Ch. Vajrābhedya (Buddha).
B, 83
Śikṣ., p. 169 gives Vajrapramardin.
Cf. Vajrābhedya (Buddha). A, 1A33
Avalokiteśvara. Ch. vajrābhedya (Avalokiteśvara).
B, 177
Vajragāndhārī (fo-mu). A, 6A24; B, 262
Cf. Sādhana, p. 403.
Vajraghaṇṭā. A, 2B13
Vajracakra (Bodhisattva). A, 5A29
Vajracatuḥpīṭha. B, 57; D, 70
Cf. Cordier 1, 99.

Vajracarcikā. Ch. Carcikā (fo-mu). B, 257
Cf. Sādhana, pp. 395–396.
Vajracaryāpāramitā. A, 4B35
Vajrajvālānalārka.
Cf. Jvālānala.
Vajraḍāka. C, R3c
Vajraḍākinī. A, 3A47; C, 29c; C, 141a; D, 224
anucarā. C, 070a
Vajratārā. C, 50c; C, R5a
aṣṭabhuja. A, 6B14
[vajra]pañjarabhāṣita. B, 228
Vajratīkṣṇa. Ch. adds Bodhisattva. A, 4B43; B, 184
Vajratejas. Ch. adds Bodhisattva. A, 4A9; B, 188
Vajradanta (Bodhisattva). A, 5A28
Vajradhara. Tib. prefixes Jina; Ch. prefixes mahā.
A, 2A36; B, 29
yab-yum. D, 56
Vajradharma. Ch. adds Bodhisattva. A, 4B42; B, 185
vajradharma (Avalokiteśvara). B, 163
Vajradharma (Buddha). A, 4A33
Vajradhātu. Ch. adds Buddha. A, 4M4; B, 65; D, 77
Vairocana. C, R14c
Buddha. A, 4A25
vajradhātvīśvarī (Mārīcī). B, 246
Vajranairātmā. C, R4a
dvibhuja. C, R4b
[vajra]pañjarabhāṣita (Vajratārā). B, 228
Vajrapāṇi. Ch. adds Bodhisattva. A, 1M6; A, 1A10; A, 2A39;
A, 6A26; A, 6A44; D, 146
A, 1M6 om. pāṇi; A, 6A44 om. Bodhisattva.
anuttara (bhūtaḍāmara). C, S11c
amoghatrāṇa(?) A, 2B4
ācārya(?). B, 74; C, 54c
kūṭāgāra. C, 57a
krodha. A, 2B3
Garuḍayuta. A, 2B2
caṇḍa.
khra-thogs. C, 56a

chuṅ. Cf. below siao A, 2B5 B, 73; D, 169
rakta. C, 56b
Cf. Caṇḍa (trimukhaṣaḍbhuja). Ch. adds Vajrapāṇi. B, 75
caṇḍamahāroṣaṇa (bsruṅ-baḫi-mkhar-ras-chuṅ-lugs). C, 55c
jagaddama. A, 5A5
nīla. A, 5A46
nīlāmbaradhara. B, 72; C, 55a; D, 170
ḫgro-bzaṅ-lugs. C, 56c
Cf. below shan-hsing. A, 5M6
bodhisattvaveṣa. D, 90
bhūtaḍāmara. B, 71; C, 57b
Cf. Bhūtaḍāmara.
anuttara. C, S11c
Buddha. A, 5M7
gsar-ma. C, 57c
mahācakra. A, 2A33; B, 59
Buddha. A, 2M9
rakta (caṇḍa, chuṅ). C, 56b
raudra (gsum-sgril). D, 171
lohanāḍī(?). A, 2A45
śānta. C, 84b
śyāma. C, 94a
sita. A, 4A35
sūtrakrama. C, S8c
sa-lugs. C, 55b
shan-hsing (Buddha). Tib. ḫgro-ba-bzaṅ-po. A, 5M6
Cf. above nīlambaradhara (ḫgro-bzaṅ-lugs). C, 56c
Is this for Sugati [garbha] krama?
See Cordier 1, 167, 327.
hsiao. A, 2B5
Cf. above caṇḍa (chuṅ). B, 73; C, 56b; D, 169
Vajrapātāla (krodha). D, 221
Vajrapāśī. A, 2B11; C, 49c
Vajraputtali(?) (fo-mu). A, 3B61
Vajrapraṇavā. C, 27a
Vajrabhāṣa. Ch. adds Bodhisattva. A, 4B49; B, 182
Ch. to B, 182 Vajradharmabhāṇaka.

Vajrabhūmi. A, 2A21
fo-mu. A, 3B4
Vajrabhṛkuṭī (fo-mu). A, 3B60
Cf. Sakaki 4281.
Vajrabhairava. D, 61
Vajramuṣṭi (or Vajrasandhi). Ch. adds Bodhisattva.
A, 4B54; B, 178
Vajrayakṣa. A, 2B17; B, 179 (Tib.)
Bodhisattva. A, 4B53; B, 179 (Ch.)
Vajrarakṣa. Ch. adds Bodhisattva. A, 4B52; B, 180
Vajraratna. Ch. adds Bodhisattva. A, 4A10; B, 189
Vajrarasā (fo-mu). A, 2A54
Vajrarāga. Ch. adds Bodhisattva. A, 4A13; B, 191
Vajrarāgā(?) (fo-mu). A, 3B1
Vajrarāja. Ch. adds Bodhisattva. A, 4A49; B, 192
Vajrarūpā (fo-mu). A, 2A57
Vajravārāhī. B, 54
brāhmaṇaśrīdharakrama. C, 28b
go-chaḫi. C, 20b
dpyal-lugs. C, 25a
Vajravidāraṇa. D, 173
kṛṣṇa (Buddha). A, 5M4
nīla. C, 73b
śyāmanīla. C, 73c
sita. C, 73a
Vajravidāraṇī (fo-mu). A, 6B28; B, 352
Ch. of A does not indicate the gender.
Cf. Cordier, 1, 294–296.
Vajravega. C, 24a
Vajravetāla. A, 2B1
Vajraśabdā (fo-mu). A, 2A56; A, 3B5
Vajraśānti (fo-mu). A, 3B2
Cf. Hôbôgirin, p. 118.
Vajraśṛṅkhalā. B, 347
fo-mu. A, 6A23
Vajrasattva. Ch. adds Buddha. B, 69; C, R9b; D, 74
Buddha. A, 4B27
Bodhi. Ch. Bodhisattva. B, 193
Bodhisattva. A, 4A50

pīta. C, 4a
Śaṁvara. Ch. adds rājabuddha. B, 38; C, R6c
go-chaḫi. C, 18b
Vajrasandhi.
Cf. Vajramuṣṭi.
Vajrasarasvatī.
dvibhuja. B, 254
ṣaḍbhuja. B, 253
Vajrasādhu. Ch. adds Bodhisattva. A, 4A12; B, 190
dam-can. D, 269
Cf. Grünwedel, pp. 182–186.
Dhāraṇī gives vajrasadhu for rdo-rje-legs-pa.
Vajrasūrya. A, 2B14
Cf. Hodgson, p. 34.
go-chaḫi. C, 19c
Vajrasphoṭī. A, 2B12
fo-mu. A, 5A43
Vajrahāsa. Ch. adds Bodhisattva. A, 4B40; B,186
Vajrahūṁkāra. A, 2A34; B, 56; B, 359; C, R11c
Vajrahetu. Ch. adds Bodhisattva. A, 4B44; B, 183
Vajrākṣobhya. Ch. adds Buddha. B, 141; D, 87
Cf. Akṣobhyavajra.
guhya (Buddha). A, 2A35
Vajrāgrā (fo-mu). A, 5A44
Vajrāṅkuśa. A, 2B57
Vajrāṅkuśī. A, 2B10; C, 49b
Vajrānalā. A, 2A20
Vajrānilā. A, 2A18
Vajrābhedya (Buddha). A, 1A33
Cf. Vajragarbhapramardin.
Vajrāmṛta. B, 49; C, R11b
Cf. Cordier 1, 106; 2, 538.
Vajrāsanamuni (gço-ḫkhor-gsum). C, 4b
Vajrīputra. A, 1B15; B, 276; C, 6c; D, 197
Vajrodakā. A, 2A19
Vajroṣṇīṣa. A, 2B15
Buddha. A, 4A46
Vajroṣṇīṣacakravartirāja. A, 2A10
Cf. Uṣṇīṣacakravartin. A, 2B61
Krodhoṣṇīṣacakravartin. D, 217

vanaratnakrama (Tārā, sita). C, 2a
Cf. Tāranātha, p. 263; Cordier, 2, 121, 207.
Vanavāsin. A, 1B48; B, 274; C, 6a; D, 195
varada (Tārā). C, 98b
Varuṇa (deva). A, 3B8; A, 5B39; D, 288
Varuṇa (nāgarāja). D, 290
Varuṇa. Ch. adds Buddha. A, 1A60; B, 96
Jina. D, 111
Varuṇadeva. Ch. adds Buddha. A, 1A59; B, 97
Jina. D, 112
Varṣādevī. B, 332
Varṣārājñī. D, 249
vaśaṁkara (Caturmukha, rakta). C, 132c
vaśitā.
Āyur. A, 4B18
Upapatti. A, 4B6
Ṛddhi. A, 4B7
Karma(?). A, 4B21
Citta. A, 4B19
Cittotpāda (= adhimukti?). A, 4B8
Jñāna. A, 4B22
Dharma. A, 4B23
Pariṣkāra(?). A, 4B20
Praṇidhāna. A, 4B9
vaśitottamada(?) (Tārā). C, 97a
Vasantadevī. B, 331
Vasantarājñī. D, 247
Vasiṣṭhadeva (Bodhisattva). A, 5A10
Vasudhārā. C, R16c; C, S11a; D, 182
gopāla. C, 112a
devī (dhāraṇīvinirgata). C, 111b
manohara. C, 112b
rakta. C, 71c
ẓā-ma-riḫi-lugs. C, 111c
Vasubandhu. B, 4
bhaṭṭāraka. D, 7
Vasumatī(?) (devī). A, 5B60
Vāgīśvarasumatisāgara (svāmin). B, 26
Cf. mahāpañcama.

Vāghevajra. C, R3a; C, R6a
Cf. Cordier 2, 155.
vādipramardaka (Tārā). C, 96c
vādirāṭ (Mañjughoṣa). B, 150
Cf. Śrīvādirāṭ (Bodhisattva). A, 6B55
vādisiṁha (Mañjughoṣa). C, 66b; C, S3b; D, 92
Cf. Cordier 2, 175.
Vāyu (deva). A, 5B52; D, 287
caturbhuja. A, 3B24
Vārāhī. Cf. Vajravārāhī.
devī. A, 5B31
fo-mu. A, 2B42
anucarā. C, 53a
arthasādhana. C, 26b
ūrdhvapāda. C, 27c
kūrmapādī. C, 28a
kruddha (kālī). C, 29b
nīla. C, R8b
pīta. C, R8c
prajñālokakṛtya (sita). C, 32b; C, 32c
Cf. Pad-dkar (śes-rab-gsal-byed). Ch. Vajravārāhī (sita). B, 270
rakta. C, R8a
sarvārthasādhana. Ch. Vajravārāhī. B, 271
Vikrānta (Jina). D, 128
Vikrāntagāmiśrī. Ch. Suvikrāntagāmin (Buddha). B, 113
Cf. Suvikrāntagāmin (Buddha). A, 1A51
Vikrāntoṣṇīṣa(?) (Buddha). A, 4A55
Vighnāntaka. Ch. adds vajra. A, 6B44; B, 345; C, S10a
Cf. Krodhavighnāntaka.
Cf. Sādhana, pp. 137, 558–559.
Vijaya (Bodhisattva). A, 5A37
Vijayoṣṇīṣa (Buddha). A, 4A57
Cf. Hôbôgirin, pp. 148–149.
Vijayā. Cf. Uṣṇīṣavijayā. A, 5B7; A, 5B33; C, R17b
fo-mu. A, 6M3; A, 6B26
Tārā. Ch. Trailokyavijayā. B, 212
sita. Ch. Trailokyavijayā. B, 223
devī. A, 5B42

Vitāna(?)dharā (fo-mu). A, 3B56
vidyārājñī (Grahamātṛkā). C, 77a
Vidyuddharā (fo-mu). A, 3A22
vipannirbarhaṇa(?) (Tārā). C, 99a
Vipaśyin (Buddha). B, 127; C, 82a
Vimala. Ch. adds Buddha. A, 1A43; B, 92
Cf. Weller 77, 217, 772.
Jina. D, 107
Vimalā [bhūmi] (fo-mu). A, 4A27
Vimalaprabhākumāra. A, 5B16
Vimalākāśa(?) (Bodhisattva). A, 5A41
Vimaloṣṇīṣa (Jina). D, 133
Virūḍhaka. B, 325; C, 11c; C, 140b; D, 280
Virūpa. Tib. Birbapa. A, 3B26
Cf. Cordier 1, 57, 223, 234.
Virūpākṣa. B, 326; C, 12a; C, 140c; D, 282
Viśva(?)ḍāka (Buddha). A, 3B52
Viśvaḍākinī. C, 31b; D, 228
Viśvabhū (Buddha). Tib. of B, 129 om. Buddha.
B, 129; C, 82c
Viśvamātṛ. B, 238
sita. C, 74b
Viśvā.
fo-mu (sita). A, 6A54
viśveṣa (Avalokiteśvara). C, 87a
Viṣṇu (deva). A, 3B6; A, 5A16
Vīṇādharā (fo-mu). A, 3B49
Vīṇāsarasvatī (fo-mu). B, 255
Cf. Cordier 2, 49.
Vīranandin. Ch. adds Buddha. A, 1A48; B, 87
Jina. D, 102
Vīrasena. Ch. adds Buddha. A, 1A30; B, 86
Jina. D, 101
Vīryapāramitā. A, 4A4
Vṛścika (deva). A, 3B34
Vetālī.
Cf. Sādhana, pp. 446, 479.
devī. C, 92b
fo-mu (sita). A, 3A43

vaiḍūryaprabhārāja (Bhaiṣajyaguru). Ch. adds tathāgata.	B, 139; D, 142
Vaidya (Buddha).	A, 1B9
Cf. Weller 33.	
Vairocana. Ch. adds Buddha.	A, 1A15; A, 2A44; B, 77; C, R9c
Cf. Weller 167 for A, 1A15.	
abhisambodhi.	A, 5M5; 5A36; B, 70; D, 83
Cf. Cordier 1, 290–292; 2, 544.	
Bhairavavajra.	A, 2B28
Mañjuvajra.	A, 2A31; C, R1b
Vajradhātu.	A, 4A25; C, R14c
Śākyasiṁha.	B, 66
sarvavit. Tib. Kun-rig.	A, 4M5; A, 4A36; B, 68
Cf. Sarvavit Tib. Kun-rigs.	D, 76
go-chaḫi.	C, 18c
yab-yum.	D, 55
hung-kuang.	A, 4A34
Vairocanī.	C, 27b
Vaiśravaṇa.	C, 12b; C, 51b; C, 139c; C, S10b; D, 281
aṣṭanāgaparivāra (raudra).	C, 105a–c
āyurdhara (sita).	C, 106b
āyurvardhana (sita).	B, 318; D, 264
Kubera (gsuṅ-mchog).	C, 104b
kṛṣṇa.	
nīlāśva.	C, 106a
raudra.	B, 319
gadādhara (śyāmapīta).	C, 103b
jinarṣabha.	C, 110c
nartakavara.	B, 324; C, 110b
rakta.	C, 103c
navadeva (mahāpīta).	C, 102c
nīlāśva.	
kṛṣṇa.	C, 106a
raktaśūla.	C, 103a
mahāpīta.	B, 322
navadeva.	C, 102c
mahārāja. Ch. devarāja.	B, 320
mahāsuvarṇa.	D, 263

rakta (nartakavara). C, 103c
raktaśūla. B, 321; D, 262
nīlāśva. C, 103a
raudra.
aṣṭanāgaparivāra. C, 105a–c
kṛṣṇa. B, 319
śyāma (siṁhavāhana, ẓñā-naḫi-lugs). C, 106c
śyāmapīta (gadādhara). C, 103b
siṁhavāhana (śyāma, ẓñā-naḫi-lugs). C, 106c
sita.
āyurdhara. C, 106b
āyurvardhana. B, 318; D, 264
yaṅ-gsaṅ-phyag-mçhan-bzhi-pa. C, 107a
Vyāghravaktraḍākinī. D, 187
vyāghravāhana (Mahākāla). B, 301; C, 123b; D, 259
Śaṁvara. Ch. Śaṁvararāja (Buddha).
A, 3M5; A, 3A35; C, R7a
Cf. Saṁvara.
āyuḥsādhana (sita). C, 22c
krodhabhayanāśana. C, 78b
Garuḍa. A, 3A46; B, 40
dvibhuja. C, R7b
pañcabuddha. A, 3A33
vajragaruḍa. C, 78c
Cf. Cordier 2, 102.
vajrasattva. B, 38; C, R6c
sahaja. B, 39; C, 18a
sita. A, 3M4; A, 3A34 (om. Buddha);
B, 37; C, 22b; D, 73
āyuḥsādhana. C, 22c
Śakra. A, 5B38
Cf. Śatakratu.
deva. A, 3A29
Śaṅkaravajra(?). A, 5A21
Śaṅkarī(?) (devī). A, 5B53
Śaṅkhapadmā. A, 5B8
Śaṅkhapālī (devī). B, 309; C, 135a; D, 246
Śaṅkhā [maṅgala]. D, 294
Śatakratu. B, 328; D, 277
Śatruṁjayavajra. A, 5A7

Śabarī (fo-mu). A, 3A61; A, 3B17
Cf. Sādhana, pp. 443, 445–446, 461, 479.
Śaraddevī. B, 333
Śaradrājñī. D, 250
Śaśiketu.
Cf. Candraketu.
śastradhara (Hevajrabuddha). A, 3M3
Śākyakulendra. D, 80
Śākyaprabha. B, 8
Cf. Tāranatha, p. 204.
Śākyamuni. Ch. adds Buddha. A, 1M5; A, 1A34; A, 5A57; B, 82
Jina. C, 81c; D, 2; D, 97
bkaḥ-gdams-lha-bzhiḥi-naṅ-gi. C, 12c
Śākyasiṁha. C, R15a
Buddha. A, 4A47
Vairocana. Ch. adds Buddha. B, 66
Śāṇakavāsin. B, 292
śānta.
Guhyapati (sahaja). C, 88c
Vajrapāṇi. C, 84b
Śāntiguptakrama.
Cf. Tāranātha, pp. 263, 265; Cordier, 2, 125.
Cf. mahāsiddha°.
Śāntarakṣita (śrīmat). D, 25
Cf. Cordier 2, 445; Tāranātha, pp. 204, 212.
Śāntideva. B, 10
bhaṭṭāraka. D, 24
Śāntendriya. D, 156
Cf. Waddell, p. 358.
Śābaripāda. A, 2B26
mahāsiddha. D, 10
Śāriputra. A, 1B22
Śikhin (Buddha). Tib. of B, 128 om. Buddha. B, 128; C, 82b
Śītavatī (fo-mu). A, 6A59; B, 203
Ch. of B, 203 prefixes mahā.
Cf. Mahāśītavatī.
Śīlapāramitā. A, 4A15
Śūraṅgama (Bodhisattva). A, 4B16

Śūradatta. Ch. adds Buddha. A, 1A42; B, 93
Jina. D, 108
śṛgālamukha (Piśāca). C, 133c
Śṛṅkhalā. A, 6B8(?); C, 50a
May be Sphoṭā. Cf. Sphoṭadharā.
Śailadevanātha (= Mahākāla). D, 260
Śailendrarāja (Buddha). Tib. to B, 116
Ch. Ratnapadmasupratiṣṭhitasumeruparvata(= śailendra)rāja (Buddha).
Jina. D, 130
Cf. Sumeruparvatarāja. A, 1A13
Śokanirghātanamati (Bodhisattva). A, 4B14
śokavinodana (Tārā). B, 215; C, 98c
Ch. nieh-p'an-chi-mieh.
śyāmāśva (Mārīcī). C, 91c
Śramaṇā. D, 183
devī. Ch. fo-mu. B, 267; C, 80b
fo-mu. A, 6A55
Śrī (garbhasuvarṇasūtra). C, 71b
Śrīkālacakra. D, 65
Śrīguhyasamāja. D, 62
Śrīcakrasaṁvara. Ch. Śaṁvararājabuddha. B, 36; D, 63
Śrījñāna (Paṇ-chen). D, 51
Śrīdevī (ekamātṛ). D, 236
Śrīdharakrama (Brāhmaṇa° °vajravārāhī). C, 28b
Cf. Tāranātha, p. 258.
śrīnātha.
Cf. Caturmukha (śrīnātha).
Nāgārjuna (śrīnātha).
śrīmatī (Pārvatī, rājñī). C, 134b
śrīmatī (Devī, dvibhuja). B, 311
Śrīmahācakra. D, 64
Śrīvatsā [maṅgala]. D, 295
Śrīvādirāṭ (Bodhisattva). A, 6B55
Cf. vādirāṭ (Mañjughoṣa). B, 150
Śrīhevajra. D, 66
ṣaḍakṣara (Avalokiteśvara, jo-bo-lugs). C, 33b
Ṣaḍakṣarī. C, 33c
Cf. Cordier 2, 22.
ṣaḍaṅga (Tārā, gñan). C, 2c

Ṣaḍābharaṇa (phyag-mçhan). C, R17c
Cf. Grünwedel, p. 100.
Ṣaṇmukha. Ch. adds Bhairavavajra.
Cf. Cordier 2, 540. B, 44
Bhairavavajra. A, 2B30
Buddha. A, 2M2
Saṁvara.
Cf. Cakrasaṁvara, Śaṁvara.
Saṁkusumita(?) Tib. Me-tog-cher-gyas. D, 81
Cf. Weller 567 Puṣpita. Tib. Me-tog-rgyas-pa.
saṁkusumita (Tārā).
Cf. praphulla.
saṁkṣipta (Bhairava). C, 24c
Saṁgrāmatāriṇī (fo-mu). A, 6A37
Cf. Sādhana, p. 416.
Sañcālinī (go-chaḫi). C, 21c
Cf. Sādhana, p. 498.
Sattvavajrī (fo-mu). A, 4A24; B, 265
Santrāsinī (go-chaḫi). C, 21b
Cf. Sādhana, p. 498.
saptākṣara (Lokeśvara). C, 23a
Cf. Cordier 1, 197.
Samantadarśin (Jina). Ch. Buddha. B, 143; D, 135
Cf. Weller 429.
Tib. Kun-gzigs; Ch. P'u-hui (= sarvavit?).
Cf. B, 68 where P'u-hui equals Kun-rig.
Samantadharavajra(?). A, 5A20
Samantaprabhā [bhūmi] (fo-mu). A, 4A5
Samantabhadra. Ch. adds Bodhisattva.
A, 1M9; A, 1A3; A, 2A23;
A, 4B5; B, 198; C, 85b; D, 152
hasti[vāhana]. B, 200
Samantāvabhāsa (Jina). D, 129
Samantāvabhāsavyūhaśrī. Ch. adds Buddha.
A, 1A50; B, 114
Samayaḍākini. C, 31a
Sarasvatī. A, 5B19; C, S8a; D, 157
Cf. Vajrasarasvatī.
caturbhuja (sita). C, 68a

devī. A, 5B49
rakta (fo-mu). A, 6A51; C, 68b
vīṇā (fo-mu). B, 255
ṣaḍbhuja (fo-mu). A, 6B5
sita. C, 2b
caturbhuja. C, 68a
Saraha. B, 11
mahāsiddha. D, 11
Saroruhavajra (bhaṭṭāraka). D, 26
Cf. Cordier, 1, 78.
sarvajña (Bu-ston). D, 37
Sarvaḍākinī. C, 31c
Sarvanivaraṇaviṣkambhin. Ch. adds Bodhisattva.
A, 1M2; A, 1A9; A, 2A24; B, 199; C, 86b; D, 149
anucara. C, 16a
Sarvanivaraṇaviṣkambhiṇī (devī). A, 5B1
Sarvavit. Tib. Kun-rigs. D, 76
Vairocana (Buddha). A, 4M5; A, 4A36; B, 68
sarvāntarāyasaṁgrasana (or sarvavighnavināyaka) (Mahākāla).
C, 116b
Sarvāpāyajaha (Bodhisattva). A, 5B4
sarvārthasādhana.
Tārā. A, 6A56; B, 235
sic. Ch. to B, 225, but Tib. siddhida and figure differs.
Cf. Cordier 2, 40.
Vārāhī. Ch. Vajravārāhī. B, 271
Cf. Cordier 2, 121.
sahaja.
Kālacakra. C, 23c
Guhyapati (śānta). C, 88c
Guhyasamāja. C, 17b
Śaṁvara. Ch. adds rājabuddha. B, 39; C, 18a
Cf. Cordier 1, 35, 40; 2, 268.
Hayagrīva (ekavīra, jo-boḫi-lugs). C, 58a
Hevajra. C, 23b
Cf. Cordier 2, 268.
Go-bzlog. C, 29a
sādhanakālasambaddha (Caturmukha, śrīnātha).
C, 131b

Sādhumatī [bhūmi] (fo-mu). A, 4A7
Sārthavāha (Buddha). A, 1A19
  Cf. Weller 12.
Sāhasrapramardanī (fo-mu). A, 6A57
  Cf. Mahāsāhasrapramardanī.
Siṁha (Buddha). A, 1A29
  Cf. Weller 6.
Siṁhadhvajā. A, 5B6
Siṁhanāda. C, 43b; C, S6b
  Avalokiteśvara. A, 6A34; B, 161; D, 94
  Buddha. A, 1B45
  Jina. Ch. Buddha. B, 140; D, 143
  Mañjughoṣa. B, 149
Siṁhabhayatrāṇa. C, 41a
Siṁhavaktrā (fo-mu). B, 357
  ḍākinī. D, 188
  nīla. C, 80c
  rakta. C, 81a
siṁhavāhana.
  Ṭakṣad. Ch. Mahākāla. B, 299
  Mañjuśrī. A, 6A32
  Mahākāla (trakṣad, jo-bo̱hi-lugs). C, 129a
  Vaiśravaṇa (śyāma, ẕñā-na̱hi-lugs). C, 106c
siṁhāsana (Gaṇapatinātha). C, 128a
  nātha = Mahākāla.
Sita (deva). A, 3B10
Sitātapatra (Bodhisattva). A, 5A39
Sitātapatroṣṇīṣa (Buddha). A, 4A60
  Cf. Hôbôgirin, pp. 148–149.
Sitātapatrā (fo-mu). A, 6M7; A, 6A47
  Cf. Uṣṇīṣasitātapatrā.
  ārya. B, 248; D, 162
Siddhasaṅgha. B, 24
  Cf. Svāmisiddhasaṅgha.
Siddhasvāmin.
  Cf. Paṇḍitasiddhasvāmin.
siddhida (Tārā). B, 225
siddhisambhava (Tārā). C, 102a
siddheśvara (Hūṁkāra). D, 27
sukhada (Tārā). B, 222

sukhasādhana (Tārā). C, 101a
sukhāvatī (Avalokiteśvara). C, 87c
Sudarśana. B, 296
  Cf. Rockhill, Life, p. 170.
 Bodhisattva. A, 6A6
Sudurjayā [bhūmi] (fo-mu). A, 4A20
Sudhana (anucara). C, 37a
Sudhanakumāra. A, 5B11
 anucara. C, 36a
Sunāmatathāgata (Buddha). A, 1B38
 Cf. Sunāman.
Sunāman. C, 15c
  Dhāraṇī gives full name corresponding to B, 133 below.
 Cf. Sunāmatathāgata (Buddha). A, 1B38
  Suparikīrtitanāmaśrī. D, 136
  Suparikīrtitanāmaśrīrāja. B, 133
Sunetra (Buddha). A, 1A20
 Cf. Weller 11.
Suparikīrtitanāmaśrī. D, 136
 Cf. Sunāman.
Suparikīrtitanāmaśrī. Ch. adds Buddha. A, 1A24; B, 109
 Jina (and om. su). D, 124
Suparikīrtitanāmaśrīrāja. Ch. adds tathāgata. B, 133
 Cf. Sunāman.
Suprajña (rṅog). D, 30
 Cf. Cordier 2, 321.
Sumatikalpabhadrasamudra (Jinendra). D, 50
 Cf. Kalpabhadrasamudra (Dalai Lama). B, 28
Sumatijñāna (Paṇ-chen). B, 27; D, 48
Sumatidharmadhvaja.
 rJes-paṇ-chen. B, 25
 Paṇ-chen. D, 47
Sumatiśāsanasūrya (Khri-chen). D, 52
Sumatiśrī (rJe-druṅ). D, 54
Sumatisiddhārtha (Jina). D, 45
Sumerukūṭa (Bodhisattva). A, 6A16
Sumeruparvatarāja (Buddha). A, 1A13
 Cf. Śailendrarāja.

Sumeruśikharadhararāja (Bodhisattva). A, 6A14
Suraśmi (Buddha). A, 1B35
Cf. Weller 730.
Suvarṇabhadravimala. C, 15b
Mantra adds ratnaprabhāsavrata.
Suvarṇabhadravimalaratnaprabhāsa. D, 138
Suvarṇabhadravimalaratnaprabhāsavrata. B, 135
Ch. Chin-sê-pao-kuang-miao-hsing-ch'êng-chiu ju-lai.
Suvarṇamatsyā [maṅgala]. D, 292
Suvarṇaratnaprabhātathāgata (Buddha). A, 1B40
Suvikrānta (Jina). D, 126
Suvikrāntagāmin (Buddha). A, 1A51
Cf. Vikrāntagāmiśrī.
Suvikrāntāśrī. Ch. adds Buddha. A, 1A22; B, 111
sūcisūtradhara (Mārīcī). C, 68c
Cf. Bhattacharyya, pp. 95–96.
Sūrya (deva). A, 5B40
Cf. Jih-kung t'ien A, 5A3.
sūtrakrama (Vajrapāṇi). C, S8c
Sūryagarbha (Buddha). A, 1A14
Cf. Weller 21.
Sūryadharā (fo-mu). A, 3A25
Sūryaprabha (deva). A, 3A26
Sūryavairocana. Ch. adds Bodhisattva. A, 6A27; C, 13c
Cf. BEFEO 3, 35.
sevākālasambaddha (Caturmukha, śrīnātha). C, 131a
sthiracakra (Mañjughoṣa). B, 147
Sphoṭadharā or Sphoṭā?
Cf. Śṛṅkhalā.
fo-mu. A, 3A10
yo-mu. A, 2A15
Smṛtiśrī. Ch. adds Buddha. A, 1A25; B, 108
Jina. D, 123
svapnadeśaka (Tārā). C, 51c
Svayambhū (devī). D, 251
Cf. Prāṇasādhanalohakīlasvayambhūrājñī (devī).
C, 134c

Svaraghoṣarāja. D, 137
Cf. Ābhāsvara(?)tathāgata (Buddha). A, 1B39
Ratnacandra. C, 15a
Ratnacandrapadmapratimaṇḍitapaṇḍita(?)tejaḥsvaraghoṣarāja. B, 134
Svāmiprajñāsimha. D, 44
Svāmisiddhasaṅgha. D, 43
Tib. rje-dge-ḫdun-grub.
Hayagrīva. Ch. adds vajra. A, 2A51; A, 5A47; A, 5B13; A, 6A31; C, S7b
anucara. C, 35a; C, 36c; C, 37c
ekavīra (sahaja, jo-boḫi-lugs). C, 58a
krodha. D, 213
garuḍapakṣavant (jo-boḫi-lugs). C, 58b
guhyasādhana. B, 61; D, 167
caturḍākinīparivāra (jo-bo-lugs). C, 58c
caturmukhāṣṭabhuja. A, 6A12
trimukhāṣṭabhuja (rakta). A, 6B4
padmanarteśvara. B, 62
rakta (trimukhāṣṭabhuja). A, 6B4
lohakhaḍga. B, 76; C, 61a; D, 166
sahaja (ekavīra, jo-boḫi-lugs). C, 58a
sita. C, 91a
Buddha. A, 5M3
sKyer-sgaṅ-lugs. C, 60c
Kha-che-paṇ-chen-lugs. C, 60b
Jo-boḫi-lugs-kyi. D, 168
harihariyāhana (Lokeśvara). B, 166
Ch. mounted on a wolf (?) īśvara (= Lokeśvara) Avalokiteśvara. Cf. A, 6B49.
Hastibhayatrāṇa. C, 41b
hasti[vāhana] (Samantabhadra). B, 200
Hārītī (deva). A, 3A2
Cf. Peri, Hārītī, pp. 16, 62.
Hārītī (yakṣiṇī). C, 92c
hālāhala (Lokeśvara). B, 162
Ch. mounted on a wolf (?) Avalokiteśvara. Cf. A, 6A10.

Hūṁkāra.
krodha. C, R9a
vajra. A, 2A34; B, 56; B, 359; C, R11c
siddheśvara. D, 27
hūṁsvaranādinī (Tārā). Ch. ākāśahūṁsvara. B, 211; C, 96a
Hemantadevī. B, 334
Hemantarājñī. D, 252
Heruka (kṛṣṇa, go-chaḫi). C, 19b
Cf. Raktapa.
Hevajra. B, 47; C, R5b
kapāladhara. A, 3M6
kāya. C, R3b; C, R6b
garbha(?). B, 48; C, R2b
citta. C, R2c; C, R5c
vāk. C,R3a; C, R6a
śastradhara (Buddha). A, 3M3
śrī. D, 66
sahaja. C, 23b

TIBETAN INDEX

TIBETAN INDEX

karma-ḍā-ki (ḫKhor°). C, 118c
Cf. Las-kyi-mkhaḫ-ḫgro.
kā-pa-li-tā-ra (rJe-bçun-ma°). C, 54a
Ku-ru-ku-le. B, 60; C, R4c
Ku-ru-kulle. C, 3a
Ku-ru-kulle-gsaṅ-sgrub. C, 70c
kun-dgaḫ-rgyal-mçhan (Sa-skya-paṇḍi-ta°). D, 38
Kun-dgaḫ-bo. B, 291
Kun-tu-bzaṅ-po. B, 198; C, 85b; D, 152
Kun-tu-bzaṅ-po-glaṅ-chen-po. B, 200
Kun-nas-snaṅ-ba-bkod-paḫi-dpal. B, 114
Cf. rGyal-ba-kun-nas-snaṅ-ba. D, 129
kun-gzigs (rGyal-ba°). B, 143; D, 135
Kun-rig-rnams-par-snaṅ-mẓad. B, 68
Kun-rigs. D, 76
kundha-li (Khol-po°). C, 115c
kurma-pā-dī (Phag-mo°). C, 28a
Kyai-rdo-rje. B, 47
sÑiṅ-po°. B, 48
dPal°. D, 66
gSuṅ°. C, R6a
Kyai-rdor. C, R5b
sKu°. C, R3b; C, R6b
sÑiṅ-po°. C, R2b
Thugs°. C, R2c; C, R5c
gSuṅ°. C, R3a
Kyai-rdor-lhan-skyes. C, 23b
Klu-rgyal-dgaḫ-bo. D, 289
Klu-rgyal-ñe-dgaḫ. D, 291
Klu-rgyal-wa-ru-ṇa. D, 290
Klu-rgyal-sog-ma-med. C, 115a
Klu-sgrub. B, 1
dPal-mgon°. D, 5
klu-sgrub-lugs.
Gur-yum-can°. C, 122c
mGon-po-phyag-bzhi-pa°. C, 119b

klu-brgyad-bcas (rNam-sras-drag-byed-ḫkhor°). C, 105a-c
Klu-dbaṅ-gi-rgyal-po. B, 85
rGyal-ba°. D, 100, 134
Klu-dbaṅ-rgyal-po. C, 16b
Klu-mo-re-ma-ti. C, 135c
Cf. Re-ma-ti.
klu-mo-las-byed-ma (ḫKhor°). C, 59c
Kluḫi-ḫjigs-skyobs. C, 42a
Kluḫi-sde. B, 285; C, 9c
Klu-yi-sde. D, 206
Kṣe-tra-pa-la. B, 315
Kṣe-tra-pā-la. C, 116a; D, 233
dkaḫ-ma (mGon-po-beṅ°). C, 123c
dKar-mo-ñi-zla-lcam-dral. C, 139b
dKar-mo-zla-mdaṅs-kyi-sgrol-ma. C, 95a
Cf. sGrol-ma-zla-mdaṅ-ma. B, 208
bkaḫ-gdams-lugs.
Khyuṅ-ser°. C, 79c
Mi-gyo-ba-sṅon-po°. C, 61c
bKaḫ-gdams-lha-bzhiḫi-naṅ-gi-sgrol-ma. C, 44a
bKaḫ-gdams-lha-bzhiḫi-naṅ-gi-spyan-ras-gzigs. C, 34a
bKaḫ-gdams-lha-bzhiḫi-naṅ-gi-śākya-thub-pa. C, 12c
bKra-śis-skye-baḫi-sgrol-ma. B, 217
bKra-śis-snaṅ-baḫi-sgrol-ma. C, 99b
bKra-śis-ç̣he-riṅ-ma. B, 335; C, 142b; D, 272
rkaṅ-gliṅ-can (mGon-dmar°). C, 120c
rkaṅ-thaṅ-ma (mGon-po-trakṣad°). C, 129c
rkyaṅ (Gur° °rṅog-lugs). C, 123a
skal-bzaṅ-rgya-mç̣ho (B reads rgyal-mç̣ho).
rGyal-dbaṅ-blo-bzaṅ°. D, 50
Tālaḫi-bla-ma°. B, 28
sKu-kyai-rdor. C, R3b; C, R6b
skyer-sgaṅ-lugs (rTa-mgrin°). C, 60c
skrag-byed-ma (Go-chaḫi°). C, 21b
sKrag-med-mun-bral-rgyal-po. B, 125
bskyod-byed-ma (Go-chaḫi°). C, 21c
kha-che-paṇ-chen-lugs.
mGon-po-gri-gug°. C, 126b
sGrol-dkar°. C, 44c

sGrol-ljaṅ°. C, 44b
ḫJam-dbyaṅs-dkar-po°. C, 65b
rTa-mgrin°. C, 60b
Don-zhags°. C, 36b
Kha-sarpa-ṇi. C, S6a
sPyan-ras-gzigs°. B, 160; C, 37b
khaṅ-brçegs (Phyag-rdor°). C, 57a
khab-skud-can (Ḫod-zer-can-ma°). C, 68c
Khams-gsum-rnam-rygal. D, 222
Khams-gsum-dbaṅ-ḫdus-spyan-ras-gzigs. B, 167
khu-çhur (rDo-rje°). B, 178
Khol-po-kundha-li. C, 115c
khyu-mchog (Sras-rgyal-ba°). C, 110c
Khyuṅ-khra. Cf. mkhaḫ-ldiṅ. D, 185
Dus-ḫkhor° °rgyud-lugs. C, 79a
rDo-rjes°. B, 41
Khyuṅ-khra-man-ṅag-lugs. C, 79b
Khyuṅ-nag. D, 184
khyuṅ-gśog-can.
rTa-mgrin° °jo-boḫi-lugs. C, 58b
Khyuṅ-ser-bkaḫ-gdams-lugs. C, 79c
Khyuṅ-gser-mig-ḫkhyil-ba. D, 186
khra-thogs (Phyag-rdor-gtum-po°). C, 56a
Khrag-ḫthuṅ. C, R12a
khrag-mdog (Las-gśin-dmar-po°). C, 138a
Khri-chen-ṅag-dbaṅ-mchog-ldan. D, 49
Khri-chen-blo-bzaṅ-bstan-paḫi-ñi-ma. D, 52
Khro-gñer-gyo-baḫi-sgrol-ma. C, 100a
Khro-gñer-can-ma. C, S9a
ḫKhor°. C, 35c; C, 36c; C, 37c
Lha-mo°. B, 256
khro-bo (gSaṅ-baḫi-bdag-po°). C, 89a
Khro-bo-bgegs-mthar-byed. C, 74a
Khro-bo-chen-po. C, 84a
Khro-bo-rta-mgrin. D, 213
Khro-bo-stobs-po-che. B, 342; D, 218
Khro-bo-bdud-rçi-ḫkhyil-pa. D, 215
Khro-bo-ḫdod-rgyal. D, 214
Cf. Ṭakki-rā-ẓa. B, 313; C, 116c; D, 235
ḫDod-rgyal-dmar-po. C, 3b

Khro-bo-rdo-rje-sa-ẖog. D, 221

Khro-bo-dbyug-sṅon-can. D, 216

Khro-bo-mi-gyo-ba. D, 174, 219

Khro-bo-sme-ba-brçegs-pa. D, 172

Khro-bo-sme-brçegs (B reads me). B, 356; C, S9c
Cf. Khro-mo°.

Khro-bo-sme-brçegs-ljaṅ-khu. C, 77c

Khro-bo-sme-brçegs-dud-kha. C, 77b

Khro-bo-gçug-tor-ẖkhor-bsgyur. D, 217

Khro-bo-gzhan-gyis-mi-thub-pa. C, 90c; D, 211

khro-bo-reg-çhig (bDe-mchog°). C, 78b

Khro-bo-gśin-rje-gśed. D, 212

Khro-bo-hūṁ-mẓad. C, R9a

Khro-mo-sme-brçegs. B, 351; C, 78a; D, 180
Cf. Khro-bo°.

khros (Phag-mo° °nag). C, 29b

khros-ma (sGrol-ma° °nag-mo). B, 219

mkhaẖ-ẖgro. Cf. mKhaẖ-ẖgro-ma.

ẖJig-rten°. C, 32a

Thams-cad°. C, 31c

Dam-çhig°. C, 31a

rDo-rje°. C, 141a; C, R3c; D, 224

sNa-çhogs°. C, 31b; D, 228

Padma°. C, 141c; D, 227

Ye-śes°. B, 52; C, R14a

Rin-chen°. C, 141a; D, 225

Las-kyi°. C, 141c; D, 226

Saṅs-rgyas°. C, 141b; D, 223

mKhaẖ-ẖgro-ma (spyod written below). B, 55
Cf. mkhaẖ-ẖgro, mkhaẖ-spyod, ḍā-ki.

rDo-rje°. C, 29c

ẖKhor°. C, 070a

Padma°.

ẖKhor°. C, 070c

Nub°. C, 30b

Rin-chen°.

ẖKhor°. C, 070b

Lho°. C, 30a

Las-kyi°.
ẖKhor°. C, 71a
Byaṅ°. C, 30c
mKhaẖ-ẖgro-ma-stag-gdoṅ-can. D, 187
mKhaẖ-ẖgro-ma-dom-gyi-gdoṅ-can. D, 189
mKhaẖ-ẖgro-ma-seṅ-geẖi-gdoṅ-can. D, 188
Cf. Seṅ-gdoṅ-ma. B, 357
mKhaẖ-ẖgroẖi-ẖjigs-skyobs. C, 42b
mkhaẖ-ldiṅ. Cf. Khyuṅ°.
bDe-mchog-rdo-rje°. C,78c
bDe-mchogs°. B,40
mkhaẖ-spyod. Cf. mKhaẖ-ẖgro-ma, ḍā-ki.
Nā-ro°. C, 25b; C, 28c
Mai-tri°. C, 25c
Indra°. C, 26a
mKhas-grub-rje. B, 23; C, 0c; D, 42
ẖKhon-daṅ(?)-rgyags-pa-rnam-gnon. B, 119
Cf. A, 1B50.
ẖKhor-karma-ḍā-ki. C, 118c
ẖkhor-klu-brgyad-bcas (rNam-sras-drag-byed°).
C, 105a–c
ẖKhor-klu-mo-las-byed-ma. C, 59c
ẖKhor-khro-gñer-can-ma. C, 35c; C, 36c; C, 37c
ẖKhor-sgrib-sel. C, 16a
ẖKhor-sgrol-ma. C, 36a; C, 37a
ẖkhor-chen (Phyag-rdor°). B, 59
ẖKhor-ẖjam-dpal. C, 16c
ẖKhor-rta-mgrin. C, 35a; C, 36c; C, 37c
ẖKhor-don-zhags-dmar-po. C, 35a
ẖKhor-rdo-rje-mkhaẖ-ẖgro-ma. C, 070a
ẖKhor-rdo-rje-las-byed-ma. C, 59a
ẖKhor-nor-bzaṅ. C, 37a
ẖKhor-nor-bzaṅ-gzhon-nu. C, 36a
ẖKhor-gnod-sbyin-brgyad. C, 104a
ẖKhor-gnod-sbyin-mo-brgyad. C, 104c
ẖKhor-gnod-sbyin-las-byed-ma. C, 60a
ẖKhor-padma-mkhaẖ-ẖgro-ma. C, 070c
ẖKhor-padma-ḍā-ki. C, 118c
ẖKhor-spyan-ras-gzigs. C, 16c
ẖKhor-phag-mo. C, 53a

ẖKhor-ba-ẖjig. B, 130
Saṅs-rgyas°. C, 83a
ẖKhor-buddha-ḍā-ki. C, 118a
ẖKhor-byams-pa. C, 16a
ẖKhor-ratna-ḍā-ki. C, 118a
ẖKhor-ral-gcig-ma. C, 35c; C, 53b
ẖKhor-rin-chen-mkhaẖ-ẖgro-ma. C, 070b
ẖKhor-las-kyi-mkhaẖ-ẖgro-ma. C, 71a
ẖkhor-lo-chen-po (dPal°). D, 64
ẖKhor-lo-sdom-pa.
dPal°. B, 36; D, 63
°ser-po. C, R7c
ẖKhor-lo-ma. D, 299
ẖKhor-gśin-rje-las-byed-ma. C, 59b
ẖkhor-lha-mo-çaṇḍi-ka (mGon-po-phyag-bzhi-paẖi°). C, 121a
gaṅ-ba-bzaṅ-po (gNod-sbyin°). B, 354
gaṅ-blo-maẖi-bstod-sgrub-mar-grags-pa (ẖJam-dbyaṅs°). C, 66a
gandha-ri (rDo-rje°). B, 262
gar-mkhan-mchog.
rNam-sras°. B, 324
rNam-sras-dmar-po°. C, 103c
Sras°. C, 110b
Gur-rkyaṅ-rṅog-lugs. C, 123a
Gur-gyi-mgon-po. D, 242
Cf. mGon-po-gur. B, 305
Gur-mgon-lcam-dral. C, 121c
Gur-mgon-phur-zhabs-can. C, 122b
Gur-mgon-lha-brgyad. C, 122a
Gur-yum-can-klu-sgrub-lugs. C, 122c
Gur-las-gzuṅs-paẖi-rdo-rje-sgrol-ma. B, 228
Gegs-mthar-byed. B, 345
Cf. bGegs-mthar-byed. C, S10a
Go-chaẖi-skrag-byed-ma. C, 21b
Go-chaẖi-bskyod-byed-ma. C, 21c
Go-chaẖi-rta-mchog. C, 20a
Go-chaẖi-rdo-rje-ñi-ma. C, 19c
Go-chaẖi-rdo-rje-phag-mo. C, 20b
Go-chaẖi-rdo-rje-sems-dpaẖ. C, 18b

Go-chaḫi-rnam-snaṅ. C, 18c
Go-chaḫi-padma-gar-dbaṅ. C, 19a
Go-chaḫi-rmoṅs-byed-ma. C, 21a
Go-chaḫi-çaṇḍi-ka. C, 22a
Go-chaḫi-gśin-rje-ma. C, 20c
Go-chaḫi-he-ru-ka-nag-po. C, 19b
Go-bzlog-lhan-skyes. C, 29a
gos-dkar-mo (Lha-mo°). C, 89c
gos-sṅon-can.
  Phyag-rdor°. B, 72; C, 55a; D, 170
  Phyag-rdor° °ḫgro-bzaṅ-lugs. C, 56c
Grva-ba-mṅon-śes-lugs-kyi-ẓambha-la-dmar-po.
  C, 109b
Gri-gug-mgon-po. C, S12b
  Cf. mGon-po-gri-gug°.
    mGon-po-trakṣad-gri-gug°.
Grub-chen-ḍo-mbi-pa. D, 20
Grub-chen-te-lo-pa. D, 17
Grub-chen-dril-bu-pa. D, 14
Grub-chen-nā-ro-pa. D, 16
Grub-chen-nag-po-spyod-pa. D, 15
Grub-chen-mai-tri-pa. D, 18
Grub-chen-ẓa-wa-ri-pa. D, 19
grub-chen-zhi-ba-sbas-paḫi-lugs (mGon-po-phyag-bzhi-pa°).
  C, 119a
Grub-chen-lā-li-ta-baẓra. D, 13
Grub-chen-lū-i-pa. D, 12
Grub-chen-śa-ba-ri-pa. D, 10
Grub-chen-sa-ra-ha-pa. D, 11
Grub-dbaṅ-hūṁ-ka-ra. D, 27
glaṅ-chen-po (Kun-tu-bzaṅ-po°). B, 200
Glaṅ-poḫi-ḫjigs-skyobs. C, 41b
dgaḫ-bo (Klu-rgyal°). D, 289
dGun-gyi-rgyal-mo. D, 252
dGun-gyi-lha-mo. B, 334
dge-bsñen (Hva-śaṅ°). B, 289
dGe-bsñen-dharma. C, 10c
dGe-bsñen-dharma-ta-la. B, 288
dGe-ḫdun-grub-pa. B, 24
  Cf. rJe-dge-ḫdun-grub. D, 43

dGra-nag-gśin-rje-gśed. C, R2a
Cf. gŚin-rje-gśed-dgra-nag. D, 71
dGra-nags. B, 43
bGegs-mthar-byed. C, S10a
Khro-bo°. C, 74a
Gegs-mthar-byed. B, 345
mgon.
dPal° °klu-grub. D, 5
dPal° °zhal-bzhi-pa-sgrub-dus-daṅ-ḫbrel-ba. C, 131b
dpal° °zhal-bzhi-pa-bsñen-dus-daṅ-ḫbrel-ba. C, 131a
Las° °bya-rog-gdoṅ-can. B, 304; C, 121b
mGon-dkar-yid-bzhin-nor-bu. B, 317; C, 0110a; C, 117a; D, 229
mGon-ljaṅ-çhe-bdag. C, 118b
Cf. Çhe-bdag-mgon-po. B, 316; D, 231
mgon-po.
Drag-śad°. D, 261
Brag-lha°. D, 260
Çhogs-bdag° °seṅgeḫi-gdan-can. C, 128a
Zhal-bzhi-pa-las-sbyor°. C, 131c
Lho-nub° °gri-gug-dmar-po. C, 125c
mGon-po-gur. B, 305
Cf. Gur°.
Gur-gyi-mgon-po.
Gur-mgon°.
mGon-po-gri-gug-kha-che-paṇ-chen-lugs. C, 126b
Cf. Gri-gug-mgon-po.
mGon-po-gri-gug-dpaḫ-gcig. C, 125b
mgon-po-gri-gug-dmar-po (Lho-nub°). C, 125c
mGon-po-gri-gug-ẓñā-na-lugs. C, 127a
mGon-po-gcer-bu-zaṅs-gri-can. C, 127c
mGon-po-ṭakṣad-? B, 300
Cf. Ṭakṣad.
Trakṣad.
Drag-śad-mgon-po.
mGon-po-trakṣad-rkaṅ-thaṅ-ma. C, 129c
mGon-po-trakṣad-gri-gug-sbrags-sgrub-ma. C, 129b
mGon-po-trakṣad-gños-lugs. C, 128b
mGon-po-trakṣad-dvags-poḫi-lugs. C, 128c
mGon-po-trakṣad-ḫbroṅ-zhal-can. C, 130b
Cf. ḫBroṅ-zhal-can. B, 298

mGon-po-trakṣad-ma-niṅ-ma. C, 130a
mGon-po-trakṣad-seṅ-zhon-jo-boḫi-lugs. C, 129a
Cf. Ṭakṣad-seṅge-zhon-pa. B, 299
mGon-po-trakṣad-gsaṅ-sgrub-śva-naḫi-zhal-can. C, 130c
mGon-po-stag-zhon. B, 301; D, 259
mGon-po-stag-gzhon-ma. C, 123b
mGon-po-phyag-drug-pa. B, 297; D, 230
mGon-po-phyag-bzhi-pa. B, 306; D, 243
ḫÇhal-lugs-kyi°. C, 120a
Lugs-gñis-gcig-tu-sgril-baḫi°. C, 120b
mGon-po-phyag-bzhi-pa-klu-sgrub-lugs. C, 119b
mGon-po-phyag-bzhi-pa-grub-chen-zhi-ba-sbas-paḫi-lugs. C, 119a
mGon-po-phyag-bzhi-pa-rgva-loḫi-lugs. C, 119c
mGon-po-phyag-bzhi-paḫi-ḫkhor-lha-mo-çaṇḍi-ka. C, 121a
mGon-po-bar-chad-kun-sel. C, 116b
mGon-po-beṅ. B, 303; D, 255
mGon-po-beṅ-dkaḫ-ma. C, 123c
mGon-po-beṅ-gter-ma. C, 124a
mGon-po-beṅ-nag-zaṅs-gri-can. C, 127b
mGon-po-bram-zeḫi-gzugs-can. D, 241
Cf. Zhal-bram-gzugs. B, 307
mGon-po-bzhi-sbrags. C, 126a
mGon-po-zaṅs-gri-can-gyi-ljaṅ-lugs. C, 126c
mGon-po-legs-ldan. B, 302; D, 256–58
mGon-po-legs-ldan-mched-gsum. C, 124b
mGon-po-lha-chen-dpal-ḫbar-jo-boḫi-lugs. C, 125a
mGon-po-aṁ-gho-ra. C, 124c
mGon-dmar-rkaṅ-gliṅ-can. C, 120c
mGon-dmar-dbaṅ-gi-rgyal-po. C, 0110c; C, 117c
mGon-ser-blo-ḫphel. C, 0110b; C, 117b
mgrin-sṅon-can (ḫJig-rten-dbaṅ-phyug°). B, 169
mGrin-bzaṅ-ma. D, 275
Cod-paṇ°. C, 142c
ḫGro-ba-ḫgugs-paḫi-sgrol-ma. B, 216
ḫGro-bzaṅ-ma. D, 274
gTad-dkar°. C, 142c
ḫgro-bzaṅ-lugs (Phyag-rdor-gos-sṅon-can°). C, 56c
rgva-loḫi-lugs (mGon-po-phyag-bzhi-pa°). C, 119c

rGol-ba-ḫjoms-paḫi-sgrol-ma. C, 96c
rGya-nag-rim-paḫi-sgrol-ma. B, 229
rGyan-drug-phyag-mçhan. C, R17c
rGyal-chen-rnam-thos-sras. B, 320
rGyal-mchog-rin-chen. D, 79
rgyal-po (rDo-rje°). B, 192
rgyal-po-rol-ba (ḫJams-dpal°). B, 153
rGyal-ba-kun-nas-snaṅ-ba. D, 129
Cf. Kun-nas-snaṅ-ba-bkod-paḫi-dpal. B, 114
rGyal-ba-kun-gzigs. B, 143; D, 135
rGyal-ba-klu-dbaṅ-gi-rgyal-po. D, 100; D, 134
rgyal-ba-khyu-mchog (Sras°). C, 110c
rgyal-ba-rgya-mçho (sPyan-ras-gzigs°). B, 34; C, 43c
rGyal-ba-chu-lha. D, 111
rGyal-ba-chu-lhaḫi-lha. D, 112
rGyal-ba-mthoṅ-ba-don-yod. D, 105
rGyal-ba-dran-paḫi-dpal. D, 123
rGyal-ba-dri-ma-med-pa. D, 107
rGyal-ba-rdo-rje-ḫchaṅ. B, 29
rGyal-ba-rdo-rje-sñiṅ-po. D, 98
rGyal-ba-nor-dpal. D, 122
rGyal-ba-rnam-par-gnon-pa. D, 128
rGyal-ba-padmaḫi-ḫod-zer. D, 121
rGyal-ba-dpaḫ-boḫi-sde. D, 101
rGyal-ba-dpal-dyges. D, 102
rGyal-ba-dpal-sbyin. D, 108
rGyal-ba-dpal-bzaṅ. D, 113
rGyal-ba-blo-bzaṅ-don-grub. D, 45
rGyal-ba-dbaṅ-poḫi-tog-gi-rgyal-mçhan. D, 125
Cf. dBaṅ-poḫi-tog-gi-rgyal-mçhan-gyi-rgyal-po. B, 110
rGyal-ba-me-tog-dpal. D, 119
rGyal-ba-mya-ṅan-med-paḫi-dpal. D, 117
rGyal-ba-çan-dan-dpal. D, 114
rGyal-ba-gçug-tor-dri-med. D, 133
rGyal-ba-çhaṅs-pa. D, 109
rGyal-ba-çhaṅs-paḫi-ḫod-zer. D, 120
rGyal-ba-çhaṅs-pas-sbyin. D, 110
rGyal-ba-çhe-dpag-med. D, 85
rGyal-ba-mçhan-dpal-yoṅs-sgrags. D, 124

rGyal-ba-gzi-brjid-mthaẖ-yas. D, 115
rGyal-ba-ẖod-dpag-med. D, 132
rGyal-ba-ẖod-dpal. D, 116
rgyal-baẖi-ẖbyuṅ-gnas (ẖBrom-ston°). D, 28
rGyal-ba-gyul-las-rgyal-ba. D, 127
rGyal-ba-ri-dbaṅ-gi-rgyal-po. D, 130
rGyal-ba-rin-chen-padma. D, 131
rGyal-ba-rin-chen-me. D, 103
rGyal-ba-rin-chen-zla-ba. D, 106
rGyal-ba-rin-chen-zla-ẖod. D, 104
rGyal-ba-rin-chen-ẖod-ẖphro. D, 99
rGyal-ba-śākya-thub-pa. C, 81c; D, 2; D, 97
rGyal-ba-śin-tu-rnam-par-gnon-pa. D, 126
rGyal-ba-seṅ-geẖi-ṅa-ro. B, 140; D, 143
rGyal-ba-sred-med-kyi-bu. D, 118
rGyal-dbaṅ-lṅa-pa-chen-po. D, 46
rGyal-dbaṅ-blo-bzaṅ-skal-bzaṅ-rgya-mçho. D, 50
Cf. Tālaẖi-bla-ma-skal-bzaṅ-rgya-mçho (reads rgyal-mçho). B, 28
rgyal-mo.
dGun-gyi°. D, 252
sTon-gyi°. D, 250
dPal-ldan-dmag-zor°. C, 134b
dPyid-kyi°. D, 247
dByar-gyi°. D, 249
gZaẖ-yum-rig-paẖi°. C, 77a
Yid-bzhin° °phyag-bzhi-ma. B, 231
Lha-mo-srog-sgrub-lcags-phur-ma-raṅ-byuṅ°. C, 134c
rGyal-çhab-rje̹. B, 22; C, 0a; D, 40
rgyal-mçhan (rDo-rje°). B, 187
rGyal-mçhan-rçe-moẖi-dpuṅ-rgyan. B, 260; C, 92a; D, 191
rGyal-mçhan-ma. D, 296
rgyu (rDo-rje°). B, 183
rgyud-lugs (Dus-ẖkhor-khyuṅ-khra°). C, 79a
sgam-po-pa (rJe-bçun°). D, 33
sGyu-ẖphrul-dra-baẖi-rim-paẖi-spyan-ras-gzigs. B, 170
sGra-gcan-ẖzin. B, 281; D, 202
sGra-gcan-zin. C, 8b

sGra-dbyaṅs-rgyal-po. D, 137
Cf. Rin-chen-zla-ba. C, 15a
Saṅs-rgyas-rin-po-che-daṅ-zla-ba-daṅ-padmas-rab-tu-brgyan-pa-mkhas-pa-gzi-brjid-sgra-dbyaṅs-kyi-rgyal-po. B, 134
sgra-bzaṅ-dbaṅ-phyug-rgyal-po (ḫJam-dbyaṅs°). B, 152
sGrib-pa-rnam-sel. B, 199; C, 86b; D, 149
Cf. ḫKhor-sgrib-sel. C, 16a
sgrub-dus-daṅ-ḫbrel-ba (dPal-mgon-zhal-bzhi-pa°). C, 131b
sgrol (gÑan° °yan-lag-drug-pa). C, 2c
sGrol-dkar. C, S6c; D, 160
Jo-lugs°. C, 1a
gÑan-lugs°. C, 1c
Nags-rin-lugs-kyi°. C, 2a
sGrol-dkar-kha-che-paṇ-chen-lugs. C, 44c
sGrol-dkar-phyag-drug-ma. B, 232
sGrol-dkar-ba-riḫi-lugs. C, 1b
sGrol-dkar-yid-bzhin-gyi-ḫkhor-lo. B, 230
Sgrol-ljaṅ. C, S7a
ḫPhags-ma°. C, 94b
sGrol-ljaṅ-kha-che-paṇ-chen-lugs. C, 44b
sGrol-ma. Cf. tā-ra. C, 52a
bKaḫ-gdams-lha-bzhiḫi-naṅ-gi°. C, 44a
bKra-śis-skye-baḫi°. B, 217
bKra-śis-snaṅ-baḫi°. C, 99b
Khro-gñer-gyo-baḫi°. C, 100a
ḫKhor°. C, 36a; C, 37a
Gur-las-gzuṅs-paḫi-rdo-rje°. B, 228
ḫGro-ba-ḫgugs-paḫi°. B, 216
rGol-ba-ḫjoms-paḫi°. C, 96c
rGya-nag-rim-paḫi°. B, 229
Ṅan-soṅ-las-sgrol-baḫi°. B, 234
dṄos-grub-sçol-baḫi°. B, 225
Chags-pa-ḫjoms-paḫi°. B, 221; C, 100c
mChog-sçol-baḫi°. C, 98b
ḫJig-rten-gsum-las-rnam-par-rgyal-baḫi°. C, 96b
Dug-nag-sel-baḫi°. B, 227
Don-thams-cad-sgrub-paḫi°. B, 235

Driẖi°. C, 49a
bDug-pa°. C, 48b
bDe-ba-sbyin-paẖi°. B, 222
rDo-rje°. C, 50c; C, R5a
Padma°. C, 47b
Phoṅs-pa-sel-baẖi°. C, 99a
Phyag-brgyad°. C, 53c
dBaṅ-mchog-ster-bahi°. C, 97a
Mar-me°. C, 48c
Me-tog°. C, 48a
Mya-ṅan-sel-baẖi°. B, 215; C, 98c
Myur-zhiṅ-dpaẖi°. B, 207
rMi-lam-ston-paẖi°. C, 51c
gÇug-tor°. B, 210
gÇug-tor-rnam-par-rgyal-baẖi°. C, 95c
Zhi-ba-chen-moẖi° (B reads baẖi). B, 220; C, 100b
Rab-tu-dpaẖ-baẖi°. C, 94c
Rin-chen°. C, 47a
Saṅs-rgyas°. C, 47c
Seṅ-ldeṅ-nags-kyi° (B reads nag-ẖbye; D om. kyi). B, 206; C, 97c; D, 161
O-rgyan° °gnas-kyi-dbaṅ-phyug-ma. C, 45b
sGrol-ma-khros-ma-nag-mo. B, 219
sGrol-ma-dṅos-grub-ẖbyuṅ-ma. C, 102a
sGrol-ma-ñin-zhi-mçhan-khro. C, 45a
sGrol-ma-bdud-ẖjoms-ma. B, 214
sGrol-ma-bde-sgrub-ma. C, 101a
sGrol-ma-sdug-bsṅal-bsreg-ma. C, 101c
Cf. sDug-bsṅal-bsregs-paẖi-sgrol-ma. B, 224
sGrol-ma-nor-sbyin-ma. B, 233; C, 46b
sGrol-ma-rnam-par-rgyal-ma-dkar-mo. B, 223
Cf. rNam-par-rgyal-baẖi-sgrol-ma. B, 212
sGrol-ma-dmar-mo-sa-lugs. C, 46a
sGrol-ma-smin-byed-ma. B, 218
Cf. Yoṅs-su-smin-par-mẓad-paẖi-sgrol-ma. C, 99c
sGrol-ma-gzhan-gyis-mi-thub-pa. B, 213
sGrol-ma-zla-mdaṅ-ma. B, 208
Cf. dKar-mo-zla-mdaṅs-kyi-sgrol-ma. C, 95a
sGrol-ma-yid-bzhin-nor-bu. C, 45c

sGrol-ma-yoṅs-rẓogs-byed-ma.   C, 102b
  Cf. Yoṅs-su-rẓogs-paẖi-sgrol-ma.   B, 226
sGrol-ma-rab-rgyas-ma.   C, 101b
sGrol-ma-ser-mo.   C, 46c
sGrol-ma-gser-mdog-ma.   B, 209
  Cf. gSer-mdog-can-gyi-sgrol-ma.   C, 95b
sGrol-ma-hūṁ-sgra-sgrogs-ma.   B, 211
  Cf. Hūṁ-sgra-sgrog-paẖi-sgrol-ma.   C, 96a
brGya-byin (D reads sbyin).   B, 328; D, 277
ṅag-gi-rgyal-po (ẖJam-dbyaṅ°).   B, 150
ṅag-dbaṅ-mchog-ldan (Khri-chen°).   D, 49
ṅag-dbaṅ-blo-bzaṅ-rgya-mçho (rJe°) (reads rgyal-po for rgya·
          B, 26
Ṅan-soṅ-sbyoṅs-rgyal.   D, 78
Ṅan-soṅ-las-sgrol-baẖi-sgrol-ma.   B, 234
dṅos-grub-ẖbyuṅ-ma (sGrol-ma°).   C, 102a
dṄos-grub-sçol-baẖi-sgrol-ma.   B, 225
mṄon-mkhyen-rgyal-po.   C, 14b; D, 141
  Cf. Chos-rgya-mçho-mchog-gi-blos-rnam-par-rol-bar-mṅoı
      mkhyen-paẖi-rgyal-po.   B, 138
mṅon-par-mkhyen-pa.
  Padmaẖi-ẖod-zer-rnam-par-rol-bas°.   B, 106
  Çhaṅs-paẖi-ẖod-zer-rnam-par-rol-bas°.   B, 105
mNon-phyogs-dmar-po.   D, 285
mṅon-ẖphags-rgyal-po (Saṅs-rgyas°).   B, 118
mṅon-byaṅ (rNam-snaṅ°) (B reads byaṅs and rnams).
          B, 70; D, 83
mṅon-śes-lugs-kyi (Grva-ba° °ẓambha-la-dmar-po).
          C, 109b
rṅog-lugs (Gur-rkyaṅ°).   C, 123a
rṄog-legs-paẖi-śes-rab.   D, 30
lṅa-pa-chen-po (rGyal-dbaṅ°).   D, 46
ce-spyaṅ-gdoṅ (Śa-za°).   C, 133c
Cod-paṇ-mgrin-bzaṅ-ma.   C, 142c
gcer-bu (mGon-po° °zaṅs-gri-can).   C, 127c
bCu-gcig-zhal.   B, 173
  Thugs-rje-chen-po°.   C, S5b; D, 95
  sPyan-ras-gzigs° °dpal-mo-lugs.   C, 34b
bCu-gcig-zhal-ẖjigs-pa-brgyad-skyobs.   C, 40a
bCom-ldan-reg-çhig.   B, 358

lcags-kyu (sPyan-ras-gzigs-don-yod°). C, 88a
lcags-kyu-ma(rDo-rje°). C, 49b
lCags-sgrog-ma. C, 50a
rDo-rje°. B, 347
lcags-phur-ma (Lha-mo-srog-sgrub° °raṅ-byuṅ-rgyal-ṁo). C, 134c
lcags-ral-can (rTa-mgrin°). B, 76; C, 61a; D, 166
lcaṅ-skya-rol-paḫi-rdo-rje (rJe°). D, 53
lcam-dral.
dKar-mo-ñi-zla°. C, 139b
Gur-mgon°. C, 121c
Pu-tra°. C, 138c
chags-pa (rDo-rje°). B, 191
Chags-pa-ḫjoms-paḫi-sgrol-ma. B, 221; C, 100c
Chad-paḫi-ḫjigs-skyobs. C, 41c
Chuḫi-ḫjigs-skyobs. C, 40c
Chu-lha. B, 96; D, 288
rGyal-ba°. D, 111
Chu-lhaḫi- ha. B, 97
rGyal-ba°. D, 112
chuṅ. Cf. gtum-chuṅ.
cher-rgyas (Me-tog°). D, 81
chos.
rDo-rje°. B, 185
sPyan-ras-gzigs-rdo-rje°. B, 163
Chos-kyi-rdo-rje-ma. B, 263
Chos-grags. B, 6
rJe-bçun°. D, 9
Chos-rgya-mçho-mchog-gi-blos-rnam-par-rol-bar-mṅon-par-mkhyen-paḫi-rgyal-po. B, 138
Cf. mṄon-mkhyen-rgyal-po. C, 14b; D, 141
Chos-rgyal. B, 312
Chos-rgyal-naṅ-sgrub. D, 239
Chos-rgyal-phyi-sgrub. D, 238
Chos-rgyal-las-kyi-gśin-rje-mthiṅ-ga. C, 137b
Chos-rgyal-gsaṅ-sgrub. D, 240
Chos-sgrags-rgya-mçhoḫi-dbyaṅs (B reads dbyaṅ). B, 137; D, 140
Chos-bsgrags-rgya-mçho. C, 14a

Chos-dbyiṅ-gsuṅ-gi-dbaṅ-phyug. B, 67
ḫJam-dbyaṅs° °brgyad-pa. B, 151
Chos-dbyiṅs-gsuṅ-dbaṅ. C, R15b
mched-gsum (mGon-po-legs-ldan°). C, 124b
mChog-sçol-baḫi-sgrol-ma. C, 98b
mchod-paḫi-nor-bu (sPyan-ras-gzigs-don-yod°).
C, 88b
ḫChi-med-rdo-rje-lha-mo. C, 65a
Jo-bo-chen-po-dpal-ldan-a-ti-śa. D, 29
jo-boḫi-lugs.
mGon-po-trakṣad-seṅ-zhon°. C, 129a
mGon-po-lha-chen-dpal-ḫbar°. C, 125a
rTa-mgrin-khyuṅ-gśog-can°. C, 58b
rTa-mgrin-dpaḫ-gcig-lhan-skyes°. C, 58a
rTa-mgrin-śva-na-bzhi-skor°. C, 58c
sPyan-ras-gzigs-yi-ge-drug-pa°. C, 33b
Çhogs-bdag-dkar-po-phyag-bzhi-pa°. C, 114b
Ẓambha-la-dkar-po-lha-lṅa°. C, 108c
Jo-boḫi-lugs-kyi-rta-mgrin. D, 168
Jo-lugs-sgrol-dkar. C, 1a
Jo-a-ti-śa. B, 19
ḫJam-dkar. Cf. ḫJam-dbyaṅs-dkar-po.
°śes-rab-ḫkhor-lo. C, 66c
Cf. ḫJam-dbyaṅs-śes-rab-ḫkhor-lo-daṅ-po.
B, 156
ḫjam-rdor.
rNam-snaṅ°. C, R1b
gSaṅ-ḫdus°. C, 17a; C, R1a; D, 68
ḫjam-paḫi-rdo-rje (gSaṅ-ḫdus°). B, 30
ḫJam-paḫi-dbyaṅs. Cf. ḫJam-dbyaṅs. D, 145
rJe-bçun°. D, 3
ḫjam-dpal.
ḫKhor°. C, 16c
ḫPhags-pa°. C, 93b
ḫJams-dpal-rgyal-po-rol-ba. B, 153
ḫJam-dpal-nā-ga-rakṣa. C, 81b
ḫJam-dpal-rnon-po. B, 157
ḫJam-dpal-gzhon-nur-gyur-ba. B, 146; D, 93
ḫJam-dpal-bśes-gñen. D, 21

ẖjam-dbyaṅs. Cf. ẖJam-paẖi-dbyaṅs.
Cf. ẖJig-gsum-lhag-par-dbaṅ-du-byed-paẖi°. B, 154
mÇhan-brjod-kyi° °phyag-bzhi-pa. B, 155
ẖJam-dbyaṅs-dkar-po. B, 145; C, S2c; D, 91
Cf. ẖJam-dkar.
ẖJam-dbyaṅs-dkar-po-kha-che-paṇ-chen-lugs. C, 65b
ẖJam-dbyaṅs-gaṅ-blo-maẖi-bstod-sgrub-mar-grags-pa. C, 66a
ẖJam-dbyaṅs-sgra-bzaṅ-dbaṅ-phyug-rgyal-po. B, 152
ẖJam-dbyaṅ-ṅag-gi-rgyal-po. B, 150
ẖJam-dbyaṅs-chos-dbyiṅs-gsuṅ-gi-dbaṅ-phyug-brgyad-pa. B, 151
ẖJam-dbyaṅs-brtan-paẖi-ẖkhor-lo. B, 147
ẖJam-dbyaṅs-nag-po. C, 80a
ẖJam-dbyaṅs-naṅ-sgrub. B, 31
ẖJam-dbyaṅs-dmar-ser. D, 88
ẖJam-dbyaṅs-smra-baẖi-seṅge. C, 66b; C, S3b
ẖJam-dbyaṅs-smra-seṅ. D, 92
ẖJam-dbyaṅs-śes-rab-ẖkhor-lo-daṅ-po. B, 156
Cf. ẖJam-dkar-śes-rab-ẖkhor-lo. C, 66c
ẖJam-dbyaṅ-seṅgeẖi-sgra. B, 149
ẖJam-dbyaṅ-gsaṅ-sgrub. B, 148
ẖJam-dbyaṅs-a-ra-pa-ça-na. C, S3a
ẖJam-dbyaṅs-a-ra-pa-ça-na-dmar-ser-sa-lugs. C, 65c
ẖJig-rten-mkhaẖ-ẖgro. C, 32a
ẖjigs-rten-dbaṅ-phyug (gSaṅ-ẖdus°). B, 33
ẖJig-rten-dbaṅ-phyug-mgrin-sṅon-can. B, 169
ẖJig-rten-dbaṅ-phyug-dmar-po-phyag-bzhi-pa. B, 168
ẖJig-rten-dbaṅ-phyug-yi-ge-bdun-pa. C, 23a
ẖJig-rten-dbaṅ-phyug-gsaṅ-sgrub. C, 39a
ẖJig-rten-dbaṅ-phyug-ha-ri-ha-ri-la-zhon-pa. B, 166
ẖJig-rten-dbaṅ-phyug-halhala. B, 162
ẖJig-rten-gsum-rgyal. B, 343
ẖJig-rten-gsum-las-rnam-par-rgyal-baẖi-sgrol-ma. C, 96b
ẖJig-gsum-lhag-par-dbaṅ-du-byed-paẖi-ẖjam-dbyaṅs. B, 154

ẖjigs-skyobs.
Kluẖi°. C, 42a
mKhaẖ-ẖgroẖi°. C, 42b
Glaṅ-poẖi°. C, 41b
Chad-paẖi°. C, 41c
Chuẖi°. C, 40c
Mi-rgod°. C, 42c
Meẖi°. C, 40b
Seṅ-geẖi°. C, 41a
ẖjigs-pa-brgyad-skyob.
bCu-gcig-zhal°. C, 40a
sPyan-ras-gzigs°. C, 86c
ẖJigs-byed. B, 42
rDo-rje°. D, 61
ẖJigs-byed-bsdus-pa. C, 24c
ẖJigs-byed-dpaẖ-gcig. B, 46
ẖJur-ẖgegs-sel-baẖi-çhogs-bdag. C, 114a
rJe-dge-ẖdun-grub. D, 43
rJe-ṅag-dbaṅ-blo-bzaṅ-rgya-mçho (reads rgyal-po for rgya-mçho)
B, 26
rJe-lcaṅ-skya-rol-paẖi-rdo-rje. D, 53
rJe-druṅ-blo-bzaṅ-dpal-ldan. D, 54
rJes-pan-chen-blo-bzaṅ-chos-kyis-rgyal-mçhan.
B, 25
Cf. Paṇ-chen-blo-bzaṅ-chos-rgyal-mçhan. D, 47
rJe-bçun-sgam-po-pa. D, 33
rJe-bçun-chos-grags. D, 9
rJe-bçun-ẖjam-paẖi-dbyaṅs. D, 3
rJe-bçun-thogs-med. D, 6
rJe-bçun-phyogs-glaṅ. D, 8
rJe-bçun-byams-pa. C, S4b; D, 1
rJe-bçun-dbyig-gñen. D, 7
rJe-bçun-ma-kā-pa-li-tā-ra. C, 54a
rJe-bçun-ma-thod-pa-rgyan. C, 72b
rJe-bçun-mar-pa. D, 32
rJe-bçun-mi-la. D, 31
rJe-bçun-mçho-skye-rdo-rje. D, 26
rJe-bçun-zhi-ba-lha. D, 24
rJe-bçun-zla-ba-grags-pa. D, 22
rJe-bçun-saṅs-rgyas-bskyaṅs. D, 23

rJe-bçun-arya-de-ba. D, 4
rJe-rin-po-che. C, 0b; D, 41
Cf. bÇoṅ-kha-pa-chen-po. B, 21
rJe-śes-rab-seṅ-ge. D, 44
rjes-su-spyod-pa (Saṅs-rgyas°). B, 117
ñams-sgrol (Zhal-bzhi-pa-sṅon-po°). C, 133a
Ñi-ltar-snaṅ-byed. C, 13c
ñi-ma (Go-chaḫi-rdo-rje°). C, 19c
ñi-zla-lcam-dral (dKar-mo°). C, 139b
ñin-zhi-mçhan-khro (sGrol-ma°). C, 45a
ñe-dgaḫ (Klu-rgyal°). D, 291
Ñer-sbas. B, 293
gÑan-sgrol-yan-lag-drug-pa. C, 2c
gÑan-lugs-sgrol-dkar. C, 1c
gños-lugs (mGon-po-trakṣad°). C, 128b
sñiṅ-gi-gser-thig-can (dPal-mo°). C, 71b
sÑiṅ-po-kyai-rdo-rje. B, 48
sÑiṅ-po-kyai-rdor. C, R2b
bsñen-dus-daṅ-ḫbrel-ba (dPal-mgon-zhal-bzhi-pa°).
C, 131a
Ṭakki-rā-ẓa. B, 313; C, 116c; D, 235
Cf. ḫDod-rgyal-dmar-po. C, 3b
Khro-bo-ḫdod-rgyal. D, 214
Ṭakṣad.
Cf. mGon-po-ṭakṣad.
mGon-po-trakṣad.
Trakṣad.
Drag-śad-mgon-po.
Ṭakṣad-nag-po. B, 308
Cf. Trakṣad-nag-po. D, 237
Ṭakṣad-seṅge-zhon-pa. B, 299
Cf. mGon-po-trakṣad-zen-zhon-jo-boḫi-lugs.
C, 129a
ḍā-ki. Cf. mKhaḫ-ḫgro-ma, mkhaḫ-spyod.
Cf. ḫKhor-karma°. C, 118c
ḫKhor-padma°. C, 118c
ḫKhor-buddha°. C, 118a
ḫKhor-ratna°. C, 118a
Ḍo-mbi-pa. B, 16
Grub-chen°. D, 20

tā-ra. Cf. sGrol-ma.
rJe-bçun-ma-kā-pa-li°. C, 54a
ḫPhags-ma-çunda°. C, 54b
Tālaḫi-bla-ma-skal-bzaṅ-rgya-mçho (reads rgyal for rgya). B, 28
Cf. rGyal-dbaṅ-blo-bzaṅ-skal-bzaṅ-rgya-mçho. D, 50
ti-nu (Lha-mo°). C, 72a
For Chinese ti-mu?
Te-lo-pa. B, 17
Grub-chen°. D, 17
Trakṣad. C, 116c
Cf. mGon-po-ṭakṣad.
mGon-po-trakṣad.
Takṣad.
Drag-śad-mgon-po.
Trakṣad-nag-po. D, 237
Cf. Ṭakṣad-nag-po. B, 308
gTad-dkar-ḫgro-bzaṅ-ma. C, 142c
gtum-chuṅ.
Phyag-rdor°. B, 73; D, 169
Phyag-rdor° °dmar-po. C, 56b
gtum-chen-bsruṅ-baḫi-mkhar-ras-chuṅ-lugs (Phyag-rdor°). C, 55c
gtum-po (Phyag-rdor° °khra-thogs). C, 56a
gTum-po-zhal-gsum-phyag-drug-pa. B, 75
gter-ma (mGon-po-beṅ°). C, 124a
rTa-mgrin. C, S7b
Khro-bo°. D, 213
ḫKhor°. C, 35a; C, 36c; C, 37c
Jo-boḫi-lugs-kyi°. D, 168
rTa-mgrin-dkar-po. C, 91a
rTa-mgrin-skyer-sgaṅ-lugs. C, 60c
rTa-mgrin-kha-che-paṇ-chen-lugs. C, 60b
rTa-mgrin-khyuṅ-gśog-can-jo-boḫi-lugs. C, 58b
rTa-mgrin-lcags-ral-can. B, 76; C, 61a; D, 166
rTa-mgrin-padma-gar-dbaṅ. B, 62
rTa-mgrin-dpaḫ-gcig-lhan-skyes-jo-boḫi-lugs. C, 58a
rTa-mgrin-śva-na-bzhi-skor-jo-bo-lugs. C, 58c
rTa-mgrin-gsaṅ-sgrub. B, 61; D, 167

rta-snon-can.
rNam-sras-mduṅ-dmar°. C, 103a
rNam-sras-nag-po°. C, 106a
rta-mchog (Go-chaḫi°). C, 20a
rta-ljaṅ-can (Ḫod-zer-can-ma°). C, 91c
stag-gdoṅ-can (mKhaḫ-ḫgro-ma°). D, 187
stag-zhon (mGon-po°). B, 301; D, 259
stag-gzhon-ma (mGon-po°). C, 123b
sToṅ-chen-mo. B, 201; D, 175
sTon-gyi-rgyal-mo. D, 250
sTon-gyi-lha-mo. B, 333
sTobs-po-che. C, S9b
Khro-bo°. B, 342; D, 218
brtan-paḫi-ḫkhor-lo (ḫJam-dbyaṅs°). B, 147
brtan-ma (Saḫi-lha-mo°). B, 323
bstod-sgrub-mar-grags-pa (ḫJam-dbyaṅs-gaṅ-blo-maḫi°). C, 66a
Thams-cad-skyob. B, 129
Saṅs-rgyas°. C, 82c
Thams-cad-mkhaḫ-ḫgro. C, 31c
thams-cad-mkhyen-pa (Bu-ston°). D, 37
Thugs-kyai-rdor. C, R2c; C, R5c
Thugs-rje-chen-po-bcu-gcig-zhal. C, S5b; D, 95
Thub-pa-dam-çhig-gsum-bkod. C, 4c; C, 70b; D, 86
Thub-pa-rdo-rje-gdan-pa-gço-ḫkhor-gsum. C, 4b
Thub-pa-gnas-bcus-bskor-pa. C, S1a–c
Thub-pa-me-ru-śe-ṣa. C, 69b
Mantra has me-ru-śe-ṣa-ra-kū-ṭa-pra-bhu-rā-ẓā.
Thub-dbaṅ. C, 5a
the-çhom-gcod-mẓad (Daṅ-po-sems-skyed°). B, 126
Thogs-med. B, 2
rJe-bçun°. D, 6
thod-pa-rgyan (rJe-bçun-ma°). C, 72b
Thod-smyon-bsam-grub. D, 36
mThiṅ-gi-zhal-bzaṅ-ma. C, 142a; D, 271
mThoṅ-ba-don-yod. B, 90
rGyal-ba°. D, 105
dvags-poḫi-lugs (mGon-po-trakṣad°). C, 128c
Daṅ-po-sems-skyed-the-çhom-gcod-mẓad. B, 126
Dam-can-rdo-rje-legs-pa. D, 269

Dam-çhig-mkhaẖ-ẖgro. C, 31a
dam-çhig-gsum-bkod (Thub-pa°). C, 4c; C, 70b; D, 86
Dug-nag-sel-baẖi-sgrol-ma. B, 227
Dug-sel-ma. D, 181
ẖPhags-ma°. B, 236
duṅ-skyoṅ-ma (Lha-mo°) (D reads skyoṅs; B reads doṅ). B, 309; C, 135a; D, 246
dud-kha (Khro-bo-sme-brçegs°). C, 77b
Duṅ-ma. D, 294
dud-sol-ma (Lha-mo°) (B reads doṅ). B, 310; C, 134a; D, 245
Dur-khrod-bdag-po. B, 337; C, 138b; D, 253
Dus-kyi-ẖkhor-lo. B, 35
dPal°. D, 65
Dus-ẖkhor. C, R14b
Dus-ẖkhor-khyuṅ-khra-rgyud-lugs. C, 79a
dus-ẖkhor-lugs (Ẓambha-la-ljaṅ-khu°). C, 109c
Dus-ẖkhor-lhan-skyes. C, 23c
Dus-ldan. B, 275; C, 6b; D, 196
don-grub (Phag-mo°). C, 26b
Don-ẖgrub. B, 81
Cf. Don-yod-grub-pa. C, R11a
Don-ẖgrub-yab-yum. D, 60
don-thams-cad-sgrub-pa (Phag-mo°). B, 271
Don-thams-cad-sgrub-paẖi-sgrol-ma. B, 235
don-zhags. Cf. Don-yod-zhags-pa.
ẖKhor° °dmar-po. C, 35a
Don-zhags-kha-che-paṇ-chen-lugs. C, 36b
Don-zhags-ser-po. C, 35b
Don-zhags-lha-lṅa-ba-ri-lugs. C, 34c
Don-yod-grub-pa. C, R11a
Cf. Don-ẖgrub.
don-yod-lcags-kyu (sPyan-ras-gzigs°). C, 88a
don-yod-mchod-paẖi-nor-bu (sPyan-ras-gzigs°). C, 88b
Don-yod-zhags-pa. Cf. don-zhags. B, 171
ẖPhags-pa°. D, 96
dom-gyi-gdoṅ-can (mKhaẖ-ẖgro-ma°). D, 189
drag-po (Phyag-rdor° °gsum-sgril). D, 171
drag-byed.

rNam-sras° °ẖkhor-klu-brgyad-bcas. C, 105a–c
rNam-sras° °nag-po. B, 319
Drag-śad-mgon-po. D, 261
Cf. mGon-po-ṭakṣad.
mGon-po-trakṣad.
Ṭakṣad.
Trakṣad.
Dran-paẖi-dpal. B, 108
rGyal-ba°. D, 123
Dri-ma-med-pa. B, 92
rGyal-ba°. D, 107
Driẖi-sgrol-ma. C, 49a
Dril-bu-pa. B, 13
Grub-chen°. D, 14
Dril-bu-ma. C, 50b
gdan-bzhi (rDo-rje°). B, 57; D, 70
gdugs-dkar-(po-can).
ẖPhags-ma°. B, 248; D, 162
gÇug-tor°. C, 75a; C, S2a
gDugs-ma. D, 293
gDul-dkaẖ-sṅon-po. D, 283
gdoṅ-gñan-can (Zhal-bzhi-pa°). C, 133b
gDoṅ-po-drug-pa. B, 44
bDag-med. B, 53
Cf. rDo-rje°.
bDug-pa-sgrol-ma. C, 48b
bdud-ẖjoms-ma (sGrol-ma°). B, 214
bdud-daṅ-yid-gñis-kun-ẖjoms(?) (Saṅs-rgyas°). B, 121
Cf. A, 1B52.
bdud-ẖdul.
Cf. Zhaṅ-blon-rdo-rje°.
bDud-mo-re-ma-ti. C, 135b
Cf. Re-ma-ti.
bdud-rçi (rDo-rje°) (B reads rçis). C, R11b; B, 49
bDud-rçi-ẖkhyil-pa. B, 346; C, R12b
Khro-bo°. D, 215
bdud-rçuẖi-ma (H̱od-zer-can°). B, 245
bde-sgrub-ma (sGrol-ma°). C, 101a
bDe-mchog. C, R7a
Cf. sdom-pa.

bDe-mchog-dkar-po (B reads mchogs). B, 37; C, 22b; D, 73
bDe-mchog-dkar-po-çhe-sgrub. C, 22c
bDe-mchog-khro-bo-reg-çhig. C, 78b
bDe-mchogs-mkhaẖ-ldiṅ. B, 40
bDe-mchog-rdo-rje-mkhaẖ-ldiṅ. C, 78c
bDe-mchog-rdo-rje-sems-dpaẖ. C, R6c
bDe-mchogs-rdor-sems. B, 38
bDe-mchog-phyag-gñis. C, R7b
bDe-mchog-lhan-skyes (B reads mchogs). B, 39; C, 18a
bDe-ba-sbyin-paẖi-sgrol-ma. B, 222
mduṅ-dmar-can (rNam-sras°) (B reads mdoṅ-dmar). B, 321; D, 262
mduṅ-dmar-rta-sṅon-can (rNam-sras°). C, 103a
mdo-lugs (Phyag-rdor°). C, S8c
ẖDod-khams-dbaṅ-phyug-dmag-zor-ma. D, 248
ẖDod-rgyal-dmar-po. C, 3b
Cf. Khro-bo-ẖdod-rgyal. D, 214
Ṭakki-rā-za. B, 313; C, 116c; D, 235
rDo-rje-khu-çhur. B, 178
rDo-rjes-khyuṅ-khra. B, 41
rDo-rje-mkhaẖ-ẖgro. C, 141a; C, R3c; D, 224
rDo-rje-mkhaẖ-ẖgro-ma. C, 29c
ẖKhor°. C, 070a
rdo-rje-mkhaẖ-ldiṅ (bDe-mchog°). C, 78c
rDo-rje-gandha-ri. B, 262
rDo-rje-rgyal-po. B, 192
rDo-rje-rgyal-mçhan. B, 187
rDo-rje-rgyu. B, 183
rDo-rje-sgrol-ma. C, 50c; C, R5a
Gur-las-gzuṅs-paẖi°. B, 228
rDo-rje-lcags-kyu-ma. C, 49b
rDo-rje-lcags-sgrog. B, 347
rDo-rje-chags-pa. B, 191
rDo-rje-chos. B, 185
sPyan-ras-gzigs°. B, 163
rDo-rje-ẖchaṅ-yab-yum. D, 56
Cf. rGyal-ba-rdo-rje-ẖchaṅ. B, 29
rDo-rje-ẖjigs-byed. D, 61
rdo-rje-ñi-ma (Go-chaẖi°). C, 19c

rdo-rje-sñiṅ-po.
rGyal-ba°. D, 98
sPyan-ras-gzigs°. C, 43a
rdo-rje-gdan-pa-gço-ẖkhor-gsum (Thub-pa°). C, 4b
rDo-rje-gdan-bzhi. B, 57; D, 70
rDo-rje-bdag-med-pa. C, R4a
rDo-rje-bdag-med-phyag-gñis-ma. C, R4b
rDo-rje-bdud-rçi (B reads rçis). B, 49; C, R11b
rDo-rje-gnod-sbyin. B, 179
rDo-rje-rnam-ẖjoms. B, 352
rDo-rje-rnam-ẖjoms-dkar-po. C, 73a
rDo-rje-rnam-ẖjoms-ljaṅ-sṅon. C, 73c
rDo-rje-rnam-ẖjoms-mthiṅ-kha. C, 73b
rDo-rje-rnam-par-ẖjoms-pa. D, 173
rDo-rje-rnon-po. B, 184
rDo-rje-phag-mo. B, 54
Go-chaẖi°. C, 20b
Bram-ze-dpal-ẖẓin-lugs-kyi°. C, 28b
dPyal-lugs°. C, 25a
rDo-rje-bur-nas-gsuṅs-paẖi-so-sor-ẖbraṅ-ma.
C, 74c
rDo-rje-dbyaṅs-can-ma-phyag-gñis-ma. B, 254
rDo-rje-dbyaṅs-can-ma-phyag-drug-ma. B, 253
rDo-rje-dbyiṅs. B, 65
Cf. Rdor-dbyiṅs.
rdo-rje-dbyiṅs-kyi-dbaṅ-phyug-ma (H̱od-zer-can°).
B, 246
rDo-rje-mi-ẖkhrugs-pa. B, 141; D, 87
rDo-rje-moẖi-bu. B, 276; C, 6c; D, 197
rDo-rje-smra-ba. B, 182
rDo-rje-ça-rçiga. B, 257
rDo-rje-zhags-pa-ma. C, 49c
rDo-rje-bzhad-pa. B, 186
rDo-rje-gzi-brjid. B, 188
rDo-rjeẖi-sñiṅ-pos-rab-tu-ẖjoms-pa. B, 83
sPyan-ras-gzigs°. B, 177
rDo-rje-rab-sṅags-ma. C, 27a
rDo-rje-rin-chen. B, 189
rDo-rje-las. B, 181
rdo-rje-las-byed-ma (ẖKhor°). C, 59a

rDo-rje-legs-pa. B, 190
Dam-can°. D, 269
rDo-rje-śugs. C, 24a
rdo-rje-gśog-rgod-ma (Re-ma-ti°). C, 136b
rdo-rje-sa-ḫog (Khro-bo°). D, 221
rDo-rje-sems-dpaḫ. Cf. rdor-sems.
B, 69; C, R9b; D, 74
Go-chaḫi°. C, 18b
bDe-mchog°. C, R6c
Byaṅ-chub°. B, 193
rDo-rje-sems-dpaḫ-ser-po. C, 4a
rDo-rje-bsruṅ. B, 180
rDo-rje-hūṁ-mẓad. B, 56; B, 359; C, R11c
rDor-dbyiṅs. Cf. rDo-rje-dbyiṅs. D, 77
sNaṅ-mẓad°. C, R14c
rdor-seṁs (bDe-mchogs°). B, 38
Cf. rDo-rje-sems-dpaḫ.
sDug-bsṅal-bsregs-paḫi-sgrol-ma. B, 224
Cf. sGrol-ma-sdug-bsṅal-bsreg-ma. C, 101c
sdom-pa. Cf. bDe-mchog.
ḫKhor-lo° °ser-po. C, R7c
dPal-ḫkhor-lo°. B, 36; D, 63
bsdus-pa (ḫJigs-byed°). C, 24c
dharma (dGe-bsñen°). C, 10c
Dharma-ta-la. D, 209
dGe-bsñen°. B, 288
Dhi-dhi-ka. B, 294
nā-ga-rakṣa (ḫJam-dpal°). C, 81b
Nā-ro-mkhaḫ-spyod. C, 25b; C, 28c
Nā-ro-pa. B, 18
Grub-chen°. D, 16
Nag-po. B, 295
Nag-po-spyod-pa. B, 14
Grub-chen°. D, 15
Nags-na-gnas. B, 274; C, 6a; D, 195
Nags-rin-lugs-kyi-sgrol-dkar. C, 2a
naṅ-sgrub.
Chos-rgyal°. D, 239
ḫJam-dbyaṅs°. B, 31
Zhaṅ-blon-rdo-rje-bdud-ḫdul°. C, 113a

nam-mkhaẖ-rgyal-mçhan (Lho-brag°). D, 39
nam-mkhaẖi-gos-can (Lha-mo°). C, 137a
Nam-mkhaẖ-rgyal-po (reads mkhas). B, 174
  sPyan-ras-gzigs°. C, 39b
Nam-mkhaẖi-sñiṅ-po. B, 196; C, 85c; D, 150
Nub-padma-mkhaẖ-ẖgro-ma. C, 30b
Nor-rgyun-ma. C, R16c; C, S11a; D, 182
  Yid-hphrog°. C, 112b
  gZuṅs-las-byuṅ-baẖi-lha-mo°. C, 111b
Nor-rgyun-ma-ba-laṅ-rẓi. C, 112a
Nor-rgyun-ma-dmar-mo. C, 71c
Nor-rgyun-ma-ẓā-ma-riẖi-lugs. C, 111c
Nor-dpal. B, 107
  rGyal-ba°. D, 122
nor-ẖphel (Zhal-bzhi-ser-po°). C, 132b
Nor-bu-ẖẓin-pa. C, 33a
nor-bu-bzaṅ-po (gNod-sbyin°). C, 110a
Nor-sbyin-ma. B, 268
  sGrol-ma°. B, 233; C, 46b
nor-bzaṅ (ẖKhor°). C, 37a
nor-bzaṅ-gzhon-nu (ẖKhor°). C, 36a
gnam-zhabs-ma (Phag-mo°). C, 27c
gnas-kyi-dbaṅ-phyug-ma (O-rgyan-sgrol-ma°).
  C, 45b
gnas-bcus-bskor-pa (Thub-pa°). C, S1a–c
gnod-sbyin (rDo-rje°). B, 179
gNod-sbyin-gaṅ-ba-bzaṅ-po. B, 354
gnod-sbyin-brgyad (ẖKhor°). C, 104a
gNod-sbyin-nor-bu-bzaṅ-po. C, 110a
gnod-sbyin-mo-brgyad (ẖKhor°). C, 104c
gNod-sbyin-mo-ẖphrog-ma. C, 92c
gNod-sbyin-re-ma-ti. C, 136a
  Cf. Re-ma-ti.
gnod-sbyin-las-byed-ma (ẖKhor°). C, 60a
gNod-sbyin-a-pa-ra-ẓi-ta. C, 113c
rNam-rgyal-ma. C, R17b
  gÇug-tor°. B, 247; C, 64c
    phyag-gñis-ma C, 90a
  gÇug-tor-rnam-par-rgyal-ma. D, 164

rNam-bcu-dbaṅ-ldan. C, S12a
  Tib. supplied from Abhandlungen der
  Bayerischen Akademie XXIX, 3, p. 97.

rnam-ẖjoms or rnam-par-ẖjoms-pa.
  Cf. rDo-rje°.

rNam-thos-sras. Cf. rNam-sras, Sras.
  C, 12b; C, 51b; C, 139c; D, 281
  rGyal-chen°. B, 320

rnam-gnon. Cf. rnam-par-gnon-pa.
  ẖKhon-daṅ(?)-rgyags-pa°. B, 119

rNam-snaṅ. Cf. rNam-par-snaṅ-mẓad. B, 77
  Go-chaẖi°. C, 18c

rNam-snaṅ-mṅon-byaṅ (B reads byaṅs, rnams).
  B, 70; D, 83

rNam-snaṅ-ẖjam-rdor. C, R1b

rNam-snaṅ-ma. C, 27b

rNam-snaṅ-yab-yum. D, 55

rNams-snaṅ-śākya-seṅ-ge. B, 66

rNam-par-rgyal-baẖi-sgrol-ma. B, 212
  Cf. sGrol-ma-rnam-par-rgyal-ma-dkar-mo.
  B, 223
    ẖJig-rten-gsum-las°. C, 96b

rnam-par-gnon-pa. Cf. rnam-gnon.
  rGyal-ba°. D, 128
  Rin-chen-padmas°. B, 115

rNam-par-gnon-paẖi-gśegs-paẖi-dpal. B, 113

rNam-par-snaṅ-mẓad. Cf. rNam-snaṅ. C, R9c
  Kun-rig°. B, 68

rnam-par-rol-bas-mṅon-par-mkhyen-pa.
  Chos-rgya-mçho-mchog-gi-blos° °ẖi-rgyal-po (reads bar for bas).
  B, 138
  Padmaẖi-ẖod-zer.° B, 106
  Çhaṅs-paẖi-ẖod-zer°. B, 105

rnam-gzigs (Saṅs-ṛgyas°). B, 127; C, 82a

rNam-sras. Cf. rNam-thos-sras, Sras. C, S10b

rNam-sras-dkar-po-çhe-ẖphel. D, 264
  Cf. rNam-sras-çhe-ẖphel-dkar-po. B, 318

rNam-sras-dkar-po-çhe-ẖẓin. C, 106b

rNam-sras-gar-mkhan-mchog. B, 324
Cf. rNam-sras-dmar-po-gar-mkhan-mchog. C, 103c
Sras-gar-mkhan-mchog. C, 110b
rNam-sras-ljaṅ-gu-seṅ-zhon-ma-ẓñā-naḫi-lugs. C, 106c
rNam-sras-ljaṅ-ser-be-con-can. C, 103b
rNam-sras-drag-byed-ḫkhor-klu-brgyad-bcas. C, 105a–c
rNam-sras-drag-byed-nag-po. B, 319
rNam-sras-mduṅ-dmar-can (B reads mdoṅ-dmar). B, 321; D, 262
rNam-sras-mduṅ-dmar-rta-sṅon-can. C, 103a
rNam-sras-nag-po-rta-sṅon-can. C, 106a
rNam-sras-dmar-po-gar-mkhan-mchog. C, 103c
rNam-sras-çhe-ḫphel-dkar-po. B, 318
Cf. rNam-sras-dkar-po-çhe-ḫphel. D, 264
rNam-sras-yaṅ-gsaṅ-phyag-mçhan-bzhi-pa. C, 107a
rNam-sras-ser-chen. B, 322
rNam-sras-ser-chen-lha-dgu. C, 102c
rNam-sras-gsuṅ-mchog-lus-ṅan-po. C, 104b
rNam-sras-gser-chen. D, 263
rNal-ḫbyor-nam-mkhaḫ. B, 58; C, R13c
rnon-po.
ḫJam-dpal°. B, 157
rDo-rje°. B, 184
sNa-çhogs-mkhaḫ-ḫgro. C, 31b; D, 228
sna-çhogs-dbaṅ-po (sPyan-ras-gzigs°). C, 87a
sNa-çhogs-yum. B, 238
sNa-çhogs-yum-dkar-mo. C, 74b
sNaṅ-mthaḫ. C, R10b
Cf. Ḫod-dpag-med.
sNaṅ-mẓad-rdor-dbyiṅs. C, R14c
Paṇ-chen-dpal-ldan-ye-śes. D, 51
Paṇ-chen-blo-bzaṅ-chos-rgyal-mçhan. D, 47
Cf. rJes-pan-chen-blo-bzaṅ-chos-kyis-rgyal-mçhan. B, 25
Paṇ-chen-blo-bzaṅ-ye-śes. B, 27; D, 48
Pad-dkar-śes-rab-gsal-byed. B, 270
Cf. Phag-dkar°.
Padma-mkhaḫ-ḫgro. C, 141c; D, 227

padma-mkhaẖ-ẖgro-ma. Cf. padma-ḍā-ki.
ẖKhor°. C, 070c
Nub°. C, 30b
padma-gar-dbaṅ.
Go-chaẖi°. C, 19a
rTa-mgrin°. B, 62
sPyan-ras-gzigs° °phyag-gñis-pa. B, 164
Padma-gar-dbaṅ-phyag-bco-brgyad-pa. B, 165
Padma-sgrol-ma. C, 47b
padma-ḍā-ki (ẖKhor°). C, 118c
Cf. Padma-mkhaẖ-ẖgro-ma.
padma-dbaṅ-ẖbyed (sPyan-ras-gzigs°). B, 159
Padma-ma. D, 298
padmaẖi-phyag (sPyan-ras-gzigs°). C, 87b
padmaẖi-ẖod-zer (rGyal-ba°). D, 121
Padmaẖi-ẖod-zer-rnam-par-rol-bas-mṅon-par-mkhyen-pa. B, 106
Pi-waṅ-dbyaṅs-can-ma. B, 255
Pu-tra-lcam-dral. C, 138c
pus-bçugs-ma (Mi-gyo-sṅon-po°). C, 61b
dpaẖ-gcig.
mGon-po-gri-gug°. C, 125b
ẖJigs-byed°. B, 46
rTa-mgrin° °lhan-skyes-jo-boẖi-lugs. C, 58a
dPaẖ-bo-chig-sgrub-las-byuṅ-baẖi-ẓambha-la-lha-maṅ. C, 108a
dPaẖ-boẖi-sde. B, 86
rGyal-ba°. D, 101
dPal-kyai-rdo-rje. D, 66
dPal-ẖkhor-lo-chen-po. D, 64
dPal-ẖkhor-lo-sdom-pa. B, 36; D, 63
dPal-dgyes. B, 87
rGyal-ba°. D, 102
dPal-mgon-klu-grub. D, 5
dPal-mgon-zhal-bzhi-pa-sgrub-dus-daṅ-ẖbrel-ba. C, 131b
dPal-mgon-zhal-bzhi-pa-bsñen-dus-daṅ-ẖbrel-ba. C, 131a
dpal-chen-mo (Lha-mo°). C, 111a
Pal-dus-kyi-ẖkhor-lo. D, 65

dPal-ldan-dmag-zor-rgyal-mo. C, 134b
dPal-ldan-zhi-ba-ḫçho. D, 25
dpal-ldan-ye-śes (Paṇ-chen°). D, 51
dPal-ldan-lha-mo-phyag-gñis-ma. B, 311
dpal-ldan-a-ti-śa (Jo-bo-chen-po°). D, 29
dPal-be-ma. D, 295
dPal-byin. B, 93
Cf. rGyal-ba-dpal-sbyin. D, 108
dpal-ḫbar (mGon-po-lha-chen° °jo-boḫi-lugs). C, 125a
dPal-mo-sñiṅ-gi-gser-thig-can. C, 71b
dpal-mo-lugs (sPyan-ras-gzigs-bcu-gcig-zhal°). C, 34b
dpal-ḫẓin-lugs-kyi (Bram-ze° °rdo-rje-phag-mo). C, 28b
dPal-bzaṅ. B, 98
rGyal-ba°. D, 113
dPal-gsaṅ-ba-ḫdus-pa. D, 62
dpal-lha-mo (Ma-cig°). D, 236
dPyal-lugs-rdo-rje-phag-mo. C, 25a
dPyid-kyi-rgyal-mo. D, 247
dPyid-kyi-lha-mo. B, 331
spun-gsum (dByug-gum°). C, 115b
sPyan-mi-bzaṅ. B, 326; C, 140c
Cf. Mig-mi-bzaṅ.
sPyan-ras-gzigs. C, 93c; D, 147
bKaḫ-gdams-lha-bzhiḫi-naṅ-gi°. C, 34a
Khams-gsum-dbaṅ-ḫdus°. B, 167
ḫKhor°. C, 16c
sGyu-ḫphrul-dra-baḫi-rim-paḫi°. B, 170
sPyan-ras-gzigs-kha-sar-pa-ni. B, 160
sPyan-ras-gzigs-kha-sarba-ṇi. C, 37b
sPyan-ras-gzigs-rgyal-ba-rgya-mçho. B, 34; C, 43c
sPyan-ras-gzigs-bcu-gcig-zhal-dpal-mo-lugs. C, 34b
sPyan-ras-gzigs-ḫjigs-pa-brgyad-skyob. C, 86c
sPyan-ras-gzigs-don-yod-lcags-kyu. C, 88a
sPyan-ras-gzigs-don-yod-mchod-paḫi-nor-bu. C, 88b
sPyan-ras-gzigs-rdo-rje-chos. B, 163
sPyan-ras-gzigs-rdo-rje-sñiṅ-po. C, 43a

sPyan-ras-gzigs-rdo-rjeḫi-sñiṅ-pos-rab-tu-ḫjoms-pa. B, 177
Cf. rDo-rjeḫi-sñiṅ-pos-rab-tu-ḫjoms-pa. B, 83
sPyan-ras-gzigs-nam-mkhaḫi-rgyal-po. C, 39b
sPyan-ras-gzigs-sna-çhogs-dbaṅ-po. C, 87a
sPyan-ras-gzigs-padma-gar-dbaṅ-phyag-gñis-pa. B, 164
sPyan-ras-gzigs-padma-dbaṅ-ḫbyed. B, 159
sPyan-ras-gzigs-padmaḫi-phyag. C, 87b
sPyan-ras-gzigs-phyag-bzhi-pa. B, 158; C, S5c; D, 89
sPyan-ras-gzigs-bhu-kham-dmar-po. B, 172
sPyan-ras-gzigs-yi-ge-drug-pa-jo-bo-lugs. C, 33b
sPyan-ras-gzigs-yi-ge-phyed-daṅ-bzhi-pa. C, 69c
sPyan-ras-gzigs-yid-bzhin-ḫkhor-lo. C, 39c
sPyan-ras-gzigs-yid-bzhin-nor-bu. B, 176
sPyan-ras-gzigs-yid-bzhin-nor-bu-lha-lṅa. C, 38b
sPyan-ras-gzigs-su-kha-wa-ti. C, 87c
sPyan-ras-gzigs-seṅgeḫi-sgra (D reads seṅ-ge-sgra). B, 161; D, 94
sPyan-ras-gzigs-sems-ñid-ṅal-gso. B, 175; C, 38a; C, 38c
sPyan-ras-gzigs-gsaṅ-grub. D, 75
sPyod-rgyud-çhe-dpag-med. D, 82
sprul-sku (Çhe-dpag-med°). C, 63b
spreḫu-brgyad-pa (Mi-gyo-ba°). B, 348
spreḫu-brgyad-ma (Mi-gyo-ba°). C, 63a
Pha-dam-pa. D, 34
Phag-dkar-śes-rab-gsal-byed. C, 32b; C, 32c
Cf. Pad-dkar°.
phag-mo. Cf. rDo-rje-phag-mo.
ḫKhor°. C, 53a
Phag-mo-kurma-pā-dī. C, 28a
Phag-mo-khros-nag. C, 29b
Phag-mo-sṅon-mo. C, R8b
Phag-mo-don-grub. C, 26b
Phag-mo-don-thams-cad-sgrub-pa. B, 271
Phag-mo-gnam-zhabs-ma. C, 27c
Phag-mo-dmar-mo. C, R8a
Phag-mo-ser-mo. C, R8c
phur-zhabs-can (Gur-mgon°). C, 122b
Phoṅs-pa-sel-baḫi-sgrol-ma. C, 99a

Phyag-brgyad-sgrol-ma. C, 53c
Phyag-rdor-khaṅ-brçegs. C, 57a
Phyag-rdor-ḫkhor-chen. B, 59
Phyag-rdor-gos-sṅon-can. B, 72; C, 55a; D, 170
Phyag-rdor-gos-sṅon-can-ḫgro-bzaṅ-lugs. C, 56c
Phyag-rdor-gtum-chuṅ. B, 73; D, 169
Phyag-rdor-gtum-chuṅ-dmar-po. C, 56b
Phyag-rdor-gtum-chen-bsruṅ-baḫi-mkhar-ras chuṅ-lugs.
C, 55c
Phyag-rdor-gtum-po-khra-thogs. C, 56a
Phyag-rdor-drag-po-gsum-sgril. D, 171
Phyag-rdor-mdo-lugs. C, S8c
Phyag-rdor-ḫbyuṅ-po-ḫdul-byed. B, 71; C, 57b
Bla-med°. C, S11c
Phyag-rdor-ḫbyuṅ-po-ḫdul-byed-gsar-ma. C, 57c
Phyag-rdor-sa-lugs. C, 55b
Phyag-rdor-sems-dpaḫi-cha-lugs-can. D, 90
Phyag-rdor-u-ça-rya. B, 74; C, 54c
Phyag-na-rdo-rje. D, 146
Phyag-na-rdo-rje-ljaṅ-khu. C, 94a
Phyag-na-rdo-rje-zhi-ba. C, 84b
phyag-mçhan.
rGyan-drug°. C, R17c
rNam-sras-yaṅ-gsaṅ° °bzhi-pa. C, 107a
phyi-sgrub.
Chos-rgyal°. D, 238
Zhaṅ-blon-rdo-rje-bdud-ḫdul°. C, 112c
Phyir-mi-ldog-paḫi-ḫkhor-lo-ḫbyuṅ-baḫi-dpal.
B, 122
Phyir-bzlog-ma. D, 190
Phyir-bzlog-ma-chen-mo (D om. ma). B, 259; D, 220
Phyogs-glaṅ. B, 5
rJe-bçun°. D, 8
ḫPhags-skyes-po (D reads skye-bo).
B, 325; C, 11c; C, 140b; D, 280
ḫPhags-pa-ḫjam-dpal. C, 93b
ḫPhags-pa-don-yod-zhags-pa. D, 96
ḫPhags-pa-lha. B, 3
ḫPhags-ma-sgrol-ljaṅ. C, 94b
ḫPhags-ma-dug-sel-ma. B, 236

ẖPhags-ma-gdugs-dkar. D, 162
ẖPhags-ma-gdugs-dkar-po-can. B, 248
ẖPhags-ma-çunda-tā-ra. C, 54b
ẖphrog-ma (gNod-sbyin-mo°). C, 92c
Ba-ku-la. B, 280; C, 8a; D, 201
Ba-ra-dhva-ẓa-gser-can. B, 279
Cf. Bha-ra°. C, 7c; D, 200
Ba-ra-dhva-ẓa-bsod-sñoms-len. B, 283
Cf. Bha-ra°. C, 9a; D, 204
ba-riẖi-lugs.
sGrol-dkar°. C, 1b
Don-zhags-lha-lṅa°. C, 34c
Çhe-dpag-med°. C, 63c
ba-laṅ-rẓi (Nor-rgyun-ma°). C, 112a
Bha-ra-dhva-ẓa-gser-can. C, 7c; D, 200
Cf. Ba-ra°. B, 279
Bha-ra-dhva-ẓa-bsod-sñoms-len. C, 9a; D, 204
Cf. Ba-ra°. B, 283
bar-chad-kun-sel (mGon-po°). C, 116b
buddha-ḍā-ki (ẖKhor°). C, 118a
Bu-ston-thams-cad-mkhyen-pa. D, 37
bhu-kham-dmar-po (sPyan-ras-gzigs°). B, 172
Bum-pa-ma. D, 297
be-con-can (rNam-sras-ljaṅ-ser°). C, 103b
Bekçe. D, 254
Beg-çe. B, 336
beṅ.
mGon-po°. B, 303; D, 255
mGon-po° °dkaẖ-ma. C, 123c
mGon-po° °gter-ma. C, 124a
mGon-po° °nag-zaṅs-gri-can. C, 127b
baiḍūryaẖi-ẖod-kyi-rgyal-po (sMan-gyi-bla°) (D reads be-ḍurya). B, 139; D, 142
bya-rog-gdoṅ-can (Las-mgon°). B, 304; C, 121b
Byaṅ-chub-rdo-rje-sems-dpaẖ. B, 193
Byaṅ-las-kyi-mkhaẖ-ẖgro-ma. C, 30c
byaṅ-sems-ẖdul-ba (Saṅs-rgyas°). B, 124
Byams-pa. C, 67c; C, 85a; D, 151
ẖKhor°. C, 16a
rJe-bçun°. C, S4b; D, 1

Byams-pa-phyag-gñis-pa. B, 195
Byams-pa-phyag-bzhi-pa. B, 194
Brag-lha-mgon-po. D, 260
Bran(?)-bdud-gśin-rje-nag-po. C, 139a
Bram-ze-dpal-ẖẓin-lugs-kyi-rdo-rje-phag-mo. C, 28b
bram-zeẖi-gzugs-can (mGon-po°). D, 241
Cf. Zhal-bram-gzugs. B, 307
Bla-med-phyag-rdor-ẖbyuṅ-po-ẖdul-byed. C, S11c
blo-ẖphel (mGon-ser°). C, 0110b; C, 117b
blo-bzaṅ-skal-bzaṅ-rgya-mçho (rGyal-dbaṅ°).
D, 50
Cf. Tālaẖi-bla-ma-skal-bzaṅ°. B, 28
blo-bzaṅ-chos-rgyal-mçhan.
Paṇ-chen°. D, 47
rJes-pan-chen°. B, 25
blo-bzaṅ-bstan-paẖi-ñi-ma (Khri-chen°). D, 52
blo-bzaṅ-don-grub (rGyal-ba°). D, 45
blo-bzaṅ-dpal-ldan (rJe-druṅ°). D, 54
blo-bzaṅ-ye-śes (Paṇ-chen°). B, 27; D, 48
Blo-bzaṅ-ma. D, 273
dbaṅ-gi-rgyal-po (mGon-dmar°). C, 0110c; C, 117c
dBaṅ-mchog-ster-baẖi-sgrol-ma. C, 97a
dbaṅ-sdud (Zhal-bzhi-dmar-po°). C, 132c
dBaṅ-po-zhi. D, 156
dBaṅ-poẖi-tog-gi-rgyal-mçhan-gyi-rgyal-po. B, 110
Cf. rGyal-ba-dbaṅ-poẖi-tog-gi-rgyal-mçhan.
D, 125
dBu-bcad-ma. C, 26c
dByaṅs-can-ma. C, S8a; D, 157
rDo-rje° °phyag-gñis-ma. B, 254
rDo-rje° °phyag-drug-ma. B, 253
Pi-waṅ°. B, 255
dByaṅs-can-ma-dkar-po. C, 2b
dByaṅs-can-ma-dkar-mo-phyag-bzhi-pa. C, 68a
dByaṅs-can-ma-dmar-mo. C, 68b
dByar-gyi-rgyal-mo. D, 249
dByar-gyi-lha-mo. B, 332
dByig-gñen. B, 4
rJe-bçun°. D, 7
dbyug-sṅon-can (Khro-bo°). D, 216

dByug-gum (or gu-ma) -spun-gsum. C, 115b
ẖByuṅ-po-ẖdul-byed. C, R15c; D, 84
Phyag-rdor°. B, 71; C, 57b
°gsar-ma. C, 57c
Bla-med-phyag-rdor°. C, S11c
ẖbrug-zhon (Ẓam-bha-la-dkar-po°). B, 355
ẖBroṅ-zhal-can. B, 298
mGon-po-trakṣad°. C, 130b
ẖBrom-ston-rgyal-baẖi-ẖbyuṅ-gnas. D, 28
ẖBrom-ston-pa. B, 20
sBed-byed. C, 10a; D, 207
sBed-byed-pa. B, 286
sbrags-sgrub-ma (mGon-po-trakṣad-gri-gug°). C, 129b
Ma-cig-dpal-lha-mo. D, 236
Ma-cig-lab-sgron. D, 35
ma-niṅ-ma (mGon-po-trakṣad°). C, 130a
ma-ru-rçe-bzhis-bskor-pa (Las-gśin-dmar-po°). C, 137c
Ma-pham-pa. B, 273; C, 5c; D, 194
Mahā-ma-ya. B, 50; C, 17c; C, R13b; D, 67
mā-ma-ki (Lha-mo°). C, 89b
man-ṅag-lugs (Khyuṅ-khra°). C, 79b
mar-pa (rJe-bçun°). D, 32
Mar-me-sgrol-ma. C, 48c
mi-bskyod-rdo-rje (gSaṅ-ẖdus°). B, 32
Mi-bskyod-pa. Cf. Mi-ẖkhrugs-pa. B, 78; C, R10c
gSaṅ-ẖdus°. C, R1c
Mi-bskyod-pa-yab-yum. D, 57
Mi-ẖkhrugs-pa. Cf. Mi-bskyod-pa. C, S8b
rDo-rje°. B, 141; D, 87
Mi-rgod-ẖjigs-skyobs. C, 42c
mi-traẖi-lugs (Çhe-dpag-med-dkar-po°). C, 64b
Mi-phyed. C, 10b
Mi-phyed-pa. B, 287; D, 208
Mi-gyo-glaṅ-bzaṅ-ma. C, 142a
Mi-gyo-sṅon-po-pus-bçugs-ma. C, 61b
mi-gyo-ba (Khro-bo°). D, 174; D, 219
Mi-gyo-ba-dkar-po. B, 340; C, 62a; C, S4c
Mi-gyo-ba-sṅon-po. B, 338; C, S5a

Mi-gyo-ba-sṅon-po-bkaḫ-gdams-lugs. C, 61c
Mi-gyo-ba-spreḫu-brgyad-pa. B, 348
Mi-gyo-ba-spreḫu-brgyad-ma. C, 63a
Mi-gyo-ba-phyag-bzhi-pa. B, 350; C, 62b
Mi-gyo-ba-dmar-po. C, 91b
Mi-gyo-ba-zhabs-bzhi-pa. C, 62c
mi-la (rJe-bçun°). D, 31
Mig-mi-bzaṅ. C, 12a; D, 282
Cf. sPyan-mi-bzaṅ.
mun-bral-rgyal-po (sKrag-med°). B, 125
Me-tog-sgrol-ma. C, 48a
Me-tog-cher-rgyas. D, 81
Me-tog-dpal. B, 104
rGyal-ba°. D, 119
Me-ltar-ḫbar-ba. B, 349
Meḫi-ḫjigs-skyobs. C, 40b
me-ru-śe-ṣa (Thub-pa°). C, 69b
Mantra has me-ru-śe-ṣa-ra-kū-ṭa-pra-bhu-rā-ẓā.
Me-lha. D, 286
Mai-tri-mkhaḫ-spyod. C, 25c
mai-tri-pa (Grub-chen°). D, 18
Mya-ṅan-med-mchog. C, 14c
Mya-ṅan-med-mchog-dpal (B reads mchogs).
B, 136; D, 139
Mya-ṅan-med-paḫi-dpal. B, 102
rGyal-ba°. D, 117
Mya-ṅan-sel-baḫi-sgrol-ma. B, 215; C, 98c
Myur-zhiṅ-dpaḫi-sgrol-ma. B, 207
dmag-zor-ma.
ḫDod-khams-dbaṅ-phyug°. D, 248
dPal-ldan° °rgyal-mo. C, 134b
dmar-chen (Çhogs-bdag°). B, 360; C, 3c
rMa-bya-chen-mo. B, 202; D, 178
rMi-lam-ston-paḫi-sgrol-ma. C, 51c
rmoṅs-byed-ma (Go-chaḫi°). C, 21a
sMan-gyi-lha-mo. D, 276
sMan-gyi-bla-baiḍūryaḫi-ḫod-kyi-rgyal-po (D reads be-ḍurya).
B, 139; D, 142
sMan-bla. C, 13b

smin-byed-ma (sGrol-ma°). B, 218
Cf. Yoṅs-su-smin-par-mẓad-paẖi-sgrol-ma. C, 99c
sme-brçegs or sme-ba-brçegs-pa.
Cf. Khro-bo°.
Khro-mo°.
sMon-lam-blo-gros. D, 155
smra-ba (rDo-rje°). B, 182
smra-seṅ (ẖJam-dbyaṅs°). D, 92
smra-baẖi-seṅge (ẖJam-dbyaṅs°). C, 66b; C, S3b
ça-rçiga (rDo-rje°). B, 257
Çan-dan-dpal. B, 99
rGyal-ba°. D, 114
çaṇḍi-ka.
Go-chaẖi°. C, 22a
mGon-po-phyag-bzhi-paẖi-ẖkhor-lha-mo°. C, 121a
Lha-mo°. B, 330; D, 244
Çunda. D, 159
ẖPhags-ma° °tā-ra. C, 54b
Lha-mo° °dkar-mo. C, 90b
Lha-mo° °phyag-maṅ. B, 241
Lha-mo° °phyag-bzhi-ma. B, 240
gçug-tor-ẖkhor-bsgyur (Khro-bo°). D, 217
gÇug-tor-sgrol-ma. B, 210
gÇug-tor-can. B, 128
Rin-chen°. B, 144; D, 144
Saṅs-rgyas°. C, 82b
gÇug-tor-gdugs-dkar. C, 75a; C, S2a
gçug-tor-dri-med (rGyal-ba°). D, 133
gÇug-tor-rnam-rgyal-phyag-gñis-ma. C, 90a
gÇug-tor-rnam-rgyal-ma (B reads rnams). B, 247; C, 64c
gÇug-tor-rnam-rgyal-lha-dgu. C, S2b
gÇug-tor-rnam-par-rgyal-baẖi-sgrol-ma. C, 95c
gÇug-tor-rnam-par-rgyal-ma. D, 164
gÇug-tor-ẖbar-ba. D, 192
gço-rkyaṅ (Ẓambha-la-ser-po°). C, 107b
gço-ẖkhor-gsum (Thub-pa-rdo-rje-gdan-pa°). C, 4b
bÇoṅ-kha-pa-chen-po. B, 21
Cf. rJe-rin-po-che. C, 0b; D, 41
Cf. A, 1A36.

Çhaṅs-pa. B, 94; B, 329; D, 278
rGyal-ba°. D, 109
Çhaṅs-paẖi-ẖod-zer-rnam-par-rol-bas-mṅon-par-mkhyen-pa. B, 105
Cf. rGyal-ba-çhaṅs-paẖi-ẖod-zer. D, 120
Çhaṅs-pas-byin. B, 95
rGyal-ba°. D, 110
Çhe-ẖgugs-lha-mo. D, 300
çhe-sgrub (bDe-mchog-dkar-po°). C, 22c
Çhe-bdag-mgon-po. B, 316; D, 231
Cf. mGon-ljaṅ-çhe-bdag. C, 118b
Çhe-dpag-med. B, 64
rGyal-ba°. D, 85
sPyod-rgyud°. D, 82
Çhe-dpag-med-dkar-po. C, 64a
Çhe-dpag-med-dkar-po-mi-traẖi-lugs. C, 64b
Çhe-dpag-med-sprul-sku. C, 63b
Çhe-dpag-med-phyag-bzhi-pa. B, 63
Çhe-dpag-med-ba-ri-lugs. C, 63c
çhe-ẖphel.
rNam-sras-dkar-po°. D, 264
rNam-sras° °dkar-po. B, 318
Zhal-bzhi-dkar-po°. C, 132a
çhe-ẖzin (rNam-sras-dkar-po°). C, 106b
çhe-riṅ-ma (bKra-śis°). B, 335; C, 142b; D, 272
çhogs-bdag (ẖJur-ẖgegs-sel-baẖi°). C, 114a
Çhogs-bdag-dkar-po-phyag-bzhi-pa-jo-boẖi-lugs. C, 114b
Çhogs-bdag-mgon-po-seṅgeẖi-gdan-can. C, 128a
Çhogs-bdag-dmar-chen. B, 360; C, 3c
Çhogs-bdag-dmar-po-phyag-bzhi-pa. C, 114c
Çhogs-bdag-ser-po. C, 93a
mÇhan-brjod-kyi-ẖjam-dbyaṅs-phyag-bzhi-pa. B, 155
mÇhan-dpal-śin-tu-yoṅs-bsgrags. B, 109
Cf. rGyal-ba-mçhan-dpal-yoṅs-sgrags. D, 124
mÇhan-legs. C, 15c
mÇhan-legs-yoṅs-grags-dpal. D, 136
mÇhan-legs-yoṅs-grags-dpal-gyi-rgyal-po. B, 133
mçho-skye-rdo-rje (rJe-bçun°). D, 26

ẖÇhal-lugs-kyi-mgon-po-phyag-bzhi-pa. C, 120a

ẓa-wa-ri-pa (Grub-chen°). D, 19

ẓā-ma-riẖi-lugs (Nor-rgyun-ma°). C, 111c

Ẓambha-la. C, S10c

Ẓam-bha-la-dkar-po. D, 266

Ẓam-bha-la-dkar-po-ẖbrug-zhon. B, 355

Ẓambha-la-dkar-po-lha-lṅa-jo-boẖi-lugs. C, 108c

Ẓambha-la-ljaṅ-khu-dus-ẖkhor-lugs. C, 109c

Ẓam-bha-la-nag-po. B, 344; C, 108b; D, 267

Ẓam-bha-la-phyag-drug-pa. B, 341

Ẓambha-la-dmar-po-sa-lugs. C, 109a

  Cf. Grva-ba-mṅon-śes-lugs-kyi-ẓambha-la-dmar-po. C, 109b

Ẓam-bha-la-ser-po. B, 339; C, 51a; D, 265

  gSaṅ-ẖdus-las-byuṅ-baẖi°. C, 107c

Ẓambha-la-ser-po-gço-rkyaṅ. C, 107b

ẓambha-la-lha-maṅ (dPaẖ-bo-chig-sgrub-las-byuṅ-baẖi°). C, 108a

Ẓam-dmar-srog-sgrub. D, 268

Ẓam-lha-zhal-gsum-phyag-drug-pa. D, 270

Ẓi-na-mi-tra. B, 314; C, 116a; D, 234

ẓñā-na-lugs.

  mGon-po-gri-gug°. C, 127a

  rNam-sras-ljaṅ-gu-seṅ-zhon-ma°. C, 106c

wa-ru-ṇa (Klu-rgyal°). D, 290

zhags-pa-ma (rDo-rje°). C, 49c

Zhaṅ-blon-rdo-rje-bdud-ẖdul. B, 353

Zhaṅ-blon-rdo-rje-bdud-ẖdul-naṅ-sgrub. C, 113a

Zhaṅ-blon-rdo-rje-bdud-ẖdul-phyi-sgrub. C, 112c

Zhaṅ-blon-rdo-rje-bdud-ẖdul-gsaṅ-sgrub. C, 113b

Zhal-bram-gzugs. B, 307

  Cf. mGon-pa-bram-zeẖi-gzugs-can. D, 241

Zhal-bzhi-dkar-po-çhe-ẖphel. C, 132a

zhal-bzhi-pa.

  dPal-mgon° °sgrub-dus-daṅ-ẖbrel-ba. C, 131b

  dPal-mgon° °bsñen-dus-daṅ-ẖbrel-ba. C, 131a

Zhal-bzhi-pa-sṅon-po-ñams-sgrol. C, 133a

Zhal-bzhi-pa-gdoṅ-gñan-can. C, 133b

Zhal-bzhi-pa-las-sbyor-mgon-po. C, 131c

Zhal-bzhi-dmar-po-dbaṅ-sdud. C, 132c

Zhal-bzhi-ser-po-nor-ẖphel. C, 132b

zhi-ba.
Phyag-na-rdo-rje°. C, 84b
gSaṅ-bdag-lhan-skyes°. C, 88c
Zhi-ba-chen-moẖi-sgrol-ma (B reads baẖi). B, 220; C, 100b
zhi-ba-sbas-paẖi-lugs (mGon-po-phyag-bzhi-pa-grub-chen°). C, 119a
zhi-ba-ẖçho (dPal-ldan°). D, 25
Zhi-ba-lha. B, 10
rJe-bçun°. D, 24
gzhan-gyis-mi-thub-pa.
Khro-bo°. C, 90c; D, 211
sGrol-ma°. B, 213
gZhan-gyis-mi-thub-ma. B, 261
gzhon-nur-gyur-ba (ẖJam-dpal°). B, 146; D, 93
bzhad-pa (rDo-rje°). B, 186
bzhi-sbrags (mGon-po°). C, 126a
zaṅs-gri-can.
mGon-po° °gyi-ljaṅ-lugs. C, 126c
mGon-po-gcer-bu°. C, 127c
mGon-po-beṅ-nag°. C, 127b
Zla-ltar-snaṅ-byed. C, 13a
zla-mdaṅ-ma (sGrol-ma°). B, 208
zla-mdaṅs-kyi-sgrol-ma (dKar-mo°). C, 95a
Zla-ba-grags-pa. B, 9
rJe-bçun°. D, 22
gZaẖ-yum. B, 269
gZaẖ-yum-rig-pa-chen-mo. C, R17a
gZaẖ-yum-rig-paẖi-rgyal-mo. C, 77a
gzi-brjid (rDo-rje°). B, 188
gZi-brjid-mthaẖ-yas. B, 100
rGyal-ba°. D, 115
gZuṅs-las-byuṅ-baẖi-ẖod-zer-can-ma. C, 69a
gZuṅs-las-byuṅ-baẖi-lha-mo-nor-rgyun-ma. C, 111b
bZaṅ-po. B, 277; C, 7a; D, 198
H̱od-kyi-tog. D, 154
H̱od-dpag-med. Cf. sNaṅ-mthaẖ. B, 80; C, 84c
rGyal-ba°. D, 132
H̱od-dpag-med-yab-yum. D, 59
H̱od-dpal. B, 101
rGyal-ba°. D, 116

H̱od-zer(?)-kun-ẖphags-dpal-brçegs-rgyal-po. B, 142
H̱od-zer-can-bdud-rçuẖi-ma. B, 245
H̱od-zer-can-rdo-rje-dbyiṅs-kyi-dbaṅ-phyug-ma. B, 246
H̱od-zer-can-phyag-brgyad-ma. B, 243
H̱od-zer-can-phyag-bcu-ma. B, 242
H̱od-zer-can-phyag-gñis-ma. B, 244
H̱od-zer-can-ma. C, 52c; C, 97b; C, R16a; C, S4a; D, 163
gZuṅs-las-byuṅ-baẖi°. C, 69a
H̱od-zer-can-ma-khab-skud-can. C, 68c
H̱od-zer-can-ma-rta-ljaṅ-can. C, 91c
H̱od-bsruṅ. B, 132
Saṅs-rgyas°. C, 83c
H̱od-bsruṅ-chen-po. B, 290
yaṅ-gsaṅ-phyag-mçhan-bzhi-pa (rNam-sras°). C, 107a
yan-lag-drug-pa (gÑan-sgrol°). C, 2c
Yan-lag-ẖbyuṅ. B, 272; C, 5b; D, 193
yi-ge-drug-pa (sPyan-ras-gzigs° °jo-bo-lugs). C, 33b
Yi-ge-drug-ma. C, 33c
yi-ge-bdun-pa (ẖJig-rten-dbaṅ-phyug°). C, 23a
yi-ge-phyed-daṅ-bzhi-pa (sPyan-ras-gzigs°). C, 69c
Yid-ẖphrog-nor-rgyun-ma. C, 112b
Yid-bzhin-rgyal-mo-phyag-bzhi-ma. B, 231
yid-bzhin-gyi-ẖkhor-lo.
sGrol-dkar°. B, 230
sPyan-ras-gzigs°. C, 39c
yid-bzhin-nor-bu.
mGon-dkar°. B, 317; C, 0110a; C, 117a; D, 229
sGrol-ma°. C, 45c
sPyan-ras-gzigs°. B, 176
sPyan-ras-gzigs° °lha-lṅa. C, 38b
Yul-ẖkhor-bsruṅ. B, 327; C, 11b; C, 140a; D, 284
ye-śes.
Paṇ-chen-dpal-ldan°. D, 51
Paṇ-chen-blo-bzaṅ°. B, 27; D, 48
Ye-śes-mkhaẖ-ẖgro. B, 52; C, R14a

Ye-śes-bla-ma. D, 153
Yoṅs-su-rẓogs-paẖi-sgrol-ma. B, 226
Cf. sGrol-ma-yoṅs-rẓogs-byed-ma. C, 102b
Yoṅs-su-smin-par-mẓad-paẖi-sgrol-ma. C, 99c
Cf. sGrol-ma-smin-byed-ma. B, 218
Yon-tan-hod. B, 7
gYul-las-śin-tu-rnam-par-rgyal-ba. B, 112
Cf. rGyal-ba-gyul-las-rgyal-ba. D, 127
Raṅ-byuṅ-lha-mo. D, 251
Cf. Lha-mo-srog-sgrub-lcags-phur-ma-raṅ-byuṅ-rgyal-mo.
ratna-ḍā-ki (ẖKhor°). C, 118a
Cf. Rin-chen-mkhaẖ-ẖgro.
rab-rgyas-ma (sGrol-ma°). Ç, 101b
rab-sṅags-ma (rDo-rje°). C, 27a
Rab-tu-dpaẖ-baẖi-sgrol-ma. C, 94c
Ral-gcig-ma. Cf. e-ka-ẓa-ti. C, 98a
ẖKhor°. C, 35c; C, 53b
Lha-mo°. B, 239
Lha-mo° °phyag-ñi-śu-rça-bzhi-ma. B, 237
ras-chuṅ-lugs (Phyag-rdor-gtum-chen-bsruṅ-baẖi-mkhar°). C, 55c
Ri-khrod-ma-lo-ma-gyon-ma-nag-mo. C, 76b
Ri-khrod-lo-ma-gyon-ma.
Cf. Lo-ma-gyon-ma.
Ri-khrod-lo-ma-gyon-ma-sṅon-po. C, 76a
Ri-khrod-lo-ma-gyon-ma-ljaṅ-gu. C, 76c
Ri-khrod-lo-ma-gyon-ma-dmar-mo. C, 75c
Ri-khrod-lo-ma-gyon-ma-ser-mo. C, 75b
ri-dbaṅ-gi-rgyal-po.
rGyal-ba°. D, 130
Saṅs-rgyas°. B, 116
rig-pa-chen-mo (gZaẖ-yum°). C, R17a
rig-paẖi-rgyal-mo (gZaẖ-yum°). C, 77a
rin-chen.
rGyal-mchog°. D, 79
rDo-rje°. B, 189
Rin-chen-mkhaẖ-ẖgro. C, 141a; D, 225
rin-chen-mkhaẖ-ẖgro-ma. Cf. ratna-ḍā-ki.
ẖKhor°. C, 070b
Lho°. C, 30a

Rin-chen-sgrol-ma. C, 47a
rin-chen-gdugs-ḫphags (Saṅs-rgyas°). B, 123
Rin-chen-rdo-rje-ma. B, 266
Rin-chen-padmas-rnam-par-gnon-pa. B, 115
Cf. rGyal-ba-rin-chen-padma. D, 131
Rin-chen-me. B, 88
rGyal-ba°. D, 103
Rin-chen-gçug-tor-can. B, 144; D, 144
Rin-chen-zla-ba. C, 15a
Cf. sGra-dbyaṅs-rgyal-po. D, 137
Saṅs-rgyas-rin-po-che-daṅ-zla-ba-daṅ-padmas-rab-tu-brgyan-pa-mkhas-pa-gzi-brjid-sgra-dbyaṅs-kyi-rgyal-po. B, 134
Rin-chen-zla-ba. B, 91
rGyal-ba°. D, 106
Rin-chen-zla-ḫod. B, 89
rGyal-ba°. D, 104
rin-chen-gzugs-bkod-ḫod-snaṅ (Saṅs-rgyas°). B, 120
Rin-chen-ḫod-ḫphros. B, 84
Cf. rGyal-ba-rin-chen-ḫod-ḫphro. D, 99
rin-po-che-daṅ-zla-ba-daṅ-padmas-rab-tu-brgyan-pa-mkhas-pa-gzi-brjid-sgra-dbyaṅs-kyi-rgyal-po (Saṅs-rgyas°). B, 134
Cf. sGra-dbyaṅs-rgyal-po. D, 137
Rin-chen-zla-ba. C, 15a
Rin-ḫbyuṅ. B, 79; C, R10a
Rin-ḫbyuṅ-yab-yum. D, 58
Re-ma-ti-rdo-rje-gśog-rgod-ma. C, 136b
Cf. Klu-mo-re-ma-ti. C, 135c
bDud-mo-re-ma-ti. C, 135b
gNod-sbyin-re-ma-ti. C, 136a
reg-çhig.
bCom-ldan°. B, 358
bDe-mchog-khro-bo°. C, 78b
ro-laṅs-ma (Lha-mo°). C, 92b
rol-paḫi-rdo-rje (rJe-lcaṅ-skya°). D, 53
Rluṅ-lha. D, 287
La-li-ta. B, 15
Cf. Grub-chen-lā-li-ta-baẓra. D, 13
lab-sgron (Ma-cig°). D, 35

Lam-bstan. B, 284; C, 9b; D, 205
Lam-phran. B, 282
Lam-phran-bstan. C, 8c; D, 203
las (rDo-rje°). B, 181
Las-kyi-mkhaḫ-ḫgro. Cf. karma-ḍā-ki. C, 141c; D, 226
las-kyi-mkhaḫ-ḫgro-ma.
ḫKhor°. C, 71a
Byaṅ°. C, 30c
Las-kyi-rdo-rje-ma. B, 264
las-kyi-gśin-rje-mthiṅ-ga (Chos-rgyal°). C, 137b
Cf. Las-gśin°.
Las-mgon-bya-rog-gdoṅ-can. B, 304; C, 121b
las-byed-ma.
ḫKhor-klu-mo°. C, 59c
ḫKhor-rdo-rje°. C, 59a
ḫKhor-gnod-sbyin°. C, 60a
ḫKhor-gśin-rje°. C, 59b
las-sbyor-mgon-po (Zhal-bzhi-pa°). C, 131c
Las-gśin-dmar-po-khrag-mdog. C, 138a
Cf. las-kyi-gśin-rje°.
Las-gśin-dmar-po-ma-ru-rçe-bzhis-bskor-pa. C, 137c
Lu-hi-pa. B, 12
Cf. Grub-chen-lū-i-pa. D, 12
Lugs-gñis-gcig-tu-sgril-baḫi-mgon-po-phyag-bzhi-pa.
C, 120b
lus-ṅan-po (rNam-sras-gsuṅ-mchog°). C, 104b
Legs-mthoṅ. B, 296
legs-ldan.
mGon-po°. B, 302; D, 256–258
mGon-po° °mched-gsum. C, 124b
legs-pa (rDo-rje°). B, 190
legs-paḫi-śes-rab (rṄog°). D, 30
Lo-ma-gyon-ma. C, S7c; D, 165
Cf. Ri-khrod°.
Lo-ma-gyon-ma-phyag-drug-ma. B, 249
Lo-ma-gyoṅ-ma-phyag-bzhi-ma. B, 250
Śa-naḫi-gos-can. B, 292
śa-ba-ri-pa (Grub-chen°). D, 10
Śa-za-ce-spyaṅ-gdoṅ. C, 133c
śva-na-bzhi-skor (rTa-mgrin° °jo-bo-lugs). C, 58c

śva-naḫi-zhal-can (mGon-po-trakṣad-gsaṅ-sgrub°). C, 130c
Śā-kya-thub-pa. B, 82
rGyal-ba°. C, 81c; D, 2; D, 97
bKaḫ-gdams-lha-bzhiḫi-naṅ-gi°. C, 12c
Śākya-rigs-dbaṅ. D, 80
Śākya-ḫod. B, 8
Śākya-seṅ-ge. C, R15a
rNams-snaṅ°. B, 66
Śin-tu-rnam-par-gnon-paḫi-dpal. B, 111
Cf. rGyal-ba-śin-tu-rnam-par-gnon-pa. D, 126
śugs (rDo-rje°). C, 24a
Śer-phyin-dkar-mo. C, 67a
Śer-phyin-phyag-gñis-ma. B, 251
Śer-phyin-phyag-bzhi-ma. B, 252
Śer-phyin-ma. C, S11b; D, 158
Śer-phyin-ser-mo C, 67b
śes-rab-ḫkhor-lo.
ḫJam-dkar°. C, 66c
ḫJam-dbyaṅs° °daṅ-po. B, 156
Śes-rab-ral-gri. C, S12c
śes-rab-seṅ-ge (rJe°). D, 44
śes-rab-gsal-byed.
Pad-dkar°. B, 270
Phag-dkar°. C, 32b; C, 32c
Śra-ma-ṇa. D, 183
Lha-mo°. B, 267; C, 80b
gśin.
Las° °dmar-po-khrag-mdog. C, 138a
Las° °dmar-po-ma-ru-rçe-bzhis-bskor-pa. C, 137c
gśin-rje.
Chos-rgyal-las-kyi° °mthiṅ-ga. C, 137b
Bran-bdud° °nag-po. C, 139a
gśin-rje-ma (Go-chaḫi°). C, 20c
gśin-rje-las-byed-ma-(ḫKhor°). C, 59b
gśin-rje-gśed (Khro-bo°). D, 212
gŚin-rje-gśed-dgra-nag. D, 71
Cf. dGra-nag-gśin-rje-gśed. C, R2a
gŚin-rje-gśed-dmar (B reads rjes). B, 45; D, 72
gŚed-dmar. C, 24b

gśog-rgod-ma (Re-ma-ti-rdo-rje°). C, 136b
Sa-skya-paṇḍi-ta-kun-dgaḫ-rgyal-mçhan. D, 38
Saḫi-sñiṅ-po. B, 197; C, 86a
Saḫi-lha-mo. D, 279
Saḫi-lha-mo-brtan-ma. B, 323
sa-ḫog (Khro-bo-rdo-rje°). D, 221
Sa-yi-sñiṅ-po. D, 148
Sa-ra-ha. B, 11
 Grub-chen°. D, 11
sa-lugs.
 sGrol-ma-dmar-mo°. C, 46a
 ḫJam-dbyaṅs-a-ra-pa-ça-na-dmar-ser°. C, 65c
 Phyag-rdor°. C, 55b
 Ẓambha-la-dmar-po°. C, 109a
saṅs-rgyas-bskyaṅs (rJe-bçun°). D, 23
Saṅs-rgyas-mkhaḫ-ḫgro. C, 141b; D, 223
Saṅs-rgyas-ḫkhor-ba-ḫjig. C, 83a
Saṅs-rgyas-sgrol-ma. C, 47c
Saṅs-rgyas-mṅon-ḫphags-rgyal-po. B, 118
Saṅs-rgyas-rjes-su-spyod-pa. B, 117
Saṅs-rgyas-thams-cad-skyob. C, 82c
Saṅs-rgyas-thod-pa. B, 51; C, R12c; C, R13a; D, 69
Saṅs-rgyas-bdud-daṅ-yid-gñis-kun-ḫjoms(?). B, 121
 Cf. A, 1B52.
Saṅs-rgyas-rnam-gzigs. B, 127; C, 82a
Saṅs-rgyas-spyan-ma. C, 70a
Saṅs-rgyas-byaṅ-sems-ḫdul-ba. B, 124
 Cf. A, 1B55.
Saṅs-rgyas-gçug-tor-can. C, 82b
Saṅs-rgyas-ḫod-sruṅ. C, 83c
Saṅs-rgyas-ri-dbaṅ-gi-rgyal-po. B, 116
 Cf. rGyal-ba-ri-dbaṅ-gi-rgyal-po. D, 130
Saṅs-rgyas-rin-chen-gdugs-ḫphags. B, 123
Saṅs-rgyas-rin-chen-gzugs-bkod-ḫod-snaṅ. B, 120
Saṅs-rgyas-rin-po-che-daṅ-zla-ba-daṅ-padmas-rab-tu-brgyan-pa-mkhas-pa-gzi-brjid-sgra-dbyaṅs-kyi-rgyal-po. B, 134
 Cf. sGra-dbyaṅs-rgyal-po. D, 137
 Rin-chen-zla-ba. C, 15a
Saṅs-rgyas-gser-thub. C, 83b

su-kha-wa-ti (sPyan-ras-gzigs°). C, 87c
Seṅge-sgra. C, 43b; C, S6b
ḫJam-dbyaṅ°. B, 149
sPyan-ras-gzigs°. B, 161; D, 94
seṅ-geḫi-ṅa-ro (rGyal-ba°). B, 140; D, 143
Seṅ-geḫi-ḫjigs-skyobs. C, 41a
seṅgeḫi-gdan-can (Çhogs-bdag-mgon-po°). C, 128a
Seṅ-gdoṅ-ma. B, 357
Cf. mKhaḫ-ḫgro-ma-seṅ-geḫi-gdoṅ-can. D, 188
Seṅ-gdoṅ-ma-sṅon-mo. C, 80c
Seṅ-gdoṅ-ma-dmar-mo. C, 81a
Seṅ-ldeṅ-nags-kyi-sgrol-ma. B, 206; C, 97c; D, 161
(B reads nag-ḫbye for nags-kyi; D om. kyi).
seṅ-zhon (mGon-po-trakṣad° °jo-boḫi-lugs). C, 129a
seṅ-zhon-ma (rNam-sras-ljaṅ-gu° °ẓñā-naḫi-lugs).
C, 106c
seṅge-zhon-pa (Ṭakṣad°). B, 299
sems-ñid-ṅal-gso (sPyan-ras-gzigs°). B, 175; C, 38a; C, 38c
sems-dpaḫi-cha-lugs-can (Phyag-rdor°). D, 90
Sems-ma-rdo-rje-ma. B, 265
ser-chen.
rNam-sras°. B, 322
rNam-sras° °lha-dgu. C, 102c
So-sor-ḫbraṅ-ma (B reads ḫbrans). Cf. Sor-ḫbraṅs°.
B, 205; C, 52b; C, R16b; D, 176
rDo-rje-bur-nas-gsuṅs-paḫi°. C, 74c
So-sor-ḫbraṅ-ma-lha-lṅa. C, S3c
sog-ma-med (Klu-rgyal°). C, 115a
Sor-ḫbraṅs-phyag-gñis-ma. B, 258
Sras.
Cf. rNam-sras, rNam-thos-sras.
Sras-gar-mkhan-mchog. C, 110b
Cf. rNam-sras-gar-mkhan-mchog.
Sras-rgyal-ba-khyu-mchog. C, 110c
Sred-med-kyi-bu. B, 103
rGyal-ba°. D, 118
srog-sgrub (Ẓam-dmar°). D, 268
srog-sgrub-lcags-phur-ma-raṅ-byuṅ-rgyal-mo (Lha-mo°).
C, 134c

gsaṅ-sgrub.
Ku-ru-kulle°. C, 70c
mGon-po-trakṣad° °śva-naḫi-zhal-can. C, 130c
Chos-rgyal°. D, 240
ḫJam-dbyaṅ°. B, 148
ḫJig-rten-dbaṅ-phyug°. C, 39a
rTa-mgrin°. B, 61; D, 167
sPyan-ras-gzigs°. D, 75
Zhaṅ-blon-rdo-rje-bdud-ḫdul°. C, 113b
gSaṅ-sṅags-chen-mo. D, 177
gSaṅ-sṅags-rjes-ḫẓin. B, 204
gSaṅ-bdag-lhan-skyes-zhi-ba. C, 88c
gSaṅ-ḫdus-ḫjam-rdor. C, 17a; C, R1a; D, 68
gSaṅ-ḫdus-ḫjam-paḫi-rdo-rje. B, 30
gSaṅ-ḫdus-ḫjigs-rten-dbaṅ-phyug. B, 33
gSaṅ-ḫdus-mi-bskyod-pa. C, R1c
gSaṅ-ḫdus-mi-bskyod-rdo-rje. B, 32
gSaṅ-ḫdus-las-byuṅ-baḫi-ẓambha-la-ser-po. C, 107c
gSaṅ-ḫdus-lhan-skyes. C, 17b
gsaṅ-ba-ḫdus-pa (dPal°). D, 62
gSaṅ-ba-ye-śes. C, 72c
gSaṅ-baḫi-bdag-po-khro-bo. C, 89a
gsar-ma (Phyag-rdor-ḫbyuṅ-po-ḫdul-byed°). C, 57c
gSuṅ-kyai-rdo-rje. C, R6a
gSuṅ-kyai-rdor. C, R3a
gsuṅ-gi-dbaṅ-phyug.
Chos-dbyiṅ°. B, 67
ḫJam-dbyaṅs-chos-dbyiṅs° °brgyad-pa. B, 151
gsuṅ-mchog (rNam-sras° °lus-ṅan-po). C, 104b
gsuṅ-dbaṅ (Chos-dbyiṅs°). C, R15b
gsum-sgril (Phyag-rdor-drag-po°). D, 171
gser-chen (rNam-sras°). D, 263
gSer-ña-ma. D, 292
gSer-thub. B, 131
Saṅs-rgyas°. C, 83b
gSer-mdog-can-gyi-sgrol-ma. C, 95b
Cf. sGrol-ma-gser-mdog-ma. B, 209
gSer-beḫu. B, 278; C, 7b; D, 199
gser-mig-ḫkhyil-ba (Khyuṅ°). D, 186
gSer-bzaṅ-dri-med. C, 15b

gSer-bzaṅ-dri-med-rin-chen-snaṅ. D, 138
gSer-bzaṅ-dri-med-rin-chen-snaṅ-brtul-zhugs-pa.
B, 135
bSil-baẖi-ç̣hal. B, 203
bSil-baẖi-ç̣hal-chen-mo. D, 179
bsruṅ (rDo-rje°). B, 180
bsruṅ-baẖi-mkhar (Phyag-rdor-gtum-chen° °ras-chuṅ-lugs).
C, 55c
ha-ri-ha-ri-la-zhon-pa (ẖJig-rten-dbaṅ-phyug°).
B, 166
Hva-śaṅ. C, 11a; D, 210
Hva-śaṅ-dge-bsñen. B, 289
halhala (ẖJig-rten-dbaṅ-phyug°). B, 162
hūṁ-ka-ra (Grub-dbaṅ°). D, 27
Hūṁ-sgra-sgrog-paẖi-sgrol-ma. C, 96a
Cf. sGrol-ma-hūṁ-sgra-sgrogs-ma. B, 211
hūṁ-mẓad.
Khro-bo°. C, R9a
rDo-rje°. B, 56; B, 359; C, R11c
he-ru-ka-nag-po (Go-chaẖi°). C, 19b
lha-dgu.
rNam-sras-ser-chen°. C, 102c
gÇug-tor-rnam-rgyal°. C, S2b
lha-brgyad (Gur-mgon°). C, 122a
lha-lṅa.
Don-zhags° °ba-ri-lugs. C, 34c
sPyan-ras-gzigs-yid-bzhin-nor-bu°. C, 38b
Ẓambha-la-dkar-po° °jo-boẖi-lugs. C, 108c
Ṡo-sor-ẖbraṅ-ma°. C, S3c
lha-chen (mGon-po° °dpal-ẖbar-jo-boẖi-lugs).
C, 125a
lha-maṅ (dPaẖ-bo-chig-sgrub-las-byuṅ-baẖi-ẓambha-la°).
C, 108a
Lha-mo. C, 116b; D, 232
dGun-gyi°. B, 334
ẖChi-med-rdo-rje°. C, 65a
sTon-gyi°. B, 333
dPal-ldan° °phyag-gñis-ma. B, 311
dPyid-kyi°. B, 331
dByar-gyi°. B, 332

Ma-cig-dpal°. D, 236
sMan-gyi°. D, 276
Çhe-ḫgugs°. D, 300
gZuṅs-las-byuṅ-baḫi° °nor-rgyun-ma. C, 111b
Raṅ-byuṅ°. D, 251
Saḫi°. D, 279
°brtan-ma. B, 323
Lha-mo-khro-gñer-can. B, 256
Lha-mo-gos-dkar-mo. C, 89c
Lha-mo-ti-nu. C, 72a
For Chinese ti-mu?
Lha-mo-duṅ-skyoṅ-ma (B reads doṅ; D reads skyoṅs).
B, 309; C, 135a; D, 246
Lha-mo-dud-sol-ma (B reads doṅ). B, 310; C, 134a; D, 245
Lha-mo-nam-mkhaḫi-gos-can. C, 137a
lha-mo-nor-rgyun-ma (gZuṅs-las-byuṅ-baḫi°).
C, 111b
Lha-mo-dpal-chen-mo. C, 111a
Lha-mo-mā-ma-ki. C, 89b
Lha-mo-çaṇḍi-ka. B, 330; D, 244
mGon-po-phyag-bzhi-paḫi-ḫkhor°. C, 121a
Lha-mo-çunda-dkar-mo. C, 90b
Lha-mo-çunda-phyag-maṅ. B, 241
Lha-mo-çunda-phyag-bzhi-ma. B, 240
Lha-mo-ral-gcig-ma. B, 239
Lha-mo-ral-gcig-ma-phyag-ñi-śu-rça-bzhi-ma.
B, 237
Lha-mo-ro-laṅs-ma. C, 92b
Lha-mo-śra-ma-ṇa. B, 267; C, 80b
Lha-mo-srog-sgrub-lcags-phur-ma-raṅ-byuṅ-rgyal-mo.
C, 134c
Cf. Raṅ-byuṅ-lha-mo. D, 251
Lha-mo-e-ka-ẓa-ti. C, 136c
lhan-skyes.
Kyai-rdor°. C, 23b
Go-bzlog°. C, 29a
rTa-mgrin-dpaḫ-gcig° °jo-boḫi-lugs. C, 58a
Dus-ḫkhor°. C, 23c
bDe-mchog°. B, 39; C, 18a

gSaṅ-bdag° °zhi-ba. C, 88c
gSaṅ-ẖdus°. C, 17b
Lho-brag-nam-mkhaẖ-rgyal-mçhan. D, 39
Lho-nub-mgon-po-gri-gug-dmar-po. C, 125c
Lho-rin-chen-mkhaẖ-ẖgro-ma. C, 30a
a-ti-śa.
Jo°. B, 19
Jo-bo-chen-po-dpal-ldan°. D, 29
a-pa-ra-ẓi-ta (gNod-sbyin°). C, 113c
a-ra-pa-ça-na.
ẖJam-dbyaṅs°. C, S3a
ẖJam-dbyaṅs° °dmar-ser-sa-lugs. C, 65c
aṁ-gho-ra (mGon-po°). C, 124c
arya-de-ba (rJe-bçun°). D, 4
Indra-mkhaẖ-spyod. C, 26a
u-ça-rya (Phyag-rdor°). B, 74; C, 54c
e-ka-ẓa-ti. Cf. Ral-gcig-ma.
Lha-mo°. C, 136c
O-rgyan-sgrol-ma-gnas-kyi-dbaṅ-phyug-ma. C, 45b

CHINESE INDEX

CHINESE INDEX

一切成就救度佛母
1. I-ch'ieh-ch'êng-chiu Chiu-tu fo-mu
B, 235. cf. 338

⊙⊙⊙⊙金剛亥⊙
2. I-ch'ieh-ch'êng-chiu Chin-kang-hai-mu
B, 271

⊙勇威羅瓦金剛
3. I-yung Wei-lo-wa-chin-kang
A, 2B29; B, 46

⊙髻佛母
I-chi fo-mu
cf. 17, 18

上樂王
Shang-lo-wang
cf. 569

⊙⊙⊙佛
4. Shang-lo-wang fo
A, 3M5; A, 3A35; B 36. cf. 28, 138, 209, 458, 570, 772

三面八臂紅馬頭金剛
5. San-mien pa-pei hung Ma-t'ou-chin-kang
A, 6B4

⊙⊙六⊙白救度佛母
6. San-mien liu-pei pai Chiu-tu fo-mu
A, 6B16

⊙⊙四背彌勒菩薩
7. San-mien ssŭ-pei Mi-lo p'u-sa
A, 6A13

不動佛
8. Pu-tung fo
A, 4A40; A, 4A51; A, 4B26; B, 78

⊙⊙⊙母
9. Pu-tung fo-mu
A, 4A8

⊙⊙性佛
10. Pu-tung-hsing fo
A, 4B38

⊙⊙金剛
11. Pu-tung-chin-kang
A, 2A49; A, 5A61. cf. 61, 147, 571, 894

⊙⊙⊙⊙佛
Pu-tung-chin-kang fo
cf. 694, 766

⊙⊙⊙⊙秘密佛
12. Pu-tung-chin-kang pi-mi fo
B, 32. cf. 604, 694

⊙廻吉祥輪佛
13. Pu-hui-chi-hsiang-lun fo
A, 1B53; B, 122

⊙空羂索自在觀世音菩薩
14. Pu-k'ung-chüan-so tzŭ-tsai Kuan-shih-yin p'u-sa
A, 6B54. cf. 341

⊙虛超越菩薩
15. Pu-hsü-ch'ao-yüeh p'u-sa
A, 6A7

九頂佛
16. Chiu-ting fo
A, 4M9

二十四臂一髻佛母
17. Êrh-shih-ssŭ-pei I-chi fo-mu
B, 237

⊙臂一髻佛母
18. Êrh-pei I-chi fo-mu
A, 6B59; B, 239

⊙⊙天母護法
19. Êrh-pei T'ien-mu hu-fa
B, 311

⊙⊙彌勒
20. Êrh-pei Mi-lo
B, 195

⊙⊙法界妙音佛
21. Êrh-pei Fa-chieh-miao-yin fo
A, 6B57

⊙⊙積光佛母
22. Êrh-pei Chi-kuang fo-mu
B, 244

⊙⊙般若⊙⊙
23. Êrh-pei Pan-jo fo-mu
B, 251

⊙⊙葉衣⊙⊙
24. Êrh-pei Yeh-i fo-mu
B, 250

⊙⊙蓮花妙舞自在觀世音
25. Êrh-pei Lien-hua-miao-wu-tzŭ-tsai Kuan-shih-yin
B, 164

⊙⊙金剛妙音佛母
26. Êrh-pei Chin-kang-miao-yin fo-mu
B, 254

⊙⊙隨求佛母
27. Êrh-pei Sui-ch'iu fo-mu
B, 258

五佛上樂王佛
28. Wu-fo Shang-lo-wang fo
A, 3A33

⊙輩達賴喇嘛
29. Wu-pei Ta-lai-la-ma
B, 26

交捥手印佛母
30. Chiao-wan-shou-yin fo-mu
A, 3A9

令安天母
31. Ling-an t'ien-mu
A, 5B53

⊙⊙金剛
32. Ling-an-chin-kang
A, 5A21

⊙甚調伏金剛
33. Ling-shên-t'iao-fu-chin-kang
A, 5A19

伏魔手持金剛
34. Fu-mo Shou-ch'ih-chin-kang
B, 71

⊙⊙⊙⊙⊙⊙佛
35. Fu-mo Shou-ch'ih-chin-kang fo
A, 5M7

伐那婆斯尊者
36. Fa-na-p'o-ssŭ tsun-chê
B, 274. cf. 351

⊙闍羅佛多尊者
37. Fa-shê-lo-fo-to tsun-chê
B, 276. cf. 349

伍嘛天母
38. Wu-ma t'ien-mu
A, 5B54. cf. 511

佛海觀世音
39. Fo-hai Kuan-shih-yin
A, 3B41; B, 34

佛海觀世音佛
40. Fo-hai Kuan-shih-yin fo
A, 3M9

⊙眼佛母
41. Fo-yen fo-mu
A, 2A61; A, 3B57; A.5M9

⊙陀嘎巴拉
42. Fo-t'o-ka-pa-la
A, 3B31

⊙⊙噶布⊙佛
43. Fo-t'o-ka-pu-la fo
A, 3M2

⊙⊙嘎巴⊙金剛
44. Fo-t'o-ka-pa-la chin-kang
B, 51

⊙⊙菩提母
45. Fo-t'o-p'u-t'i-mu
A, 4B25

⊙頂菩薩
46. Fo-ting p'u-sa
A, 5A38

使役嶽母
47. Shih-i yo-mu
A, 2A3

⊙⊙窩時麻母
48. Shih-i-wo-shih-ma-mu
A, 3A20

⊙羸延天
49. Shih-lei-yen t'ien
A, 5B51

值冬天母護法
50. Chih-tung t'ien-mu hu-fa
B, 334

⊙夏⊙⊙⊙⊙
51. Chih-hsia t'ien-mu hu-fa
B, 332

值春天母護法
52. Chih-ch'un t'ien-mu hu-fa
B, 331

⊙秋⊙⊙⊙⊙
53. Chih-ch'iu t'ien-mu hu-fa
B, 333

修藥佛
54. Hsiu-yao fo
A, 1A6

優婆倶多
55. Yu-p'o-chü-to
B, 293

光德佛
56. Kuang-tê fo
A, 1A55; B, 101

⊙燄⊙
57. Kuang-yen fo
A, 1B34

⊙輝⊙
58. Kuang-hui fo
A, 4A21. cf. 281

⊙音如來佛
59. Kuang-yin-ju-lai fo
A, 1B39. cf. 274

內成精明文殊
60. Nei-ch'êng-ching-ming Wên-shu
A, 2A46. cf. 613

八猴不動金剛
61. Pa-hou Pu-tung-chin-kang
B, 348

⊙臂法性妙語自在文殊
62. Pa-pei Fa-hsing-miao-yü-tzŭ-tsai Wên-shu
B, 151

八臂積光佛母
63. Pa-pei Chi-kuang fo-mu
B, 243

⊙⊙金剛救度佛母
64. Pa-pei Chin-kang-chiu-tu fo-mu
A, 6B14

六⊙勇保護法
65. Liu-pei Yung-pao hu-fa
B, 297

⊙⊙妙音佛母
66. Liu-pei Miao-yin fo-mu
A, 6B5

⊙⊙布祿金剛
67. Liu-pei Pu-lu-chin-kang
A, 6A52; B, 341

⊙⊙白衣救度佛母
68. Liu-pei pai-i Chiu-tu fo-mu
B, 232

⊙⊙葉衣佛母
69. Liu-pei Yeh-i fo-mu
A, 6B3; B, 249

⊙⊙金剛妙音佛母
70. Liu-pei Chin-kang-miao-yin fo-mu
B, 253

⊙面威羅瓦金剛
71. Liu-mien Wei-lo-wa-chin-kang
A, 2B30; B, 44

⊙⊙⊙⊙⊙⊙⊙佛
72. Liu-mien Wei-lo-wa-chin-kang fo
A, 2M2

初慈决疑佛
73. Ch'u-tz'ŭ-chüeh-i fo
B, 126

則喇巴喇嘎佛母
74. Tsê-la-pa-la-ka fo-mu
A, 3B58

力波羅蜜母
75. Li Po-lo-mi-mu
A, 4B33

功德佛
kung-tê fo
cf. 109, 115, 128, 450, 461, 720

⊙⊙華佛
76. Kung-tê-hua fo
A, 1A40; B, 104

⊙⊙語王菩薩
77. Kung-tê-yü-wang p'u-sa
A, 6B55

勇保護法
Yung-pao hu-fa
cf. 65, 118, 148, 201, 220, 259, 336, 361, 540, 593, 890, 903, 920, 922

⊙施佛
78. Yung-shih fo
A, 1A42; B, 93

⊙行菩薩
79. Yung-hsing p'u-sa
A, 4B16

⊙識金剛佛母
80. Yung-shih-chin-kang fo-mu
B, 265. cf. 774

勝天母
81. Shêng t'ien-mu
A, 5B41

⊙慧王如來佛
82. Shêng-hui-wang-ju-lai fo
A, 1B43. cf. 496

勝敵金剛
83. Shêng-ti-chin-kang
A, 5A7

⊙發頂菩薩
84. Shêng-fa-ting p'u-sa
A, 5A53

⊙頂佛
85. Shêng-ting fo
A, 4A53

勢成佛
86. Shih-ch'êng fo
A, 1B8

匝哷呰嘎佛母
87. Tsa-lieh-tzŭ-ka fo-mu
B, 257. cf. 110

⊙門支天母
88. Tsa-mên-chih t'ien-mu
A, 5B32

十一面大悲觀世音
89. Shih-i-mien ta-pei Kuan-shih-yin
B, 173

⊙⊙⊙觀世音
90. Shih-i-mien Kuan-shih-yin
A, 6M4

⊙⊙⊙⊙⊙⊙菩薩
91. Shih-i-mien Kuan-shih-yin p'u-sa
A, 6A36

⊙二臂積光佛母
92. Shih-êrh-pei Chi-kuang fo-mu
A, 6B2

⊙八臂蓮花妙舞自在觀世音
93. Shih-pa-pei Lien-hua-miao-wu-tzŭ-tsai Kuan-shih-yin
B, 165

十六臂觀世音菩薩
94. Shih-liu-pei Kuan-shih-yin p'u-sa
A, 6B40

⊙臂積光佛母
95. Shih-pei Chi-kuang fo-mu
A, 6B61; B, 242

千摧碎佛母
96. Ch'ien-ts'ui-sui fo-mu
A, 6A57. cf. 178

半托迦尊者
97. Pan-t'o-chia tsun-chê
B, 284. cf. 549

厄嘎達沙天
98. O-ka-ta-sha t'ien
A, 3B11

右刷哈哩母
99. Yu-shua-ha-li-mu
A, 5B9

⊙(? r. 古)穆巴天
100. Yu[? r. ku]-mu-pa t'ien
A, 3A19

吉利納
101. Chi-li-na
B, 295

⊙祥圓滿救度佛母
102. Chi-hsiang-yüan-man Chiu-tu fo-mu
B, 226

⊙⊙長壽天母護法
103. Chi-hsiang-ch'ang-shou t'ien-mu hu-fa
B, 335

⊙禮斯納巴祖師
104. Chi-li-ssŭ-na-pa tsu-shih
B, 14

名相佛
105. Ming-hsiang fo
A, 1A5
同妙髮天母
106. T'ung-miao-fa t'ien-mu
A, 5B58. cf. 236
吒噶
ch'a-ka
cf. 280
⊙⊙佛
ch'a-ka fo
cf. 697, 713
⊙⊙⊙母
ch'a-ka fo-mu
cf. 672
⊙⊙母
ch'a-ka-mu
cf. 776
⊙機尼佛母
107. Ch'a-chi-ni fo-mu
A, 3B3. cf. 754
吽威聲金剛
108. Hung-wei-shêng-chin-kang
B, 359. cf. 183, 539
和尙
Ho-shang
cf. 302
周匝莊嚴功德佛
109. Chou-tsa-chuang-yen-kung-tê fo
A, 1A50; B, 114
咂哷資噶佛母
110. Tsa-lieh-tzŭ-ka fo-mu
A, 2B41. cf. 87
哷克達卡天
111. Lieh-k'o-ta-ch'ia t'ien
A, 3A1
喇乎拉尊者
112. La-hu-la tsun-chê
A, 1B60. cf. 631, 636
⊙噶喇底佛母
113. La-ka-la-ti fo-mu
A, 2B43
善名如來佛
114. Shan-ming-ju-lai fo
A, 1B38
⊙⊙稱功德佛
115. Shan-ming-ch'êng-kung-tê fo
A, 1A24; B, 109
⊙⊙⊙吉祥王如來
116. Shan-ming-ch'êng-chi-hsiang-wang-ju-lai
B, 133
⊙天祖師
117. Shan-t'ien tsu-shih
B, 10
⊙德勇保護法
118. Shan-tê Yung-pao hu-fa
B, 302
⊙慧佛母
119. Shan-hui fo-mu
A, 4A7
⊙滅諍傲佛
120. Shan-mieh-chêng-ao fo
A, 1B50
⊙⊙⊙謸⊙
121. Shan-mieh-chêng-ao fo
B, 119
⊙⊙魔障⊙
122. Shan-mieh-mo-chang fo
A, 1B52; B, 121
⊙現菩薩
123. Shan-hsien p'u-sa
A, 6A6

善稱名揚天菩薩
124. Shan-ch'êng-ming-yang-t'ien p'u-sa
A, 5A51

⊙行手持金剛佛
125. Shan-hsing Shou-ch'ih-chin-kang fo
A, 5M6

⊙觀
126. Shan-kuan
B, 296

⊙遊步佛
127. Shan-yu-pu fo
A, 1A51; B, 113. cf. 278

⊙⊙⊙功德佛
128. Shan-yu-pu-kung-tê fo
A, 1A22; B, 111

⊙隆菩薩
129. Shan-lung p'u-sa
A, 4B61

喜心金剛
130. Hsi-hsin-chin-kang
B, 48. cf. 132

⊙樂和祖師
131. Hsi-lo-ho tsu-shih
B, 11

⊙金剛
132. Hsi-chin-kang
B, 47. cf. 130, 354

⊙⊙⊙佛
Hsi-chin-kang fo
cf. 352

嘉勒擦布祖師
133. Chia-lo-ts'a-pu tsu-shih
B, 22

嘛哈哷卒瓦哷嘛西母
134. Ma-ha-lieh-tsu-wa-lieh-ma hsi-mu
A, 6B11

⊙哷嘎嘛西母
135. Ma-lieh-ka-ma hsi-mu
A, 6B24

⊙⊙噶達天菩薩
136. Ma-lieh-ka-ta-t'ien p'u-sa
A, 5A12

⊙嘛基佛母
137. Ma-ma-chi fo-mu
A, 3B45; A, 5M1; A, 5A45

嘎嚕底上樂王佛
138. Ka-lu-ti Shang-lo-wang fo
A, 3A46. cf. 209

⊙斯嘛哩佛母
139. Ka-ssŭ-ma-li fo-mu
A, 3A42; A, 3B15

⊙班巴的
140. Ka-pan-pa-ti
A, 1B11

⊙禮嘎尊者
141. Ka-li-ka tsun-chê
A, 1B14. cf. 734

⊙那嘎拔喇危匝尊者
142. Ka-na-ka-pa-la-wei-tsa tsun-chê
A, 1B58. cf. 736

⊙⊙⊙斡斯尊者
143. Ka-na-ka-wa-ssŭ tsun-chê
A, 1B17. cf. 735

⊙⊙牙天
144. Ka-na-ya t'ien
A, 3B23

噶哷噶達天菩薩
145. Ka-lieh-ka-ta-t'ien p'u-sa
A, 5A11

四座金剛
146. Ssŭ-tso-chin-kang
B, 57

⊙臂不動金剛
147. Ssŭ-pei Pu-tung-chin-kang
A, 6A50; B, 350

⊙⊙勇保護法
148. Ssŭ-pei Yung-pao hu-fa
B, 306

⊙⊙如意自在救度佛母
149. Ssŭ-pei ju-i-tzŭ-tsai Chiu-tu fo-mu
B, 231

⊙⊙⊙⊙輪救度佛母
150. Ssŭ-pei ju-i-lun Chiu-tu fo-mu
A, 6B15. cf. 221

⊙⊙彌勒
151. Ssŭ-pei Mi-lo
B, 194

⊙⊙準提佛母
152. Ssŭ-pei Chun-t'i fo-mu
A, 6B60; B, 240

⊙⊙紅自在觀世音
153. Ssŭ-pei hung tzŭ-tsai Kuan-shih-yin
B, 168

⊙⊙般若佛母
154. Ssŭ-pei Pan-jo fo-mu
B, 252

⊙⊙觀世音
155. Ssŭ-pei Kuan-shih-yin
A, 6M6; B, 158

四臂觀音菩薩
156. Ssŭ-pei Kuan-yin p'u-sa
A, 6A35

⊙⊙陰陽無量壽佛
157. Ssŭ-pei yin-yang Wu-liang-shou fo
B, 63

⊙⊙風天
158. Ssŭ-pei Fêng-t'ien
A, 3B24

⊙面八臂馬頭金剛
159. Ssŭ-mien pa-pei Ma-t'ou-chin-kang
A, 6A12

因竭陀尊者
160. Yin-chieh-t'o tsun-chê
B, 272. cf. 424

⊙陀羅藥叉大將
161. Yin-t'o-lo yao-ch'a-ta-chiang
A, 6B35

土地
162. T'u-ti
A, 5B45

地主永寧天母
163. Ti-chu yung-ning t'ien-mu
B, 323

⊙天母
164. Ti t'ien-mu
A, 5B44

⊙拉巴
165. Ti-la-pa
A, 2B35

⊙藏王菩薩
166. Ti-tsang-wang p'u-sa
A, 1M7; A, 1A4; A, 2A40; B, 197. A, 1A4 om. 王

基哷底噶天
167. Chi-lieh-ti-ka t'ien
A, 5A14
增長天王
168. Tsêng-chang t'ien-wang
B, 325
墳主護法
169. Fên-chu hu-fa
B, 337
多瓦那達沙天
170. To-wa-na-ta-sha t'ien
A, 3B12
夜叉賢滿護法
171. Yeh-ch'a Hsien-man hu-fa
B, 354
大光佛
172. Ta-kuang fo
A, 1A17
⊙力⊙
173. Ta-li fo
A, 1A8
⊙⊙金剛
174. Ta-li-chin-kang
A, 2A11; A, 6B43; B, 342
⊙勝三界自在文殊
175. Ta-shêng-san-chieh-tzŭ-tsai Wên-shu
B, 154
⊙⊙菩薩
176. Ta-shêng p'u-sa
A, 5A27
⊙勢至菩薩
177. Ta-shih-chih p'u-sa
A, 5A31
⊙千摧碎佛母
178. Ta-ch'ien-ts'ui-sui fo-mu
B, 201. cf. 96
大脣金剛
179. Ta-ch'un-chin-kang
A, 5A26
⊙善秋月救度佛母
180. Ta-shan-ch'iu-yüeh Chiu-tu fo-mu
B, 208
⊙地紅色觀世音
181. Ta-ti hung-sê Kuan-shih-yin
B, 172
⊙⊙觀世音菩薩
182. Ta-ti Kuan-shih-yin p'u-sa
A, 6A11
⊙威吽聲金剛
183. Ta-wei-hung-shêng-chin-kang
B, 56. cf. 108
⊙孔雀佛母
184. Ta-k'ung-ch'iao fo-mu
A, 6A60; B, 202
⊙安樂⊙
185. Ta-an-lo fo
A, 4B37
⊙寒林⊙母
186. Ta-han-lin fo-mu
B, 203. cf. 264
⊙寶如意觀世音
187. Ta-pao-ju-i Kuan-shih-yin
B, 176
⊙⊙金剛佛母
188. Ta-pao-chin-kang fo-mu
B, 266. cf. 786
⊙幻⊙⊙
189. Ta-huan-chin-kang
B, 50
⊙⊙⊙⊙佛
190. Ta-huan-chin-kang fo
A, 3M7

大廻佛母
191. Ta-hui fo-mu
A, 6A39; B, 259

⊙急忿⊙
192. Ta-chi-fên-mu
A, 6B6

⊙慧菩薩
193. Ta-hui p'u-sa
A, 6A19

⊙⊙金色救度佛母
194. Ta-hui chin-sê Chiu-tu fo-mu
B, 209

⊙手佛
195. Ta-shou fo
A, 1A18

⊙持金剛
196. Ta-ch'ih-chin-kang
A, 2A36; B, 29

⊙柔善救度佛母
197. Ta-jou-shan Chiu-tu fo-mu
B, 220

⊙發頂菩薩
198. Ta-fa-ting p'u-sa
A, 5A54

⊙白文殊
199. Ta-pai Wên-shu
B, 145

⊙⊙祝壽財寶護法
200. Ta-pai chu-shou Ts'ai-pao hu-fa
B, 318

⊙紅勇保護法
201. Ta-hung Yung-pao hu-fa
B, 336

⊙聖白傘蓋佛母
202. Ta-shêng Pai-san-kai fo-mu
B, 248

大聖除毒佛母
203. Ta-shêng Ch'u-tu fo-mu
B, 236

⊙自在天
204. Ta-tzŭ-tsai t'ien
A, 5A17

⊙輪手持金剛
205. Ta-lun Shou-ch'ih-chin-kang
A, 2A33; B, 59

⊙⊙⊙⊙⊙⊙佛
206. Ta-lun Shou-ch'ih-chin-kang fo
A, 2M9

⊙迦葉
207. Ta-chia-yeh
B, 290

⊙頂佛
208. Ta-ting fo
A, 4A54; A, 4A59

⊙鵬
Ta-p'êng
cf. 635, 666, 936

⊙⊙上樂王佛
209. Ta-p'êng Shang-lo-wang fo
B, 40. cf. 138

⊙⊙金剛佛
210. Ta-p'êng-chin-kang fo
B, 41

⊙黃財寶護法
211. Ta-huang Ts'ai-pao hu-fa
B, 322

⊙黑天
212. Ta-hei t'ien
A, 3B18

⊙⊙金剛
213. Ta-hei-chin-kang
A, 2B59

大黑雄威護法
214. Ta-hei hsiung-wei hu-fa
B, 308

⊙⊙⊙⊙財寶護法
215. Ta-hei hsiung-wei Ts'ai-pao hu-fa
B, 319

天容母
216. T'ien-jung-mu
A, 5B20

⊙母護法
t'ien-mu hu-fa
cf. 19, 50, 51, 52, 53, 103, 611, 648, 900

⊙王
t'ien-wang
cf. 168, 317, 355, 721

⊙菩薩
t'ien p'u-sa
cf. 124, 136, 145, 412, 423, 665, 740, 912, 926

奇妙菩薩
217. Ch'i-miao p'u-sa
A, 5B2

奪尊母
218. To tsun-mu
A, 5B22

如來
ju-lai
cf. 116, 274, 496, 497, 519, 683, 853

⊙⊙佛
ju-lai fo
cf. 59, 82, 114, 501, 520, 682, 852

如性母
219. Ju-hsing-mu
A, 4B24

⊙意大白勇保護法
220. Ju-i ta-pai Yung-pao hu-fa
B, 317

⊙⊙寶輪白救度佛母
221. Ju-i-pao-lun pai Chiu-tu fo-mu
B, 230. cf. 150

⊙⊙觀世音
222. Ju-i Kuan-shih-yin
B, 175

⊙火熾盛救度佛母
223. Ju-huo-ch'ih-ch'êng Chiu-tu fo-mu
B, 218

妙光佛
224. Miao-kuang fo
A, 1B35

⊙寶童子
225. Miao-pao-t'ung-tzŭ
A, 5B11

⊙法金剛佛母
226. Miao-fa-chin-kang fo-mu
B, 263. cf. 816

⊙目佛
227. Miao-mu fo
A, 1A20

⊙舞佛母
228. Miao-wu fo-mu
A, 3A48; A, 4B45

⊙⊙母
229. Miao-wu-mu
A, 2B9

妙舞財寶護法
230. Miao-wu Ts'ai-pao hu-fa
B, 324

⊙華佛
231. Miao-hua fo
A, 1A26

⊙語尊帝文殊
232. Miao-yü-tsun-ti Wên-shu
B, 150

⊙醫佛
233. Miao-i fo
A, 1B9

⊙音佛母
Miao-yin fo-mu
cf. 26, 66, 70, 369, 618

⊙⊙天母
234. Miao-yin t'ien-mu
A, 5B49

⊙⊙母
234a. Miao-yin mu
A, 5B19

⊙⊙自在文殊
235. Miao-yin-tzŭ-tsai Wên-shu
B, 152

⊙髮天母
236. Miao-fa t'ien-mu
A, 5B17. cf. 106

威光蘊頂菩薩
237. Wei-kuang-yün-ting p'u-sa
A, 5A24

⊙⊙金剛
238. Wei-kuang-chin-kang
A, 2B54. cf. 791

⊙⊙頂佛
239. Wei-kuang-ting fo
A, 4A42; A, 4A58

威嚴母
240. Wei-yen-mu
A, 6B25

⊙烈三頭六臂手持金剛
241. Wei-lieh san-t'ou liu-pei Shou-ch'ih-chin-kang
B, 75

⊙⊙手持金剛
242. Wei-lieh Shou-ch'ih-chin-kang
B, 73

⊙積佛母
243. Wei-chi fo-mu
B, 351. cf. 330

⊙⊙金剛
244. Wei-chi-chin-kang
B, 356

⊙羅瓦金剛
245. Wei-lo-wa-chin-kang
A, 2B27; B, 42. cf. 3, 71, 249, 250, 283, 333, 353, 362, 378, 383, 384, 566, 619, 723, 939

⊙⊙⊙⊙⊙佛
246. Wei-lo-wa-chin-kang fo
A, 2M7. cf. 72, 620

娑你羅藥叉大將
247. So-ni-lo yao-ch'a-ta-chiang
A, 6B34

婆夷⊙⊙⊙⊙⊙
248. P'o-i-lo yao-ch'a-ta-chiang
A, 6B36

嫉威羅瓦金剛
249. Chi Wei-lo-wa-chin-kang
A, 2A26; A, 2B40

宏光佛
Hung-kuang fo
cf. 439

⊙⊙威羅瓦金剛
250. Hung-kuang Wei-lo-wa-chin-kang
A, 2B28

⊙⊙文殊金剛
251. Hung-kuang Wên-shu-chin-kang
A, 2A31

⊙⊙毘盧佛
252. Hung-kuang P'i-lu fo
A, 4A34

⊙⊙釋迦獅子佛
253. Hung-kuang Shih-chia-shih-tzŭ fo
B, 66

⊙⊙顯耀菩提佛
254. Hung-kuang-hsien-yao-p'u-t'i fo
A, 5M5; A, 5A36; B, 70

宜帝護法
255. I-ti hu-fa
B, 313

宗喀巴
256. Tsung-k'a-pa
A, 1A36

⊙⊙⊙祖師
257. Tsung-k'a-pa tsu-shih
B, 21

害彼母
258. Hai-pi-mu
A, 6B13

宮室勇保護法
259. Kung-shih Yung-pao hu-fa
B, 305

宮毘盧藥叉大將
260. Kung-p'i-lu yao-ch'a-ta-chiang
A, 6A4

密 cf. 蜜
mi mi

⊙咒隨持佛母
261. Mi-chou-sui-ch'ih fo-mu
B, 204. cf. 691

⊙那天
262. Mi-na t'ien
A, 3A27

宿王佛
263. Su-wang fo
A, 1B18. cf. 748

寒林佛母
264. Han-lin fo-mu
A, 6A59. cf. 186

實破闇慧菩薩
265. Shih-p'o-an-hui p'u-sa
A, 6A5

寶傘勝佛
266. Pao-san-shêng fo
B, 123

⊙⊙⊙光佛
267. Pao-san-shêng-kuang fo
A, 1B54

⊙光佛
268. Pao-kuang fo
A, 1A32; B, 84

⊙冠菩薩
269. Pao-kuan p'u-sa
A, 5B15

⊙勝佛
270. Pao-shêng fo
B, 79. cf. 276

寶最勝母
271. Pao-tsui-shêng-mu
A, 5B18

⊙月佛
272. Pao-yüeh fo
A, 1A44; B, 91

⊙⊙光佛
273. Pao-yüeh-kuang fo
A, 1A46; B, 89

⊙⊙智嚴光音自在王如來
274. Pao-yüeh-chih-yen-kuang-yin-tzŭ-tsai-wang-ju-lai
B, 134. cf. 59

⊙火佛
275. Pao-huo fo
A, 1A47; B, 88

⊙生⊙
276. Pao-shêng fo
A, 1B30; A, 2A43; A, 4A11; A, 4A39. cf. 270

⊙自在母
277. Pao-tzŭ-tsai-mu
A, 5B23

⊙華遊步佛
278. Pao-hua-yu-pu fo
A, 1A49; B, 115. cf. 127

⊙蓮花善住須彌山王佛
279. Pao-lien-hua-shan-chu-hsü-mi-shan-wang fo
B, 116. cf. 901

⊙貝吒噶
280. Pao-pei ch'a-ka
A, 3A37

⊙身光輝佛
281. Pao-shên-kuang-hui fo
A, 1B51; B, 120. cf. 58

寶頂佛
282. Pao-ting fo
A, 4A45; B, 144

射勢威羅瓦金剛
283. Shê-shih Wei-lo-wa-chin-kang
A, 2B32

專必尼佛母
284. Chuan-pi-ni fo-mu
A, 3A59

尊勝佛母
285. Tsun-shêng fo-mu
A, 6M3; A, 6B26; B, 247

⊙⊙天⊙
286. Tsun-shêng t'ien-mu
A, 5B42

⊙⊙母
287. Tsun-shêng-mu
A, 5B7

⊙⊙菩薩
288. Tsun-shêng p'u-sa
A, 5A37

⊙⊙頂佛
289. Tsun-shêng-ting fo
A, 4A57

⊙者
tsun-chê
cf. 36, 37, 97, 112, 141, 142, 143, 160, 298, 342, 349, 350, 351, 424, 491, 549, 592, 631, 724, 725, 729, 734, 735, 736, 753, 759, 856, 865, 866, 868, 871

⊙⊙速勇救度佛母
290. Tsun-chê su-yung Chiu-tu fo-mu
B, 207. cf. 739

尊親護法
291. Tsun-ch'in hu-fa
B, 314

導師佛
292. Tao-shih fo
A, 1A19

小手持金剛
293. Hsiao Shou-ch'ih-chin-kang
A, 2B5

尸棄佛
294. Shih-ch'i fo
B, 128

山沙喀哷天
295. Shan-sha-ou-lieh t'ien
A, 3B25

獄主
yo-chu
cf. 867, 927

⊙⊙天
296. Yo-chu t'ien
A, 3A14

⊙母
yo-mu
cf. 47, 363, 367, 374, 381, 386, 435, 874

巴哷沙雜扎天
297. Pa-lieh-sha-tsa-cha t'ien
A, 3B34

⊙沽拉尊者
298. Pa-ku-la tsun-chê
A, 1B59; B, 280

⊙達哷嘎哷嘛西母
299. Pa-ta-lieh-ka-lieh-ma hsi-mu
A, 6B12

布倫祖師
300. Pu-lun tsu-shih
B, 20

⊙田救度佛母
301. Pu-t'ien Chiu-tu fo-mu
B, 233

⊙祿金剛
Pu-lu-chin-kang
cf. 67, 924, 932, 937

⊙袋和尙
302. Pu-tai Ho-shang
B, 289

⊙達天
303. Pu-ta-t'ien
A, 3A4

帝幢王佛
Ti-ch'uang-wang fo
cf. 622, 623

⊙釋
304. Ti-shih
A, 5B38; B, 328

⊙⊙天
305. Ti-shih t'ien
A, 3A29

幢頂佛
306. Ch'uang-ting fo
A, 4A41; A, 6A41

⊙⊙膊嚴佛母
307. Ch'uang-ting-po-yen fo-mu
B, 260

⊙⊙臂⊙⊙⊙
308. Ch'uang-ting-pei-yen fo-mu
A, 6A38

幼天母
309. Yu t'ien-mu
A, 5B29

底提喀扎母
310. Ti-t'i k'a-cha-mu
A, 3A18

⊙⊙薩布達母
311. Ti-t'i sa-pu-ta-mu
A, 3A8

⊙⊙達沙母
312. Ti-t'i ta-sha-mu
A, 3A6

⊙⊙那瓦母
313. Ti-t'i na-wa-mu
A, 3A5

⊙⊙阿喀扎母
314. Ti-t'i a-k'a-cha-mu
A, 3A7

度生佛
315. Tu-shêng fo
A, 4M6; A, 4A30

⊙脫衰敗救度佛母
316. Tu-t'o-shuai-pai Chiu-tu fo-mu
B, 222

廣目天王
317. Kuang-mu t'ien-wang
B, 326

⊙臂準提佛母
318. Kuang-pei Chun-t'i fo-mu
B, 241

彌勒
Mi-lo
cf. 20, 151

⊙⊙佛
319. Mi-lo fo
A, 1B28. cf. 609

彌勒菩薩
320. Mi-lo p'u-sa
A, 1M1; A, 2A53; A, 4B46.
cf. 7, 335

微妙音菩薩
321. Wei-miao-yin p'u-sa
A, 6A15

德光佛
322. Tê-kuang fo
A, 1B21

⊙⊙祖師
323. Tê-kuang tsu-shih
B, 7

⊙念佛
324. Tê-nien fo
A, 1A25; B, 108

⊙樂巴祖師
325. Tê-lo-pa tsu-shih
B, 17

必哷斡巴
326. Pi-lieh-wa-pa
A, 3B26

忍辱波羅蜜母
327. Jên-ju Po-lo-mi-mu
A, 4A14

念佑菩薩
328. Nien-yu p'u-sa
A, 5B5

忿怒妙月金剛
329. Fên-nu-miao-yüeh-chin-kang
A, 5A42

⊙⊙威積佛母
330. Fên-nu Wei-chi fo-mu
A, 6B29

忿怒手持金剛
331. Fên-nu Shou-ch'ih-chin-kang
A, 2B3

⊙⊙母
332. Fên-nu-mu
A, 5B12. cf. 799

悋威羅瓦金剛
333. Lin Wei-lo-wa-chin-kang
A, 2A28; A, 2B38

惠施波羅蜜母
334. Hui-shih Po-lo-mi-mu
A, 4A16

慈氐(r. 氏)菩薩
335. Tz'ŭ-ti (r. shih) p'u-sa
A, 1A2; A, 6A18. cf. 320

⊙鳥面勇保護法
336. Tz'ŭ-niao-mien Yung-pao hu-fa
B, 304

慧輪文殊
337. Hui-lun Wên-shu
B, 156

成就一切救度佛母
338. Ch'êng-chiu-i-ch'ieh Chiu-tu fo-mu
A, 6A56; B, 225. cf. 1

⊙⊙佛
339. Ch'êng-chiu fo
A, 1B32; A, 2A41; A, 4M3; A, 4A38; A, 4A48; A, 4B28; A, 4B50; B, 81

⊙護手持金剛
340. Ch'êng-hu Shou-ch'ih-chin-kang
A, 2B4

成鎖觀世音
341. Ch'êng-so Kuan-shih-yin
B, 171. cf. 14

戒博迦尊者
342. Chieh-po-chia tsun-chê
B, 286. cf. 856

手持金剛
343. Shou-ch'ih-chin-kang
A, 6A44. cf. 34, 205, 241, 242, 293, 331, 340, 576, 635, 678, 711, 858, 897, 908

⊙⊙⊙⊙佛
344. Shou-ch'ih-chin-kang fo
cf. 35, 125, 206

⊙⊙⊙⊙菩薩
345. Shou-ch'ih-chin-kang p'u-sa
A, 1A10; A, 2A39; A, 6A26

拘留孫佛
346. Chü-liu-sun fo
B, 130

⊙那含牟尼佛
347. Chü-na-shê-mou-ni fo
B, 131

拉禮達祖師
348. La-li-ta tsu-shih
B, 15

拔匝哩補達喇尊者
349. Pa-tsa-li-pu-ta-la tsun-chê
A, 1B15. cf. 37

⊙達喇尊者
350. Pa-ta-la tsun-chê
A, 1B16. cf. 729

⊙那巴斯尊者
351. Pa-na-pa-ssŭ tsun-chê
A, 1B48. cf. 36

持兵器喜金剛佛
352. Ch'ih-ping-ch'i Hsi-chin-kang fo
A, 3M3

⊙劍威羅瓦金剛
353. Ch'ih-chien Wei-lo-wa-chin-kang
A, 2A5; A, 2B52

⊙嘎布拉喜金剛
354. Ch'ih-ka-pu-la Hsi-chin-kang
A, 3M6

⊙國天王
355. Ch'ih-kuo t'ien-wang
B, 327

⊙圓鼓佛母
356. Ch'ih-yüan-ku fo-mu
A, 3B50

⊙威波羅蜜母
357. Ch'ih-wei Po-lo-mi-mu
A, 4A15

⊙山王佛
358. Ch'ih-shan-wang fo
A, 1B27

⊙幔佛母
359. Ch'ih-man fo-mu
A, 3B56

⊙日⊙⊙
360. Ch'ih-jih fo-mu
A, 3A25

⊙棒勇保護法
361. Ch'ih-pang Yung-pao hu-fa
B, 303

⊙⊙威羅瓦金剛
362. Ch'ih-pang Wei-lo-wa-chin-kang
A, 2A7; A, 2B50

持棒嶽母
363. Ch'ih-pang yo-mu
A, 2A1

⊙流星佛母
364. Ch'ih-liu-hsing fo-mu
A, 3A23

⊙燈佛母
365. Ch'ih-têng fo-mu
A, 3A30

⊙⊙母
366. Ch'ih-têng mu
A, 2B24

⊙牙嶽母
367. Ch'ih-ya yo-mu
A, 2A2

⊙珠佛
368. Ch'ih-chu fo
A, 1B20

⊙琶妙音佛母
369. Ch'ih-p'a Miao-yin fo-mu
B, 255

⊙琵琶佛母
370. Ch'ih-p'i-p'a fo-mu
A, 3B49

⊙管佛母
371. Ch'ih-kuan fo-mu
A, 3B44

⊙網⊙⊙
372. Ch'ih-wang fo-mu
A, 3A55

⊙繩⊙⊙
373. Ch'ih-shêng fo-mu
A, 3A56

⊙繩嶽⊙
374. Ch'ih-shêng yo-mu
A, 2A16

持花佛母
375. Ch'ih-hua fo-mu
A, 3A53

⊙⊙母
376. Ch'ih-hua-mu
A, 2B22

⊙蓮花佛母
377. Ch'ih-lien-hua fo-mu
A, 3A12

⊙⊙⊙威羅瓦金剛
378. Ch'ih-lien-hua Wèi-lo-wa-chin-kang
A, 2A6; A, 2B51

⊙輪王佛
379. Ch'ih-lun-wang fo
A, 3M8

⊙鉤佛母
380. Ch'ih-kou fo-mu
A, 3A54

⊙⊙嶽⊙
381. Ch'ih-kou yo-mu
A, 2A17

⊙鉗佛⊙
382. Ch'ih-ch'ien fo-mu
A, 3A57

⊙錘威羅瓦金剛
383. Ch'ih-chui Wei-lo-wa-chin-kang
A, 2B49

⊙鐘⊙⊙⊙⊙⊙
384. Ch'ih-chung Wei-lo-wa-chin-kang
A, 2A8

⊙鐲佛母
385. Ch'ih-cho fo-mu
A, 3A10

持鐲嶽母
386. Ch'ih-cho yo-mu
A, 2A15

⊙鑰匙佛母
387. Ch'ih-yao-shih fo-mu
A, 3B54

⊙門佛母
388. Ch'ih-mên fo-mu
A, 3B55

⊙⊙鎖佛母
389. Ch'ih-mên-so fo-mu
A, 3B53

⊙雙燈佛母
390. Ch'ih-shuang-têng fo-mu
A, 3A24

⊙電佛母
391. Ch'ih-tien fo-mu
A, 3A22

⊙須彌峯王菩薩
392. Ch'ih-hsü-mi-fêng-wang p'u-sa
A, 6A14

⊙香佛母
393. Ch'ih-hsiang fo-mu
A, 3A40

⊙⊙母
394. Ch'ih-hsiang-mu
A, 2B23

⊙⊙水母
395. Ch'ih-hsiang-shui-mu
A, 2B25

⊙鬘佛⊙
396. Ch'ih-man fo-mu
A, 3B27; A, 4B56

⊙⊙母
397. Ch'ih-man-mu
A, 2B7

接引三塗菩薩
398. Chieh-yin-san-t'u p'u-sa
A, 4B48

摧碎金剛
399. Ts'ui-sui-chin-kang
A, 6B28. cf. 938

⊙⊙⊙⊙佛母
400. Ts'ui-sui-chin-kang fo-mu
B, 352

攝伏世間救度佛母
401. Shê-fu-shih-chien Chiu-tu fo-mu
B, 216

救度佛母
402. Chiu-tu fo-mu
A, 2A58; A, 3B47.
Cf. 1, 6, 64, 68, 102, 149, 150, 180, 194, 197, 221, 223, 290, 301, 316, 338, 401, 425, 506, 507, 577, 626, 629, 637, 638, 645, 646, 647, 650, 679, 685, 739, 792, 875, 880, 881, 893, 895, 910

⊙⊙母
403. Chiu-tu-mu
A, 5B10

⊙脫菩薩
404. Chiu-t'o p'u-sa
A, 6A28

敏捷文殊
405. Min-chieh Wên-shu
B, 157

⊙⊙⊙⊙菩薩
406. Min-chieh Wên-shu p'u-sa
A, 6A42

敏捷頂佛
407. Min-chieh-ting fo
A, 4A61

文殊
Wên-shu
cf. 60, 62, 175, 199, 232, 235, 337, 405, 484, 543, 587, 597, 600, 610, 613, 751

⊙⊙室利佛
Wên-shu-shih-li fo
cf. 602, 692

⊙⊙菩薩
408. Wên-shu p'u-sa
A, 1M4; A, 1A12; A, 2A 25; A, 6A29; A, 6A33. cf. 406, 578, 588, 601, 689, 750, 921

⊙⊙金剛
Wên-shu-chin-kang
cf. 251, 603

⊙⊙⊙⊙佛
Wên-shu-chin-kang fo
cf. 695, 805

斗母
409. Tou-mu
B, 269

斡哷希天母
410. Wa-lieh-hsi t'ien-mu
A, 5B31

⊙喇⊙佛⊙
411. Wa-la-hsi fo-mu
A, 2B42

⊙施斯叉天菩薩
412. Wa-shih-ssŭ-ch'a-t'ien p'u-sa
A, 5A10

方便波羅蜜母
413. Fang-pien Po-lo-mi-mu
A, 4A2

施勝佛母
414. Shih-shêng fo-mu
A, 6B17

⊙妙金剛
415. Shih-miao-chin-kang
A, 5B48

⊙無畏菩薩
416. Shih-wu-wei p'u-sa
A, 5B3

⊙畏金剛
417. Shih-wei-chin-kang
A, 2B60

日光天
418. Jih-kuang t'ien
A, 3A26

⊙⊙徧照菩薩
419. Jih-kuang-pien-chao p'u-sa
A, 6A27. cf. 453

⊙天
420. Jih t'ien
A, 5B40

⊙宮天
421. Jih-kung t'ien
A, 5A3

⊙藏佛
422. Jih-tsang fo
A, 1A14

昂机哩天菩薩
423. Ang-chi-li-t'ien p'u-sa
A, 5A9

⊙機達尊者
424. Ang-chi-ta tsun-chê
A, 1B46. cf. 160

明咒吽聲救度佛母
425. Ming-chou-hung-shêng Chiu-tu fo-mu
B, 221

⊙慧菩薩
426. Ming-hui p'u-sa
A, 6A17

⊙月母
427. Ming-yüeh-mu
A, 5B35

⊙照佛
428. Ming-chao fo
A, 1A15

⊙燈⊙
429. Ming-têng fo
A, 1B7

⊙燄⊙
430. Ming-yen fo
A, 1A28

⊙象祖師
431. Ming-hsiang tsu-shih
B, 5

⊙點尊母
432. Ming-tien tsun-mu
A, 5B34

時火天
433. Shih-huo t'ien
A, 3B7

⊙相⊙母
434. Shih-hsiang t'ien-mu
A, 5B28

⊙⊙嶽⊙
435. Shih-hsiang yo-mu
A, 2A4

⊙輪王佛
436. Shih-lun-wang fo
B, 35

普光佛母
437. P'u-kuang fo-mu
A, 4A5

⊙慧佛
438. P'u-hui fo
B, 143

⊙⊙宏光佛
439. P'u-hui Hung-kuang fo
B, 68

⊙⊙毘盧⊙
440. P'u-hui P'i-lu fo
A, 4M5; A, 4A36

⊙持金剛
441. P'u-ch'ih-chin-kang
A, 5A20

⊙賢菩薩
442. P'u-hsien p'u-sa
A, 1M9; A, 1A3; A, 2A23; A, 4B5; B, 198. cf. 923

智慧波羅蜜母
443. Chih-hui Po-lo-mi-mu
A, 4A17

⊙⊙空行佛⊙
444. Chih-hui-k'ung-hsing fo-mu
B, 52. cf. 608

⊙⊙頂菩薩
445. Chih-hui-ting p'u-sa
A, 4B58

⊙波羅蜜母
446. Chih Po-lo-mi-mu
A, 4B34

⊙積菩薩
447. Chih-chi p'u-sa
A, 6A8. cf. 607

智行佛母
448. Chih-hsing fo-mu
B, 60. cf. 492

⊙⊙金剛佛母
449. Chih-hsing-chin-kang fo-mu
B, 264

最上功德佛
450. Tsui-shang-kung-tê fo
A, 4M2; A, 4B31

⊙勝母
451. Tsui-shêng-mu
A, 5B33. cf. 271

⊙能散鹿菩薩
452. Tsui-nêng-san-lu p'u-sa
A, 5A25

月光徧照菩薩
453. Yüeh-kuang-pien-chao p'u-sa
A, 6A21. cf. 419

⊙⊙母
454. Yüeh-kuang-mu
A, 6B22

⊙⊙菩薩
455. Yüeh-kuang p'u-sa
A, 4B60

⊙天
456. Yüeh t'ien
A, 3A28; A, 5B55

⊙相佛
457. Yüeh-hsiang fo
A, 1B33

本生上樂王佛
458. Pên-shêng Shang-lo-wang fo
B, 39

末你羅藥叉大將
459. Mo-ni-lo yao-ch'a-ta-chiang
A, 6B33

朱杜羅藥叉大將
460. Chu-tu-lo yao-ch'a-ta-chiang
A, 6B20

栴檀功德佛
461. Chan-t'an-kung-tê fo
A, 1A57; B, 99

梵王
462. Fan-wang
B, 329

⊙⊙天
463. Fan-wang t'ien
A, 3B13; A, 5A15. cf. 465

棄諸惡趣菩薩
464. Ch'i-chu-wu-ch'ü p'u-sa
A, 5B4

梵(r. 梵)天
465. Fan-t'ien
A, 5B43. cf. 463

樂自在天
466. Lo-tzŭ-tsai t'ien
A, 3B36; A, 5A1

權衡三界觀世音
467. Ch'üan-hêng-san-chieh Kuan-shih-yin
B, 167

⊙⊙⊙⊙⊙⊙⊙菩薩
468. Ch'üan-hêng-san-chieh Kuan-shih-yin p'u-sa
A, 6B50

欲王金剛
469. Yü-wang-chin-kang
A, 2A13

歌唄佛母
470. Ko-pai fo-mu
A, 3A50; A, 4B57

歌唄母
471. Ko-pai-mu
A, 2B8

歡喜佛母
472. Huan-hsi fo-mu
A, 4A28

毒嚴金剛
473. Tu-yen-chin-kang
A, 2A9

毘婆尸佛
474. P'i-p'o-shih fo
B, 127

⊙盧佛
475. P'i-lu fo
A, 2A44; B, 77. cf. 252, 440, 824

毗羯羅藥叉大將
476. P'i-chieh-lo yao-ch'a-ta-chiang
A, 6B21

毘舍浮佛
477. P'i-shê-fou fo
B, 129

氐氐迦
478. Ti-ti-chia
B, 294

水天
479. Shui-t'ien
A, 3B8; A, 5B39

⊙⊙佛
480. Shui-t'ien fo
A, 1A60; B, 96

⊙⊙中天佛
481. Shui-t'ien-chung-t'ien fo
A, 1A59; B, 97

水月觀世音
482. Shui-yüeh Kuan-shih-yin
B, 160
⊙⊙⊙⊙⊙菩薩
483. Shui-yüeh Kuan-shih-yin p'u-sa
A, 6A45
永輪文殊
484. Yung-lun Wên-shu
B, 147
求財佛母
485. Ch'iu-ts'ai fo-mu
A, 6B27
沙斡哩
486. Sha-wa-li
A, 2B26
⊙⊙⊙佛母
487. Sha-wa-li fo-mu
A, 3A61; A, 3B17
⊙納衣
488. Sha-na-i
B, 292
⊙羅門佛母
489. Sha-lo-mên fo-mu
B, 267
⊙門佛母
490. Sha-mên fo-mu
A, 6A55
注荼半托尊者
491. Chu-ch'a-pan-t'o tsun-chê
B, 282. cf. 592
沽嚕古勒佛母
492. Ku-lu-ku-lo fo-mu
A, 3B40. cf. 448
法帝
493. Fa-ti
A, 2B34. cf. 941
法帝護法
494. Fa-ti hu-fa
B, 312
⊙性妙音自在佛
495. Fa-hsing-miao-yin-tzŭ-tsai fo
B, 67. cf. 62, 498
⊙海勝慧遊戲神通如來
496. Fa-hai-shêng-hui-yu-hsi-shên-t'ung-ju-lai
B, 138. cf. 82
⊙⊙審音如來
497. Fa-hai-shên-yin-ju-lai
B, 137
⊙界妙音自在佛
498. Fa-chieh-miao-yin-tzŭ-tsai fo
A, 4M1; A, 4A31. cf. 21, 495
⊙聲祖師
499. Fa-shêng tsu-shih
B, 6
⊙雲佛母
500. Fa-yün fo-mu
A, 4A6
⊙音如來佛
501. Fa-yin-ju-lai fo
A, 1B42
波羅蜜母
Po-lo-mi-mu
cf. 75, 327, 334, 357, 413, 443, 446, 595, 615, 675, 835, 906
消憂智菩薩
502. Hsiao-yu-chih p'u-sa
A, 4B14
淸淨佛
503. Ch'ing-ching fo
A, 1A41; B, 94

清淨光遊戲神通佛
504. Ch'ing-ching-kuang-yu-hsi-shên-t'ung fo
A, 1A39; B, 105

⊙⊙施佛
505. Ch'ing-ching-shih fo
A, 1A61; B, 95

涅槃寂滅救度佛母
506. Nieh-p'an-chi-mieh Chiu-tu fo-mu
B, 215

準提佛母
Chun-t'i fo-mu
cf. 152, 318

灌頂遵勝救度佛母
507. Kuan-ting-tsun-shêng Chiu-tu fo-mu
B, 210

火天
508. Huo t'ien
A, 3A21; A, 5A50. cf. 433

⊙餤光佛
509. Huo-yen-kuang fo
A, 4B32

⊙⊙⊙頂佛
510. Huo-yen-kuang-ting fo
A, 4A56

烏麻母
511. Wu-ma mu
A, 5B36. cf. 38

烈焰金剛
512. Lieh-yen-chin-kang
B, 349

⊙聲⊙⊙
513. Lieh-shêng-chin-kang
A, 2B55

無垢佛
514. Wu-kou fo
A, 1A43; B, 92

⊙⊙⊙母
515. Wu-kou fo-mu
A, 4A27

⊙⊙虛空菩薩
516. Wu-kou-hsü-k'ung p'u-sa
A, 5A41

⊙⊙光童子
517. Wu-kou-kuang-t'ung-tzŭ
A, 5B16

⊙憂佛
518. Wu-yu fo
A, 1B36

⊙⊙勝吉祥如來
519. Wu-yu-shêng-chi-hsiang-ju-lai
B, 136

⊙⊙如來佛
520. Wu-yu-ju-lai fo
A, 1B41

⊙⊙德佛
521. Wu-yu-tê fo
A, 1A54; B, 102

⊙我佛母
522. Wu-wo fo-mu
A, 2A60; B, 53

⊙支金剛菩薩
523. Wu-chih-chin-kang p'u-sa
A, 6B56

⊙敵佛母
524. Wu-ti fo-mu
B, 261

⊙畏滅冥佛
525. Wu-wei-mieh-ming fo
B, 125

無盡智菩薩
526. Wu-chin-chih p'u-sa
A, 4B3

⊙着祖師
527. Wu-cho tsu-shih
B, 2

⊙能勝忿怒天母
528. Wu-nêng-shêng-fên-nu t'ien-mu
A, 5B57

⊙⊙⊙⊙⊙金剛
529. Wu-nêng-shêng-fên-nu-chin-kang
A, 5B56

⊙⊙⊙母
530. Wu-nêng-shêng-mu
A, 6B7. cf. 933

⊙邊聲音菩薩
531. Wu-pien-shêng-yin p'u-sa
A, 5A40

⊙量光佛
532. Wu-liang-kuang fo
A, 2A42; A, 4B41

⊙⊙⊙菩薩
533. Wu-liang-kuang p'u-sa
A, 4B59

⊙⊙壽佛
534. Wu-liang-shou fo
A, 6M5; A, 6B38; B, 64. cf. 157

⊙⊙掬光佛
535. Wu-liang-chü-kuang fo
A, 1A56; B, 100

燄明佛
536. Yen-ming fo
A, 1B19

燃燈佛
537. Jan-têng fo
A, 1B29

牙瓦的
538. Ya-wa-ti
A, 2B33

牛(r. 吽)威聲金剛
539. Niu-(r. hung)wei-shêng-chin-kang
A, 2A34. cf. 108.

⊙首勇保護法
540. Niu-shou Yung-pao hu-fa
B, 298

牟尼佛
541. Mou-ni fo
A, 1A27. cf. 347, 763

獅吼佛
542. Shih-hou fo
A, 1B45; B, 140

⊙⊙文殊
543. Shih-hou Wên-shu
B, 149

⊙⊙觀世音
544. Shih-hou Kuan-shih-yin
B, 161

⊙⊙⊙⊙⊙菩薩
545. Shih-hou Kuan-shih-yin p'u-sa
A, 6A34

⊙子佛
546. Shih-tzŭ fo
A, 1A29. cf. 253, 764

⊙⊙幢母
547. Shih-tzŭ-ch'uang-mu
A, 5B6

獅面佛母
548. Shih-mien fo-mu
B, 357

班塔嘎尊者
549. Pan-t'a-ka tsun-chê
A, 1B2. cf. 97

⊙臣羅卜藏垂極嘉勒參
550. Pan-ch'ên lo-pu-tsang ch'ui-chi chia-lo-ts'an
B, 25

⊙⊙⊙⊙⊙葉施
551. Pan-ch'ên lo-pu-tsang yeh-shih
B, 27

現前佛母
552. Hsien-ch'ien fo-mu
A, 4A19

⊙⊙菩薩
553. Hsien-ch'ien p'u-sa
A, 5A58

⊙無愚佛
554. Hsien wu-yü fo
A, 1A45; B, 90

⊙⊙⊙菩薩
555. Hsien wu-yü p'u-sa
A, 4B47

瑜伽虛空佛
556. Yü-ch'ieh-hsü-k'ung fo
A, 3M1; A, 3B32

⊙迦⊙⊙⊙
557. Yü-chia-hsü-k'ung fo
B, 58

壁組積光⊙母
558. Pi-tsu Chi-kuang fo-mu
A, 6B1; B, 245

甘吒巴
559. Kan-ch'a-pa
A, 3A36

⊙扎⊙祖師
560. Kan-cha-pa tsu-shih
B,13

⊙露滴金剛
561. Kan-lu-ti-chin-kang
A, 2A47

⊙⊙潭⊙⊙
562. Kan-lu-t'an-chin-kang
A, 2B56; B, 346

⊙⊙金剛
563. Kan-lu-chin-kang
B, 49

田親祖師
564. T'ien-ch'in tsu-shih
B, 4

畢穆格哩底天
565. Pi-mu-ko-li-ti t'ien
A, 3B20

癡威羅瓦金剛
566. Ch'ih Wei-lo-wa-chin-kang
A, 2A29; A, 2B37

發光佛母
567. Fa-kuang fo-mu
A, 4A26

⊙心行地佛母
568. Fa-hsin-hsing-ti fo-mu
A, 4A29

⊙頂菩薩
fa-ting p'u-sa
cf. 84, 198

白上樂王
569. Pai Shang-lo-wang
A, 3A34

白上樂王佛
570. Pai Shang-lo-wang fo
A, 3M4; B, 37

⊙不動金剛
571. Pai Pu-tung-chin kang
A, 6A30; B, 340

⊙伯答哩佛母
572. Pai Po-ta-li fo-mu
A, 3A43

⊙傘蓋佛母
573. Pai-san-kai fo-mu
A, 6M7; A, 6A47. cf. 202

⊙⊙⊙菩薩
574. Pai-san-kai p'u-sa
A, 5A39

⊙⊙頂佛
575. Pai-san-ting fo
A, 4A60

⊙手持金剛
576. Pai Shou-ch'ih-chin-kang
A, 4A35

⊙救度佛母
577. Pai Chui-tu fo-mu
A, 6M2; A, 6B37

⊙文殊菩薩
578. Pai Wên-shu p'u-sa
A, 6B42

⊙明慧金剛亥母
579. Pai ming-hui Chin-kang-hai-mu
B, 270

⊙毫佛母
580. Pai-hao fo-mu
A, 5A55

白衣佛母
581. Pai-i fo-mu
A, 2A59; A, 3B46; A, 5M 8; A, 5A48

⊙諸品佛母
582. Pai Chu-p'in fo-mu
A, 6A54

⊙馬頭金剛佛
583. Pai Ma-t'ou-chin-kang fo
A, 5M3

⊙龍母
584. Pai Lung-mu
A, 5B47

⊙⊙王
585. Pai Lung-wang
A, 5B46

目建連
586. Mu-chien-lien
A, 1B23

眞實名尊四臂文殊
587. Chên-shih-ming-tsun ssŭ-pei Wên-shu
B, 155

⊙⊙⊙文殊菩薩
588. Chên-shih-ming Wên-shu p'u-sa
A, 6B47

⊙達羅藥叉大將
589. Chên-ta-lo yao-ch'a-ta-chiang
A, 6B19

眼光菩薩
590. Yen-kuang pu'-sa
A, 5A56

睺星天
591. Hou-hsing t'ien
A, 5A2

祖師
tsu-shih
cf. 104, 117, 131, 133, 257, 300, 323, 325, 348, 431, 499, 527, 560, 564, 633, 669, 693, 755, 762, 861, 869, 896, 930, 943

⊙吒班塔嘎尊者
592. Tsu-ch'a-pan-t'a-ka tsun-chê
A, 1B61. cf. 491

祝壽勇保護法
593. Chu-shou Yung-pao hu-fa
B, 316

福自在母
594. Fu-tzŭ-tsai-mu
A, 5B21

禪定波羅蜜母
595. Ch'an-ting Po-lo-mi-mu
A, 4A3

⊙⊙顯聖王佛
596. Ch'an-ting-hsien-shêng-wang fo
A, 1B56. cf. 907

秘密文殊
597. Pi-mi Wên-shu
B, 148

⊙⊙自在觀世音
598. Pi-mi tzŭ-tsai Kuan-shih-yin
A, 2A48. cf. 701

⊙⊙馬頭金剛
599. Pi-mi Ma-t'ou-chin-kang
B, 61

⊙蜜成就文殊
600. Pi-mi-ch'êng-chiu Wên-shu
A, 2A30

秘蜜成就文殊菩薩
601. Pi-mi-ch'êng-chiu Wên-shu p'u-sa
A, 2M6

⊙⊙文殊室利佛
602. Pi-mi Wên-shu-shih-li fo
A, 2M3; A, 4A32

⊙⊙⊙⊙金剛
603. Pi-mi Wên-shu-chin-kang
A, 2A32. cf. 695, 805

⊙⊙金剛不動佛
604. Pi-mi Chin-kang-pu-tung fo
A, 2A35. cf. 12, 694

積光佛母
605. Chi-kuang fo-mu
A, 6M1; A, 6A43.
cf. 22, 63, 92, 95, 558, 801, 934

⊙⊙吉祥王佛
606. Chi-kuang-chi-hsiang-wang fo
B, 142

⊙智菩薩
607. Chi-chih p'u-sa
A, 4B4. cf. 447

空行佛母
608. K'ung-hsing fo-mu
B, 55. cf. 444

站像彌勒佛
609. Chan-hsiang Mi-lo fo
A, 6A48

童子
t'ung-tzŭ
cf. 225, 517, 627

童子文殊
610. T'ung-tzŭ Wên-shu
B, 146

簪芝噶天母護法
611. Tsan-chih-ka t'ien-mu hu-fa
B, 330

⊙達里佛母
612. Tsan-ta-li fo-mu
A, 3A60; A, 3B59

精明文殊
613. Ching-ming Wên-shu
B, 31. cf. 60

⊙進喜佛
614. Ching-chin-hsi fo
A, 1A48; B, 87

⊙⊙波羅蜜母
615. Ching-chin Po-lo-mi-mu
A, 4A4

⊙⊙軍佛
616. Ching-chin-chün fo
A, 1A30; B, 86

紅四臂觀世音菩薩
617. Hung ssŭ-pei Kuan-shih-yin p'u-sa
A, 6B51

⊙妙音佛母
618. Hung Miao-yin fo-mu
A, 6A51

⊙威羅瓦金剛
619. Hung Wei-lo-wa-chin-kang
B, 45

⊙⊙⊙⊙⊙⊙佛
620. Hung Wei-lo-wa-chin-kang fo
A, 2M8

紅戟財寶護法
621. Hung-chi Ts'ai-pao hu-fa
B, 321

⊙焰帝幢王佛
622. Hung-yen Ti-ch'uang-wang fo
B, 110

⊙餤⊙⊙⊙⊙
623. Hung-yen Ti-ch'uang-wang fo
A, 1A23

⊙目星
624. Hung-mu-hsing
A, 2B20

⊙部落王金剛
625. Hung Pu-lo-wang-chin-kang
B, 360. cf. 634

紫竹林救度佛母
626. Tzŭ-chu-lin Chiu-tu fo-mu
A, 6B32

網光童子
627. Wang-kuang-t'ung-tzŭ
A, 5B14

綱⊙菩薩
628. Kang-kuang p'u-sa
A, 4B1

綠救度佛母
629. Lü Chiu-tu fo-mu
A, 6M8

羅叉
630. Lo-ch'a
A, 5B37

⊙沽羅尊者
631. Lo-ku-lo tsun-chê
B, 281. cf. 112, 636

美名佛母
632. Mei-ming fo-mu
A, 5A30

聖天祖師
633. Shêng-t'ien tsu-shih
B, 3

聚主天
634. Chü-chu t'ien
A, 5A4. cf. 625

聯續大鵬手持金剛
635. Lien-hsü-ta-p'êng Shou-ch'ih-chin-kang
A, 2B2

囉睺囉
636. Lo-hou-lo
A, 1B13. cf. 112, 631

能動三界救度佛母
637. Nêng-tung-san-chieh Chiu-tu fo-mu
B, 223

⊙勝⊙⊙⊙⊙⊙⊙
638. Nêng-shêng-san-chieh Chiu-tu fo-mu
B, 212

⊙⊙⊙⊙佛
639. Nêng-shêng-san-chieh fo
A, 4B30

⊙⊙⊙⊙菩薩
640. Nêng-shêng-san-chieh p'u-sa
A, 5A60

⊙⊙⊙⊙金剛
641. Nêng-shêng-san-chieh-chin-kang
A, 4M7; B, 343

能勝磨障金剛
642. Nêng-shêng-mo-chang-chin-kang
A, 2B53

⊙壞惡眼⊙⊙
643. Nêng-huai-wu-yen-chin-kang
A, 5A18

⊙拘天母
644. Nêng-chü t'ien-mu
A, 5B61

⊙摧怨魔救度佛母
645. Nêng-ts'ui-yüan-mo Chiu-tu fo-mu
B, 214

⊙⊙惡敵⊙⊙⊙⊙
646. Nêng-ts'ui-wu-ti Chiu-tu fo-mu
B, 213

⊙滅諸苦⊙⊙⊙⊙
647. Nêng-mieh-chu-k'u Chiu-tu fo-mu
B, 224

⊙烘⊙敵天母護法
648. Nêng-hung-chu-ti t'ien-mu hu-fa
B, 310

⊙⊙⊙障金剛
649. Nêng-hung-chu-chang-chin-kang
B, 358

⊙生吉祥救度佛母
650. Nêng-shêng-chi-hsiang Chiu-tu fo-mu
B, 217

自在天
651. Tzŭ-tsai t'ien
A, 5A23. cf. 204, 466

自在壽母
652. Tzŭ-tsai-shou-mu
A, 4B18

⊙⊙幻化母
653. Tzŭ-tsai-huan-hua-mu
A, 4B7

⊙⊙意母
654. Tzŭ-tsai-i-mu
A, 4B19

⊙⊙智⊙
655. Tzŭ-tsai-chih-mu
A, 4B22

⊙⊙法⊙
656. Tzŭ-tsai-fa-mu
A, 4B23

⊙⊙生⊙
657. Tzŭ-tsai-shêng-mu
A, 4B6

⊙⊙發心母
658. Tzŭ-tsai-fa-hsin-mu
A, 4B8

⊙⊙行母
659. Tzŭ-tsai-hsing-mu
A, 4B20; A, 4B21

⊙⊙觀世音菩薩
660. Tzŭ-tsai Kuan-shih-yin p'u-sa
A, 6A46

⊙⊙願母
661. Tzŭ-tsai-yüan-mu
A, 4B9

舍利佛
662. Shê-li-fo
A, 1B22

般若⊙母
663. Pan-jo fo-mu
A, 6A61. cf. 23, 154

般若除滅金剛
664. Pan-jo-ch'u-mieh-chin-kang
A, 2A52

花光鬘天菩薩
665. Hua-kuang-man-t'ien p'u-sa
A, 5A22

⊙大鵬
666. Hua Ta-p'êng
A, 3B42

茶桑
667. Ch'a-sang
A, 2B19

莊嚴母
668. Chuang-yen-mu
A, 5B24

⊙秘巴祖師
669. Chuang-pi-pa tsu-shih
B, 16

華氐(r. 氏)佛
670. Hua-ti (r. shih) fo
A, 1A21

葉衣佛母
Yeh-i fo-mu
cf. 24, 69

蓮花光遊戲神通佛
671. Lien-hua-kuang-yu-hsi-shên-t'ung fo
A, 1A38; B, 106

⊙⊙吒噶佛母
672. Lien-hua-ch'a-ka fo-mu
A, 3A13

⊙⊙妙舞自在觀世音菩薩
673. Lien-hua-miao-wu-tzŭ-tsai Kuan-shih-yin p'u-sa
A, 6A9. cf. 25, 93

蓮花妙舞自在馬頭金剛
674. Lien-hua-miao-wu-tzŭ-tsai Ma-t'ou-chin-kang
B, 62

⊙⊙行波羅蜜母
675. Lien-hua-hsing Po-lo-mi-mu
A, 4B36

⊙華頂佛
676. Lien-hua-ting fo
A, 4A44

薄呼羅藥叉大將
677. Po-hu-lo yao-ch'a-ta-chiang
A, 6B18

藍手持金剛
678. Lan Shou-ch'ih-chin-kang
A, 5A46

⊙救度佛母
679. Lan Chiu-tu fo-mu
A, 5A33. cf. 895

⊙棒金剛
680. Lan-pang-chin-kang
A, 2A12

藥叉大將
yao-ch'a-ta-chiang
cf. 161, 247, 248, 260, 459, 460, 476, 589, 677, 728, 737, 905

⊙⊙天
681. Yao-ch'a t'ien
A, 3B22

⊙師如來佛
682. Yao-shih-ju-lai fo
A, 1B37

⊙⊙琉璃光王如來
683. Yao-shih-liu-li-kuang-wang-ju-lai
B, 139

蘭穆達哷達那嘛西母
684. Lan-mu-ta-lieh-ta-na-ma hsi-mu
A, 6B10

虛空吽音救度佛母
685. Hsü-k'ung-hung-yin Chiu-tu fo-mu
B, 211

⊙⊙王菩薩
686. Hsü-k'ung-wang p'u-sa
B, 174

⊙⊙目⊙⊙
687. Hsü-k'ung-mu p'u-sa
A, 5A35

⊙⊙藏⊙⊙
688. Hsü-k'ung-tsang p'u-sa
A, 1M8; A, 1A1; A, 2A38; A, 4B17; B, 196

蜣(?蜂)音文殊菩薩
689. Chiang (? Fêng)-yin Wên-shu p'u-sa
A, 6B46

蜜 cf. 密
mi mi

⊙克巴
690. Mi-k'o-pa
A, 2B18

⊙咒隨持佛母
691. Mi-chou-sui-ch'ih fo-mu
A, 6A58. cf. 261

⊙德文殊室利佛
692. Mi-tê Wên-shu-shih-li fo
A, 4M8

⊙拉祖
693. Mi-la tsu
A, 1A35

蜜跡不動金剛佛
694. Mi-chi Pu-tung-chin-kang fo
A, 2M5. cf. 12, 604

⊙⊙文殊⊙⊙⊙
695. Mi-chi Wên-shu-chin-kang fo
A, 2M4. cf. 603, 805

補嘎西佛母
696. Pu-ka-hsi fo-mu
A, 3A41; A, 3B16

⊙達吒噶佛
697. Pu-ta-ch'a-ka fo
A, 3A58

西母
hsi-mu
cf. 134, 135, 299, 684, 863

⊙達天
698. Hsi-ta t'ien
A, 3B10

觀世音
Kuan-shih-yin
cf. 25, 39, 89, 90, 93, 153, 155, 181, 187, 222, 341, 467, 482, 544, 598, 765, 768, 790, 862, 898, 918, 919

⊙⊙⊙佛
Kuan-shih-yin fo
cf. 40

⊙⊙⊙菩薩
699. Kuan-shih-yin p'u-sa
A, 1M3; A, 1A11; A, 6A 20. cf. 14, 91, 94, 156, 182, 468, 483, 545, 617, 660, 673, 899, 916, 917, 935

⊙義佛
700. Kuan-i fo
A, 1B6

觀自在秘密佛
701. Kuan-tzŭ-tsai pi-mi fo
B, 33. cf. 598

⊙⊙⊙菩薩
702. Kuan-tzŭ-tsai p'u-sa
A, 5A34

解實辦才母
703. Chieh-shih-pan-ts'ai-mu
A, 4B13

⊙法實母
704. Chieh-fa-shih-mu
A, 4B10

⊙眞⊙句母
705. Chieh-chên-shih-chü-mu
A, 4B11

⊙積佛
706. Chieh-chi fo
A, 1A16

⊙義實母
707. Chieh-i-shih-mu
A, 4B12

⊙脫鬬戰佛母
708. Chieh-t'o-tou-chan fo-mu
A, 6A37

計都星天
709. Chi-tu-hsing t'ien
A, 3B9

調伏毒惡金剛
710. T'iao-fu-tu-wu-chin-kang
A, 5A6

⊙⊙生手持金剛
711. T'iao-fu-shêng Shou-ch'ih-chin-kang
A, 5A5

⊙⊙難調菩薩
712. T'iao-fu-nan-t'iao p'u-sa
A, 5A59

諸品吒噶佛
713. Chu-p'in-ch'a-ka fo
A, 3B52

⊙⊙天母
714. Chu-p'in t'ien-mu
A, 5B59. cf. 582

⊙⊙頂佛
715. Chu-p'in-ting fo
A, 4A43

⊙相佛母
716. Chu-hsiang fo-mu
B, 238

護國護法
717. Hu-kuo hu-fa
* B, 315

⊙魔金剛
718. Hu-mo-chin-kang
A, 5A8

貝(?蓮)花母
719. Pei-lien-hua-mu
A, 5B8

財功德佛
720. Ts'ai-kung-tê fo
A, 1A37; B, 107

⊙寶天王
721. Ts'ai-pao t'ien-wang
B, 320

⊙⊙護法
Ts'ai-pao hu-fa
cf. 200, 211, 215, 230, 621

⊙帛天母
722. Ts'ai-po t'ien-mu
A, 5B60

貪威羅瓦金剛
723. T'an Wei-lo-wa-chin-kang
A, 2A27; A, 2B39

賓度羅跋羅墮尊者
724. Pin-tu-lo-po-lo-to tsun-chê
B, 283

⊙達拉拔喇多匝尊者
725. Pin-ta-la-pa-la-to-tsa tsun-chê
A, 1B1

賢德佛
726. Hsien-tê fo
A, 1A58; B, 98

⊙滿護法
Hsien-man hu-fa
cf. 171

超頂佛
727. Ch'ao-ting fo
A, 4A55

跋拆羅藥叉大將
728. Po-ch'ai-lo yao-ch'a-ta-chiang
A, 6A3

⊙陀⊙尊者
729. Po-t'o-lo tsun-chê
B, 277. cf. 350

轉輪頂
730. Chuan-lun-ting
A, 2B61

迦咀延
731. Chia-chü-yen
A, 1B24

⊙舍
732. Chia-shê
A, 1B25

⊙葉佛
733. Chia-yeh fo
B, 132. cf. 207

* For 護法 see p. 169.

迦裏迦尊者
734. Chia-li-chia tsun-chê
B, 275. cf. 141

⊙諾⊙伐蹉尊者
735. Chia-no-chia-fa-ts'o tsun-chê
B, 278. cf. 143

⊙⊙⊙跋黎墮闍尊者
736. Chia-no-chia-po-li-to-shê tsun-chê
B, 279. cf. 142

迷企羅藥叉大將
737. Mi-ch'i-lo yao-ch'a-ta-chiang
A, 6A2

造哩佛母
738. Tsao-li fo-mu
A, 3A44

速勇救度佛母
739. Su-yung Chiu-tu fo-mu
A, 6B31. cf. 290

⊙急意天菩薩
740. Su-chi-i-t'ien p'u-sa
A, 5A52

達努天
741. Ta-nu t'ien
A, 3A3

⊙哷嘛達都佛母
742. Ta-lieh-ma-ta-tu fo-mu
A, 3A11

⊙⊙月⊙沙天
743. Ta-lieh-yüeh-ta-sha t'ien
A, 3B35

⊙摩多羅
744. Ta-mo-to-lo
B, 288

⊙賴喇嘛
745. Ta-lai-la-ma
A, 1B26. cf. 29, 904

達賴喇嘛噶勒藏佳穆磋
746. Ta-lai-la-ma ka-lo-tsang chia-mu-ts'o
B, 28

遍入天
747. Pien-ju t'ien
A, 3B6; A, 5A16

遊宿王佛
748. Yu-su-wang fo
A, 1A7. cf. 263

⊙戲佛母
749. Yu-hsi fo-mu
A, 2B6; A, 4B55

⊙⊙王文殊菩薩
750. Yu-hsi-wang Wên-shu p'u-sa
A, 6B45

⊙⊙神通佛
yu-hsi-shên-t'ung fo
cf. 496, 504, 671

⊙⊙自在文殊
751. Yu-hsi-tzŭ-tsai Wên-shu
B, 153

⊙步佛
yu-pu fo
cf. 127, 278

遠行⊙母
752. Yüan-hsing fo-mu
A, 4A18

那噶塞那尊者
753. Na-ka-sai-na tsun-chê
A, 1B3. cf. 759

⊙羅吒機尼佛母
754. Na-lo-ch'a-chi-ni fo-mu
A, 3A49

⊙⊙巴祖師
755. Na-lo-pa tsu-shih
B, 18

那羅延佛
756. Na-lo-yen fo
A, 1A53; B, 103

⊙⊙⊙天
757. Na-lo-yen t'ien
A, 5B50

⊙⊙⊙⊙母
758. Na-lo-yen t'ien-mu
A, 5B30

⊙迦犀尊者
759. Na-chia-hsi tsun-chê
B, 285. cf. 753

部落王金剛
Pu-lo-wang-chin-kang
cf. 625, 634

都拉天
760. Tu-la t'ien
A, 3B21

醫藥大權伏魔護法
761. I-yao-ta-ch'üan fu-mo hu-fa
B, 353

釋迦光祖師
762. Shih-chia-kuang tsu-shih
B, 8

⊙⊙牟尼佛
763. Shih-chia-mou-ni fo
A, 1M5; A, 1A34; A, 5A 57; B, 82

⊙⊙獅子⊙
764. Shih-chia-shih-tzŭ fo
A, 4A47. cf. 253

重疊廣幻觀世音
765. Chung-tieh-kuang-huan Kuan-shih-yin
B, 170

金剛不動佛
766. Chin-kang-pu-tung fo
B, 141. cf. 604

⊙⊙⊙壞⊙
767. Chin-kang-pu-huai fo
A, 1A33; B, 83

⊙⊙⊙⊙觀世音
768. Chin-kang-pu-huai Kuan-shih-yin
B, 177

⊙⊙亥母
769. Chin-kang-hai-mu
B, 54. cf. 2, 579

⊙⊙佛⊙
chin-kang fo-mu
cf. 80, 188, 226, 449

⊙⊙佑菩薩
770. Chin-kang-yu p'u-sa
A, 4B52

⊙⊙保護菩薩
771. Chin-kang-pao-hu p'u-sa
B, 180

⊙⊙勇識上樂王佛
772. Chin-kang-yung-shih Shang-lo-wang fo
B, 38

⊙⊙⊙⊙佛
773. Chin-kang-yung-shih fo
A, 4B27; B, 69

⊙⊙⊙⊙⊙母
774. Chin-kang-yung-shih fo-mu
A, 4A24. cf. 80

⊙⊙⊙⊙菩薩
775. Chin-kang-yung-shih p'u-sa
A, 4A50; B, 193

金剛吒噶母
776. Chin-kang-ch'a-ka-mu
A, 3A47

⊙⊙味佛⊙
777. Chin-kang-wei fo-mu
A, 2A54

⊙⊙喜慕菩薩
778. Chin-kang-hsi-mu p'u-sa
B, 191

⊙⊙⊙笑⊙⊙
779. Chin-kang-hsi-hsiao p'u-sa
B, 186

⊙⊙善賢⊙⊙
780. Chin-kang-shan-hsien p'u-sa
B, 190

⊙⊙因緣⊙⊙
781. Chin-kang-yin-yüan p'u-sa
B, 183

⊙⊙⊙菩薩
782. Chin-kang-yin p'u-sa
A, 4B44

⊙⊙地佛母
783. Chin-kang-ti fo-mu
A, 3B4

⊙⊙⊙母
784. Chin-kang-ti-mu
A, 2A21

⊙⊙夜叉菩薩
785. Chin-kang-yeh-ch'a p'u-sa
B, 179

⊙⊙大寶母
786. Chin-kang-ta-pao-mu
A, 6B9. cf. 188

⊙⊙⊙⊙菩薩
787. Chin-kang-ta-pao p'u-sa
B, 189

金剛大帝菩薩
788. Chin-kang-ta-ti p'u-sa
B, 192

⊙⊙妙法⊙⊙
789. Chin-kang-miao-fa p'u-sa
B, 185

⊙⊙⊙⊙觀世音
790. Chin-kang-miao-fa Kuan-shih-yin
B, 163

⊙⊙⊙音佛母
Chin-kang-miao-yin fo-mu
cf. 26, 70

⊙⊙威光菩薩
791. Chin-kang-wei-kuang p'u-sa
A, 4A9. cf. 238

⊙⊙宮室救度佛母
792. Chin-kang-kung-shih Chiu-tu fo-mu
B, 228

⊙⊙寶佛母
793. Chin-kang-pao fo-mu
A, 4A23

⊙⊙⊙菩薩
794. Chin-kang-pao p'u-sa
A, 4A10

⊙⊙尖佛母
795. Chin-kang-chien fo-mu
A, 5A44

⊙⊙幢菩薩
796. Chin-kang-ch'uang pu'-sa
A, 4B39

⊙⊙⊙蓋菩薩
797. Chin-kang-ch'uang-kai p'u-sa
B, 187

金剛德威菩薩
798. Chin-kang-tê-wei p'u-sa
B, 188

⊙⊙忿怒佛母
799. Chin-kang-fên-nu fo-mu
A, 3B60. cf. 332

⊙⊙性佛
800. Chin-kang-hsing fo
B, 65. cf. 823

⊙⊙⊙王積光佛母
801. Chin-kang-hsing-wang Chi-kuang fo-mu
B, 246

⊙⊙拳印菩薩
802. Chin-kang-ch'üan-yin p'u-sa
B, 178

⊙⊙⊙菩薩
803. Chin-kang-ch'üan p'u-sa
A, 4B54

⊙⊙敏捷菩薩
804. Chin-kang-min-chieh p'u-sa
A, 4B43; B, 184

⊙⊙救度佛母
Chin-kang-chiu-tu fo-mu
cf. 64, 792

⊙⊙文殊秘密佛
805. Chin-kang-wên-shu pi-mi fo
B, 30. cf. 603, 695

⊙⊙日
806. Chin-kang-jih
A, 2B14

⊙⊙時
807. Chin-kang-shih
A, 2B58

金剛智行菩薩
808. Chin-kang-chih-hsing p'u-sa
B, 181

⊙⊙柔善佛母
809. Chin-kang-jou-shan fo-mu
A, 3B2

⊙⊙業佛母
810. Chin-kang-yeh fo-mu
A, 4A52

⊙⊙⊙菩薩
811. Chin-kang-yeh p'u-sa
A, 4B51

⊙⊙欲佛母
812. Chin-kang-yü fo-mu
A, 3B1

⊙⊙⊙菩薩
813. Chin-kang-yü p'u-sa
A, 4A13

⊙⊙水母
814. Chin-kang-shui-mu
A, 2A19

⊙⊙法佛
815. Chin-kang-fa fo
A, 4A33

⊙⊙⊙⊙母
816. Chin-kang-fa fo-mu
A, 4A22. cf. 226

⊙⊙⊙菩薩
817. Chin-kang-fa p'u-sa
A, 4B42

⊙⊙潭
818. Chin-kang-t'an
A, 2B16

⊙⊙火母
819. Chin-kang-huo-mu
A, 2A20

金剛王菩薩
820. Chin-kang-wang p'u-sa
A, 4A49

⊙⊙甘達哩佛母
821. Chin-kang-kan-ta-li fo-mu
A, 6A24

⊙⊙⊙陀羅⊙⊙
822. Chin-kang-kan-t'o-lo fo-mu
B, 262

⊙⊙界性佛
823. Chin-kang-chieh-hsing fo
A, 4M4. cf. 800

⊙⊙⊙毘盧佛
824. Chin-kang-chieh P'i-lu fo
A, 4A25

⊙⊙畢達拉
825. Chin-kang-pi-ta-la
A, 2B1

⊙⊙笑菩薩
826. Chin-kang-hsiao p'u-sa
A, 4B40

⊙⊙繩母
827. Chin-kang-shêng-mu
A, 2B11

⊙⊙聲佛母
828. Chin-kang-shêng fo-mu
A, 2A56; A, 3B5

⊙⊙色⊙⊙
829. Chin-kang-sê fo-mu
A, 2A57

⊙⊙⊙相佛母
830. Chin-kang-sê-hsiang fo-mu
A, 3B61

⊙⊙菩薩
831. Chin-kang p'u-sa
A, 1M6

金剛藏菩薩
832. Chin-kang-tsang p'u-sa
A, 4B2

⊙⊙藥叉
833. Chin-kang-yao-ch'a
A, 2B17

⊙⊙⊙⊙菩薩
834. Chin-kang-yao-ch'a p'u-sa
A, 4B53

⊙⊙行波羅蜜母
835. Chin-kang-hsing Po-lo-mi-mu
A, 4B35

⊙⊙說法菩薩
836. Chin-kang-shuo-fa p'u-sa
B, 182

⊙⊙語菩薩
837. Chin-kang-yü p'u-sa
A, 4B49

⊙⊙賢⊙⊙
838. Chin-kang-hsien p'u-sa
A, 4A12

⊙⊙輪⊙⊙
839. Chin-kang-lun p'u-sa
A, 5A29

⊙⊙鈎
840. Chin-kang-kou
A, 2B57

⊙⊙⊙母
841. Chin-kang-kou-mu
A, 2B10

⊙⊙鈴⊙
842. Chin-kang-ling-mu
A, 2B13

⊙⊙鎖佛母
843. Chin-kang-so fo-mu
A, 5A43

金剛鐲佛母
844. Chin-kang-cho fo-mu
A, 6A23

⊙⊙⊙母
845. Chin-kang-cho-mu
A, 2B12

⊙⊙頂
846. Chin-kang-ting
A, 2B15

⊙⊙⊙佛
847. Chin-kang-ting fo
A, 4A46

⊙⊙⊙轉輪王
848. Chin-kang-ting-chuan-lun-wang
A, 2A10

⊙⊙風母
849. Chin-kang-fêng-mu
A, 2A18

⊙⊙香佛母
850. Chin-kang-hsiang fo-mu
A, 2A55

⊙⊙齒菩薩
851. Chin-kang-ch'ih p'u-sa
A, 5A28

⊙色寶光如來佛
852. Chin-sê-pao-kuang-ju-lai fo
A, 1B40

⊙⊙⊙⊙妙行成就如來
853. Chin-sê-pao-kuang-miao-hsing-ch'êng-chiu-ju-lai
B, 135

⊙鐲金剛
854. Chin-cho-chin-kang
B, 347

鈴墜天
855. Ling-chui t'ien
A, 3B19

鍋巴嘎尊者
856. Kuo-pa-ka tsun-chê
A, 1B4. cf. 342

鐵劍馬頭金剛
857. T'ieh-chien Ma-t'ou-chin-kang
B, 76

⊙管手持⊙⊙
858. T'ieh-kuan Shou-ch'ih-chin-kang
A, 2A45

⊙鎖母
859. T'ieh-so-mu
A, 6B8

長祿佛母
860. Ch'ang-lu fo-mu
B, 268

開主補祖師
861. K'ai-chu-pu tsu-shih
B, 23

⊙花觀世音
862. K'ai-hua Kuan-shih-yin
B, 159

阿哷嘎嘛西母
863. A-lieh-ka-ma hsi-mu
A, 6B23

⊙彌陀佛
864. A-mi-t'o fo
A, 1B31; B, 80

⊙必達尊者
865. A-pi-ta tsun-chê
A, 1B5. cf. 868

阿氏(r. 氏)多尊者
866. A-shih-to tsun-chê
B, 273. cf. 871

⊙瓦牛頭嶽主
867. A-wa-niu-t'ou yo-chu
A, 2B36

⊙秘特尊者
868. A-pi-t'ê tsun-chê
B, 287. cf. 865

⊙第沙祖師
869. A-ti-sha tsu-shih
B, 19

⊙說示
870. A-shuo-shih
A, 1B10

⊙資達尊考
871. A-tzŭ-ta tsun-chê
A, 1B47. cf. 866

⊙難
872. A-nan
A, 1B12; B, 291

降伏獄鬼菩薩
873. Hsiang-fu-yü-kuei p'u-sa
A, 5B27

⊙臨嶽母
874. Chiang-lin yo-mu
A, 2A14

除惡趣救度佛母
875. Ch'u-wu-ch'ü Chiu-tu fo-mu
A, 6B58; B, 234

⊙毒佛母
876. Ch'u-tu fo-mu
A, 6A53; A, 6B41.
cf. 203

除滅鬼王金剛
877. Ch'u-mieh-kuei-wang-chin-kang
A, 2A22; A, 2B45

⊙煩惱佛
878. Ch'u-fan-nao fo
A, 1B57

⊙蓋障天母
879. Ch'u-kai-chang t'ien-mu
A, 5B1

⊙諸惡毒救度佛母
880. Ch'u-chu-wu-tu Chiu-tu fo-mu
B, 227

⊙⊙⊙難⊙⊙⊙⊙
881. Ch'u-chu-wu-nan Chiu-tu fo-mu
B, 206

⊙⊙障菩薩
882. Ch'u-chu-chang p'u-sa
A, 1M2; A, 1A9; A, 2A24; B, 199

⊙魔金剛
883. Ch'u-mo-chin-kang
A, 6B44; B, 345

隆寓天
884. Lung-yü t'ien
A, 3A16

⊙衆生母
885. Lung-chung-shêng-mu
A, 5B25

隨引菩提佛
886. Sui-yin-p'u-t'i fo
B, 124

隨引菩薩(r.提)佛
887. Sui-yin p'u-sa (r. t'i) fo
A, 1B55. cf. 886

⊙應佛
888. Sui-ying fo
A, 1B44; B, 117

⊙求⊙母
889. Sui-ch'iu fo-mu
A, 6M9; A, 6B39; B, 205
cf. 27

雄威勇保護法
890. Hsiung-wei Yung-pao hu-fa
B, 300

離實天
891. Li-shih t'ien
A, 3B33

難勝佛母
892. Nan-shêng fo-mu
A, 4A20

震旦救度佛母
893. Chên-tan Chiu-tu fo-mu
A, 6B48; B, 229

青不動金剛
894. Ch'ing Pu-tung-chin-kang
A, 4B29; B, 338

⊙救度佛母
895. Ch'ing Chiu-tu fo-mu
A, 5M2. cf. 679

⊙目祖師
896. Ch'ing-mu tsu-shih
B, 9

⊙衣手持金剛
897. Ch'ing-i Shou-ch'ih-chin-kang
B, 72

青項自在觀世音
898. Ch'ing-hsiang tzŭ-tsai Kuan-shih-yin
B, 169

⊙⊙⊙⊙⊙⊙⊙菩薩
899. Ch'ing-hsiang tzŭ-tsai Kuan-shih-yin p'u-sa
A, 6B52

頂佛
ting fo
cf. 16, 85, 208, 239, 282, 289, 306, 407, 510, 575, 676, 715, 727, 847

⊙菩薩
ting p'u-sa
cf. 46, 84, 198, 237, 445

⊙螺天母護法
900. Ting-lo t'ien-mu hu-fa
B, 309

須彌山王佛
901. Hsü-mi-shan-wang fo
A, 1A13. cf. 279

⊙⊙積菩薩
902. Hsü-mi-chi p'u-sa
A, 6A16

頗羅門勇保護法
903. P'o-lo-mên Yung-pao hu-fa
B, 307

頭輩達賴喇嘛
904. T'ou-pei Ta-lai-la-ma
B, 24

額你羅藥叉大將
905. Ê-ni-lo yao-ch'a-ta-chiang
A, 6A1

願波羅蜜母
906. Yüan Po-lo-mi-mu
A, 4A1

顯聖王佛
907. Hsien-shêng-wang fo
A, 1B49; B, 118. cf. 596

⊙行手持金剛
908. Hsien-hsing Shou-ch'ih-chin-kang
B, 74

顰眉佛母
909. P'in-mei fo-mu
A, 5A32; B, 256

⊙⊙威相救度佛母
910. P'in-mei wei-hsiang Chiu-tu fo-mu
B, 219

風天
911. Fêng-t'ien
A, 5B52. cf. 158

飲光天菩薩
912. Yin-kuang-t'ien p'u-sa
A, 5A49

香象菩薩
913. Hsiang-hsiang p'u-sa
A, 4B15

馬頂(?頭)金剛
914. Ma-ting (t'ou?)-chin-kang
A, 5B13

⊙頭金剛
915. Ma-t'ou-chin-kang
A, 2A51; A, 5A47; A, 6A 31. cf. 5, 159, 599, 674, 857, 914

⊙⊙⊙⊙佛
Ma-t'ou-chin-kang fo
cf. 583

騎吼(r. 犼)自在觀世音菩薩
916. Ch'i-hou tzŭ-tsai Kuan-shih-yin p'u-sa
A, 6B49

⊙⊙(r. ⊙)觀世音菩薩
917. Ch'i-hou Kuan-shih-yin p'u-sa
A, 6A10

⊙犼自在觀世音
918. Ch'i-hou tzŭ-tsai Kuan-shih-yin
B, 166

⊙⊙觀世音
919. Ch'i-hou Kuan-shih-yin
B, 162

⊙獅勇保護法
920. Ch'i-shih Yung-pao hu-fa
B, 299

⊙⊙文殊菩薩
921. Ch'i-shih Wên-shu p'u-sa
A, 6A32

⊙虎勇保護法
922. Ch'i-hu Yung-pao hu-fa
B, 301

⊙象普賢菩薩
923. Ch'i-hsiang P'u-hsien p'u-sa
B, 200

⊙龍白布祿金剛
924. Ch'i-lung pai Pu-lu-chin-kang
B, 355

高哩佛母
925. Kao-li fo-mu
A, 2B44; A, 3A45; A, 3B 39

高達嘛天菩薩
926. Kao-ta-ma-t'ien p'u-sa
A, 5A13

髮九股嶽主
927. Fa-chiu-ku yo-chu
A, 2B21

鬭戰勝佛
928. Tou-chan-shêng fo
A, 1A52; B, 112

鬼母天
929. Kuei-mu t'ien
A, 3A2

魯兮巴祖師
930. Lu-hsi-pa tsu-shih
B, 12

麻嘎哷天
931. Ma-ka-lieh t'ien
A, 3A17

黄布祿金剛
932. Huang Pu-lu-chin-kang
A, 6A49; A, 6B30; B, 339

⊙無能勝佛母
933. Huang Wu-nêng-shêng fo-mu
A, 6A25

⊙積光佛母
934. Huang Chi-kuang fo-mu
A, 6A40

黑五面十二臂觀世音菩薩
935. Hei wu-mien shih-êrh-pei Kuan-shih-yin p'u-sa
A, 6B53

黑大鵬
936. Hei Ta-p'êng
A, 3B43

⊙布祿金剛
937. Hei Pu-lu-chin-kang
A, 6A22; B, 344

⊙摧碎⊙⊙佛
938. Hei Ts'ui-sui-chin-kang fo
A, 5M4

⊙敵威羅瓦金剛
939. Hei-ti Wei-lo-wa-chin-kang
A, 2B31; B, 43

⊙⊙金剛佛
940. Hei-ti-chin-kang fo
A, 2M1

⊙法帝
941. Hei Fa-ti
A, 5B26

龍尊王佛
942. Lung-tsun-wang fo
A, 1A31; B, 85

⊙樹祖師
943. Lung-shu tsu-shih
B, 1

⊙母
Lung-mu
cf. 584

⊙王
Lung-wang
cf. 585

護法
hu-fa cf. 169, 171, 214, 291, 494, 717, 761 and Yung-pao hu-fa (p. 128), t'ien-mu hu-fa (p. 135), Ts'ai-pao hu-fa (p. 159)

CONTENTS

Volume II — Plates

Pao-hsiang Lou Pantheon 1–222

Chu Fo P'u-sa Shêng Hsiang Tsan 225–314

PLATES

Entrance to the Tz'ŭ Ning Kung garden in which the Pao Hsiang Lou is located

Pao Hsiang Lou

第一妙吉祥大寶樓上供奉如是
佛說大乘般若經品內一切調御
丈夫天人師釋迦牟尼佛及文殊
菩薩金剛菩薩觀世音菩薩地藏
王菩薩除諸障菩薩虛空藏菩薩
彌勒菩薩普賢菩薩八大佛子等
諸如過去七佛八大藥師如來三
十五佛賢劫千佛皆可供奉其經
則三大般若華嚴寶積等以及諸
經論菩提路等大乘註疏皆宜藏
度是為最上福田功德不可思議

1A

1 B

大清乾隆年敬造
釋迦牟尼佛

1 M 5 **763**

Śākyamuni (Buddha)

1 M 1 320

Maitreya (Bodhisattva)

1 M 2 882

Sarvanivaraṇaviṣkambhin (Bodhisattva)

1 M 3 699

Avalokiteśvara (Bodhisattva)

1 M 4 408

Mañjuśrī (Bodhisattva)

1 M 6 831

Vajra[pāṇi] (Bodhisattva)

1 M 7 166

Kṣitigarbharāja (Bodhisattva)

1 M 8 688

Ākāśagarbha (Bodhisattva)

1 M 9 442

Samantabhadra (Bodhisattva)

1 A 1 688

Ākāśagarbha (Bodhisattva)

1 A 2 335

Maitreya (Bodhisattva)

1 A 3 442

Samantabhadra (Bodhisattva)

1 A 4 166

Kṣitigarbha (Bodhisattva)

1 A 5 105

Yaśaḥketu or Yaśodhvaja (Buddha)

1 A 6 54

Oṣadhi (Buddha)

遊宿王佛

1 A 7 748

Nakṣatrarājavikrīḍita (Buddha)

大力佛

1 A 8 173

Mahābala (Buddha)

1 A 9 882

Sarvanivaraṇaviṣkambhin (Bodhisattva)

1 A 10 345

Vajrapāṇi (Bodhisattva)

觀世音菩薩

1 A 11 699

Avalokiteśvara (Bodhisattva)

文殊菩薩

1 A 12 408

Mañjuśrī (Bodhisattva)

須彌山王佛

1 A 13 901

Sumeruparvatarāja or Śailendrarāja (Buddha)

日藏佛

1 A 14 422

Sūryagarbha (Buddha)

明照佛

1 A 15 428

Vairocana (Buddha)

解積佛

1 A 16 706

Muktiskandha (Buddha)

1 A 17 172

Mahāprabha (Buddha)

1 A 18 195

Mahābāhu (Buddha)

導師佛

1 A 19 292

Sārthavāha (Buddha)

妙目佛

1 A 20 227

Sunetra (Buddha)

華氏佛

1 A 21 670

Kusuma (Buddha) the second

善遊步功德佛

1 A 22 128

Suvikrāntaśrī (Buddha)

紅燄帝幢王佛

1 A 23 623

Indraketudhvajarāja (Buddha)

善名稱功德佛

1 A 24 115

Suparikīrtitanāmaśrī (Buddha)

1 A 25 **324**

Smṛtiśrī (Buddha)

大清乾隆年敬造
妙華佛

1 A 26 **231**

Kusuma (Buddha)

牟尼佛

1 A 27 **541**

Muni (Buddha)

1 A 28 **430**

Pradyota (Buddha)

獅子佛

1 A 29 546

Siṁha (Buddha)

精進軍佛

1 A 30 616

Vīrasena (Buddha)

大清乾隆年敬造
龍尊王佛

1 A 31 942

Nāgeśvararāja (Buddha)

大清乾隆年敬造
寶光佛

1 A 32 268

Ratnārcis (Buddha)

金剛不壞佛

1 A 33 767

Vajrābhedya (Buddha)

釋迦牟尼佛

1 A 34 763

Śākyamuni (Buddha)

1 A 35 693

Milaraspa

1 A 36 256

bÇoṅ-kha-pa

1 A 37 720

Dhanaśrī (Buddha)

1 A 38 671

Padmajyotirvikrīḍitābhijña (Buddha)

1 A 39 504

Brahmajyotirvikrīḍitābhijña (Buddha)

1 A 40 76

Kusumaśrī (Buddha)

1 A 41 503

Brahman (Buddha)

勇施佛

1 A 42 78

Śūradatta (Buddha)

無垢佛

1 A 43 514

Vimala (Buddha)

寶月佛

1 A 44 272

Ratnacandra (Buddha)

1 A 45 554

Amoghadarśin (Buddha)

寶月光佛

1 A 46 273

Ratnacandraprabha (Buddha)

1 A 47 275

Ratnāgni (Buddha)

精進喜佛

1 A 48 614

Vīranandin (Buddha)

1 A 49 278

Ratnapadmavikrāmin
(Buddha)

1 A 50 109

Samantāvabhāsavyūhaśrī
(Buddha)

1 A 51 127

Suvikrāntagāmin (Buddha)

鬪戰勝佛

1 A 52 928

Yuddhajaya (Buddha)

那羅延佛

1 A 53 756

Nārāyaṇa (Buddha)

無憂德佛

1 A 54 521

Aśokaśrī (Buddha)

光德佛

1 A 55 56

Prabhāsaśrī (Buddha)

1 A 56 535

Anantaujas (Buddha)

栴檀功德佛

1 A 57 **461**

Candanaśrī (Buddha)

賢德佛

1 A 58 **726**

Bhadraśrī (Buddha)

水天中天佛

1 A 59 481

Varuṇadeva (Buddha)

水天佛

1 A 60 480

Varuṇa (Buddha)

1 A 61 505

Brahmadatta (Buddha)

1 B 1 725

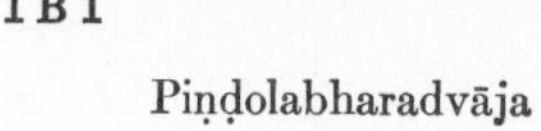

Piṇḍolabharadvāja

大清乾隆年敬造
班塔嘎尊者

1 B 2 549

Panthaka

大清乾隆年敬造
那嘎塞那尊者

1 B 3 753

Nāgasena

大清乾隆年敬造
鍋巴嘎尊者

1 B 4 856

Gopaka

阿必達尊者

1 B 5 865

Abheda

1 B 6 700

Arthadarśin (Buddha)

明燈佛

1 B 7 429

Pradīpa (Buddha)

勢成佛

1 B 8 86

Prabhūta (Buddha)

妙醫佛

1 B 9 233

Vaidya (Buddha)

阿說示

1 B 10 870

Aśvajit

嬰班巴的

1 B 11 140

Gavāmpati

阿難

1 B 12 872

Ānanda

1 B 13 636

Rāhula

1 B 14 141

Kālika

1 B 15 349

Vajrīputra

1 B 16 350

Bhadra

1 B 17 143

Kanakavatsa

宿王佛

1 B 18 263

Nakṣatrarāja (Buddha)

1 B 19 536

Jyotiṣprabha(?) (Buddha)

持珠佛

1 B 20 368

Maṇidhārin (Buddha)

1 B 21 322

Guṇaprabha (Buddha)

舍利佛

1 B 22 662

Śāriputra

目建連

1 B 23 586

Maudgalyāyana

1 B 24 731

Kātyāyana

1 B 25 732

Kāśyapa

1 B 26 745

Dalai Lama

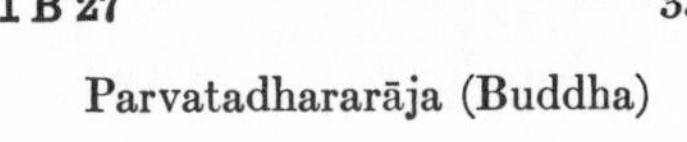
持山王佛

1 B 27 358

Parvatadhararāja (Buddha)

彌勒佛

1 B 28 319

Maitreya (Buddha)

1 B 29 537

Dīpaṅkara (Buddha)

寶生佛

1 B 30 276

Ratnasambhava (Buddha)

阿

1 B 31 864

Amitābha (Buddha)

1 B 32 339

Amoghasiddhi (Buddha)

1 B 33 457

Candraketu or Śaśiketu (Buddha)

1 B 34 57

Ābhāsaraśmi(?) (Buddha)

妙光佛

1 B 35 224

Suraśmi (Buddha)

無憂佛

1 B 36 518

Aśoka (Buddha)

1 B 37 682

Bhaiṣajyagurutathāgata (Buddha)

佛來如名善

1 B 38 114

Sunāmatathāgata (Buddha)

佛來如音光

1 B 39 59

Ābhāsvara(?)tathāgata (Buddha)

佛來如光寶色金

1 B 40 852

Suvarṇaratnaprabhātathāgata (Buddha)

1 B 41 520

Aśokatathāgata (Buddha)

法音如來佛

1 B 42 501

Dharmaghoṣatathāgata (Buddha)

勝慧王如來佛

1 B 43 82

Agra(?)matirājatathāgata (Buddha)

隨應佛

1 B 44 888

Anucārin(?) (Buddha)

獅吼佛

1 B 45 542

Simhanāda (Buddha)

昂機達尊者

1 B 46 424

Aṅgaja

阿資達尊者

1 B 47 871

Ajita

拔那巴斯尊者

1 B 48 351

Vanavāsin

顯聖王佛

1 B 49 907

Abhyudgatarāja (Buddha)

善滅諍傲佛

1 B 50 120

Shan-mieh-chêng-ao fo

寶身光輝佛

1 B 51 281

Ratnāṅgadyuti (Buddha)

善滅魔障佛

1 B 52 122

Shan-mieh-mo-chang fo

不迴吉祥輪佛

1 B 53 13

Avaivartikaśrīcakra (Buddha)

寶傘勝光佛

1 B 54 267

Ratnacchattrodgataprabha (Buddha)

隨引菩薩佛

1 B 55 887

Sui-yin-p'u-sa(read t'i) fo

禪定顯聖王佛

1 B 56 596

Dhyānābhyudgatarāja (Buddha)

除煩惱佛

1 B 57 878

Bhinnakleśa(?) (Buddha)

1 B 58 142

Kanakabharadvāja

1 B 59 298

Bakula

1 B 60 112

Rāhula

1 B 61 592

Cūḍapanthaka

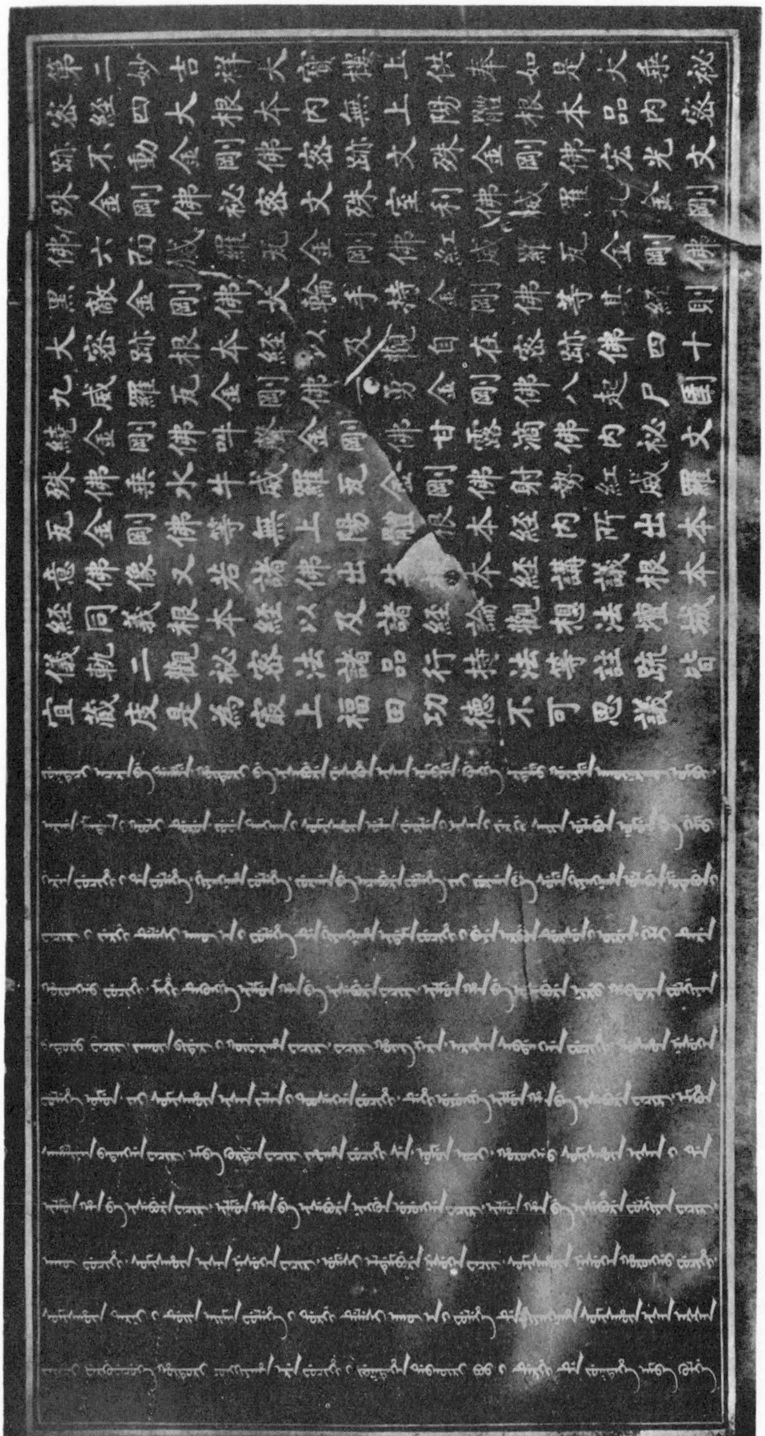

第二妙吉祥大寶樓上供奉如是大乘秘
密經四大根本內無上陽體根本品內密
跡不動金剛佛密跡文殊金剛佛宏光文
殊金剛佛秘密文殊室利佛威羅刹金剛
佛六面威羅刹金剛佛紅威羅刹金剛佛
黑敵金剛佛大輪手持金剛佛等其經則
大密跡根本經以及觀自在密跡佛四十
九威羅刹金剛佛一勇金剛佛八起尸圍
繞金剛佛吽聲金剛佛甘露滴佛內秘文
殊佛乘水牛威羅刹金剛佛射勢紅威羅
刹金剛佛等無上陽體根本經內所出本
意佛像又若諸佛出生本經講議根本
經同義根本經以及諸經論觀想法壇城
儀軌二觀秘密法諸品行持法等註疏皆
宜藏度是為寂上福田功德不可思議

2A

2 B

大清乾隆年敬造
秘密不動金剛佛

2 M 5 694

Guhya-Akṣobhyavajra (Buddha)

2 M 1 940

Kṛṣṇārivajra (Buddha)

2 M 2 72

Ṣaṇmukha-Bhairavavajra (Buddha)

2 M 3 602

Guhya-Mañjuśrī (Buddha)

2 M 4 695

Guhya-Mañjuvajra (Buddha)

2 M 6 601

Guhyasādhana-Mañjuśrī (Bodhisattva)

2 M 7 246

Bhairavavajra (Buddha)

2 M 8 620

Rakta-Bhairavavajra (Buddha)

2 M 9 206

Mahācakra-Vajrapāṇi (Buddha)

2 A 1 363

Daṇḍadharā (yo-mu)

2 A 2 367

Daṁṣṭrādharā (yo-mu)

2 A 3 47

Dūtī(?) or Ceṭī(?) (yo-mu)

2 A 4 435

Kāladhvajā(?) or Kālaketu(?) (yo-mu)

持劍威羅瓦金剛

2 A 5 353

Khaḍgadhara-Bhairavavajra

持蓮花威羅瓦金剛

2 A 6 378

Padmadhara-Bhairavavajra

持棒威羅瓦金剛

2 A 7 362

Daṇḍadhara-Bhairavavajra

持鐘威羅瓦金剛

2 A 8 384

Ghaṇṭādhara-Bhairavavajra

毒嚴金剛

2 A 9 473

Tu-yen-chin-kang

金剛頂轉輪王

2 A 10 848

Vajroṣṇīṣacakravartirāja

大力金剛

2 A 11 174

Mahābalavajra

藍棒金剛

2 A 12 680

Nīladaṇḍavajra

2 A 13 469

Kāmarājavajra

2 A 14 874

Chiang-lin (yo-mu)

2 A 15 386

Sphoṭadharā(?) (yo-mu)

2 A 16 374

Pāśadharā (yo-mu)

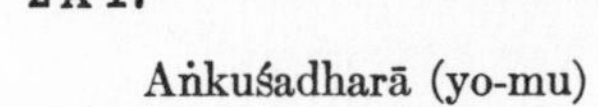

2 A 17 381

Aṅkuśadharā (yo-mu)

金剛風母

2 A 18 849

Vajrānilā

金剛水母

2 A 19 814

Vajrodakā

金剛火母

2 A 20 819

Vajrānalā

2 A 21 784

Vajrabhūmi

2 A 22 877

Yamāntakavajra

2 A 23 442

Samantabhadra (Bodhisattva)

2 A 24 882

Sarvanivaraṇaviṣkambhin (Bodhisattva)

2 A 25 408

Mañjuśrī (Bodhisattva)

2 A 26 249

Īrṣyā-Bhairavavajra

2 A 27 723

Rāga-Bhairavavajra

2 A 28 333

Mātsarya(?)-Bhairavavajra

大清乾隆年敬造

2 A 29 566

Moha-Bhairavavajra

2 A 30 600

Guhyasādhana-Mañjuśrī

大清乾隆年敬造
宏光文殊金剛

2 A 31 251

Vairocana-Mañjuvajra

2 A 32 603

Guhya-Mañjuvajra

大清乾隆年敬造

2 A 33 205

Mahācakra-Vajrapāṇi

大清乾隆年敬造

2 A 34 539

Hūṁkāravajra

大清乾隆年敬造
秘密金剛不動佛

2 A 35 604

Guhya-Vajrākṣobhya (Buddha)

大清乾隆年敬造
大持金剛

2 A 36 196

Mahāvajradhara

2 A 38 688

Ākāśagarbha (Bodhisattva)

2 A 39 345

Vajrapāṇi (Bodhisattva)

地藏王

2 A 40 166

Kṣitigarbharāja (Bodhisattva)

成就佛

2 A 41 339

Amoghasiddhi (Buddha)

2 A 42 532

Amitābha (Buddha)

2 A 43 276

Ratnasambhava (Buddha)

2 A 44 475

Vairocana (Buddha)

2 A 45 858

Lohanāḍī(?)-Vajrapāṇi

2 A 46 60

Antarasādhana-Mañjughoṣa

2 A 47 561

Amṛtabinduvajra

2 A 48 598

Guhya-īśvara(= Lokeśvara)-
Avalokiteśvara

2 A 49 11

Akṣobhyavajra

2 A 51 915 

Hayagrīvavajra

2 A 52 664

Prajñāntakavajra

2 A 53 320

Maitreya (Bodhisattva)

2 A 54 777

Vajrarasā (fo-mu)

2 A 55 850

Vajragandhā (fo-mu)

2 A 56 828

Vajraśabdā (fo-mu)

2 A 57 829

Vajrarūpā (fo-mu)

2 A 58 402

Tārā (fo-mu)

2 A 59 581

Pāṇḍaravāsinī (fo-mu)

無我佛母

2 A 60 522

Nairātmā (fo-mu)

佛眼佛母

2 A 61 41

Buddhalocanā (fo-mu)

2 B 1 825

Vajravetāla

2 B 2 635

Garuḍayuta-Vajrapāṇi

2 B 3 331

Krodha-Vajrapāṇi

2 B 4 340

Amoghatrāṇa(?)-Vajrapāṇi

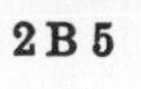

2 B 5 293

Hsiao-Vajrapāṇi

2 B 6 749

Lāsyā (fo-mu)

2 B 7 397

Mālyā

2 B 8 471

Gītā

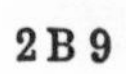

2 B 9 229

Nṛtyā

2 B 10 841

Vajrāṅkuśī

2 B 11 827

Vajrapāśī

2 B 12 845

Vajrasphoṭī

2 B 13 842

Vajraghaṇṭā

2 B 14 806

Vajrasūrya

2 B 15 846

Vajroṣṇīṣa

2 B 16 818

Vajrakuṇḍalin

2 B 17 833

Vajrayakṣa

2 B 18 690

Mi-k'o-pa

2 B 19 667

Ch'a-sang

2 B 20 624

Aṅgāraka

2 B 21 **927**

Fa-chiu-ku yo-chu

2 B 22 **376**

Puṣpā

2B 23 **394**

Dhūpā

2 B 24 **366**

Dīpā

2 B 25 395

Gandhā

2 B 26 486

Śābari [pāda]

2 B 27 245

Bhairavavajra

2 B 28 250

Vairocana-Bhairavavajra

大清乾隆年敬造

2 B 29 3

Ekavīra-Bhairavavajra

大清乾隆年敬造

2 B 30 71

Ṣaṇmukha-Bhairavavajra

大清乾隆年敬造

2 B 31 939

Kṛṣṇāri-Bhairavavajra

大清乾隆年敬造

2 B 32 283

Pratyālīḍha-Bhairavavajra

大清乾隆年敬造

2 B 33 538

Ya-wa-ti

大清乾隆年敬造

2 B 34 493

Dharmarāja

大清乾隆年敬造

2 B 35 165

Ti-la-pa

2 B 36 867

A-wa-niu-t'ou yo-chu

2 B 37 566

Moha-Bhairavavajra

2 B 38 333

Mātsarya(?)-Bhairavavajra

2 B 39 723

Rāga-Bhairavavajra

2 B 40 249

Īrṣyā-Bhairavavajra

2 B 41 110

Carcikā (fo-mu)

2 B 42 411

Vārāhī (fo-mu)

2 B 43 113

La-ka-la-ti (fo-mu)

2 B 44 925

Gaurī (fo-mu)

2 B 45 877

Yamāntakavajra

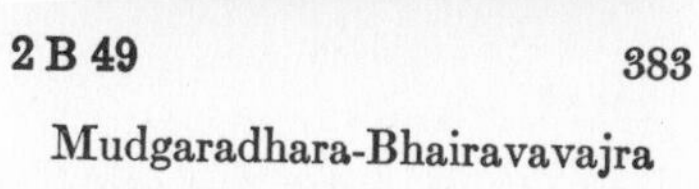

2 B 49 383

Mudgaradhara-Bhairavavajra

2 B 50 362

Daṇḍadhara-Bhairavavajra

2 B 51 378

Padmadhara-Bhairavavajra

2 B 52 353

Khaḍgadhara-Bhairavavajra

2 B 53 642

Nêng-shêng-mo-chang-chin-kang

2 B 54 238

Tejo(?)vajra

2 B 55 513

Lieh-shêng-chin-kang

2 B 56 562

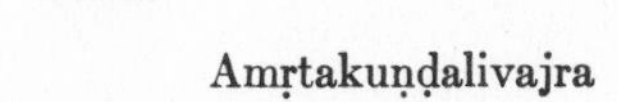

Amṛtakuṇḍalivajra

2 B 57 840

Vajrāṅkuśa

2 B 58 807

Vajrakāla

2 B 59 213

Mahākālavajra

2 B 60 417

Bhayadavajra

2 B 61 730

Uṣṇīṣacakravartin

第三妙吉祥大寶樓上供奉如是大乘祕
密經四大根本內無上陰體根本品內上
樂王佛白上樂王佛持嘴巴拉喜金剛佛
持兵器喜金剛佛大幻金剛佛佛陀噶巴
拉佛時輪王佛瑜伽虛空佛佛海觀世音
佛等共經則大上樂王根本經以及本生
上樂王佛黑大鵬上樂王佛空行佛母金
剛亥母智行佛母花大鵬金剛佛黑大鵬
金剛佛白空行佛母獅像佛母等無上陰
體根本經內所出本意佛像又若諸佛出
生根本經講議根本經同義根本經及諸
經論觀想法壇城儀軌二觀祕密法諸品
行持法等註疏皆宜藏度是為最上福田
功德不可思議

3 A

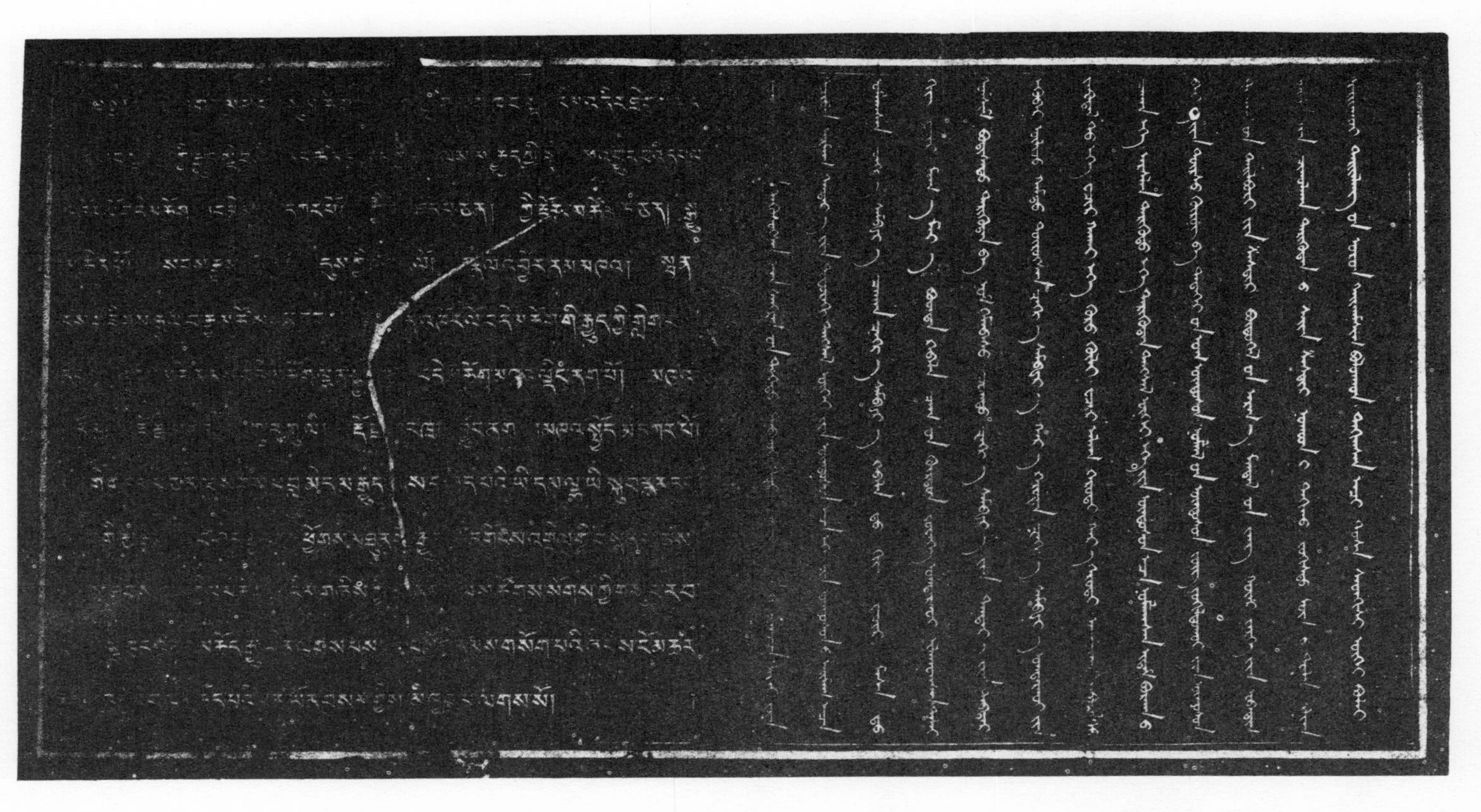

3 B

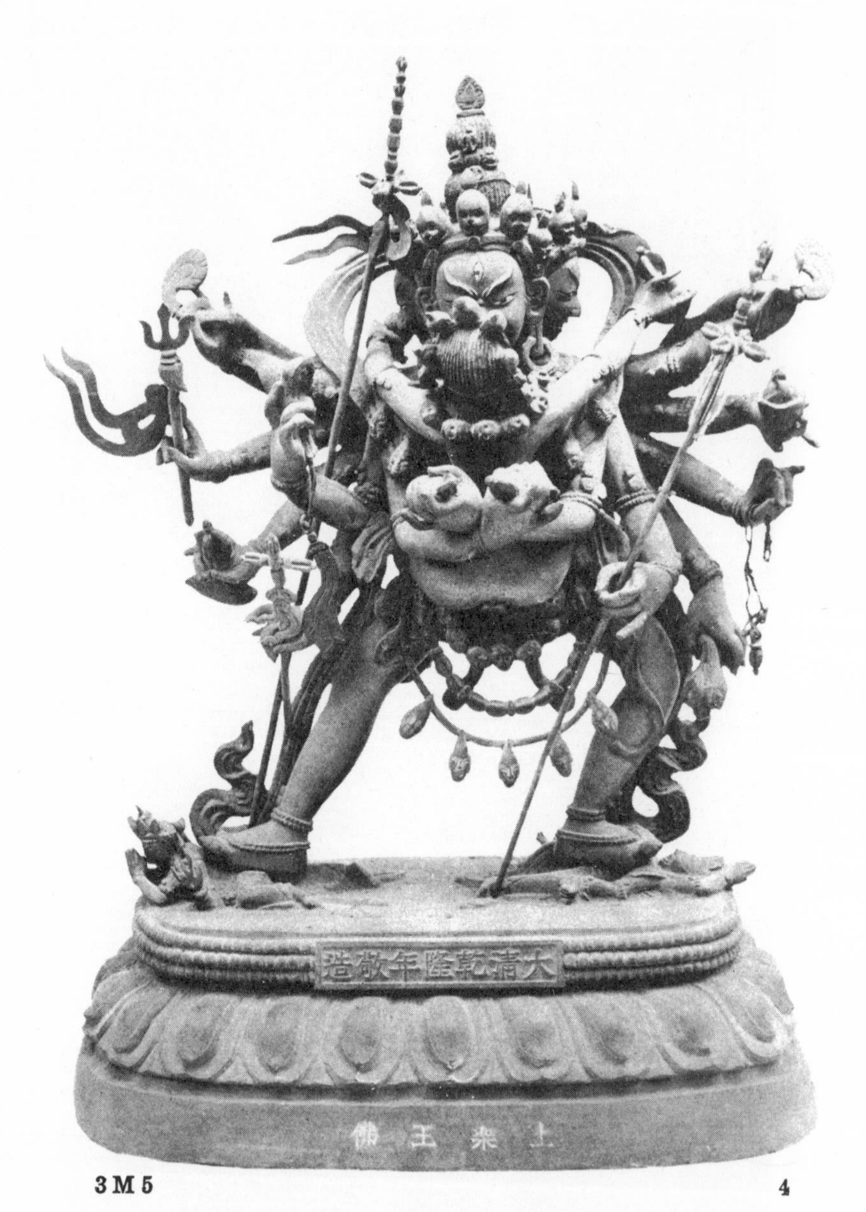
大清乾隆年敬造
上楽王佛

3 M 5 4

Śaṁvararāja (Buddha)

3 M 1 556

Yogāmbara (Buddha)

3 M 2 43

Buddhakapāla (Buddha)

3 M 3 352

Śastradhara-Hevajra (Buddha)

3 M 4 570

Sita-Śaṁvararāja (Buddha)

3 M 6 354

Kapāladhara-Hevajra

3 M 7 190

Mahāmāyāvajra (Buddha)

3 M 8 379

Cakradhararāja (Buddha)

3 M 9 40

Jinasāgara-Avalokiteśvara (Buddha)

3 A 1 111

Lieh-k'o-ta-ch'ia t'ien

3 A 2 929

Hārītī (deva)

3 A 3 741

Dhanus (deva)

3 A 4 303

Budha (deva)

3 A 5 **313**

Navamī Tithi

3 A 6 **312**

Daśamī Tithi

3 A 7 **314**

Aṣṭamī Tithi

3 A 8 **311**

Saptamī Tithi

3 A 9 30

Chiao-wan-shou-yin (fo-mu)

3 A 10 385

Sphoṭadharā (fo-mu)

3 A 11 742

Dharmadhātu (fo-mu)

3 A 12 377

Padmadharā (fo-mu)

3 A 13 672

Padmaḍākinī (fo-mu)

3 A 14 296

Yo-chu t'ien

3 A 16 884

Lung-yü t'ien

3 A 17 931

Makara (deva)

3 A 18 310

Ṣaṣṭhī Tithi

3 A 19 100

Kumbha(?) (deva)

3 A 20 48

Shih-i-wo-shih-ma-mu

3 A 21 508

Agni (deva)

3 A 22 391

Vidyuddharā (fo-mu)

3 A 23 364

Ulkādharā (fo-mu)

3 A 24 390

Dīpayugmadharā (fo-mu)

3 A 25 360

Sūryadharā (fo-mu)

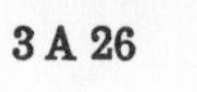

3 A 26 418

Sūryaprabha (deva)

3 A 27 262

Mīna (deva)

3 A 28 456

Candra (deva)

3 A 29 305

Śakra (deva)

3 A 30 365

Dīpā (fo-mu)

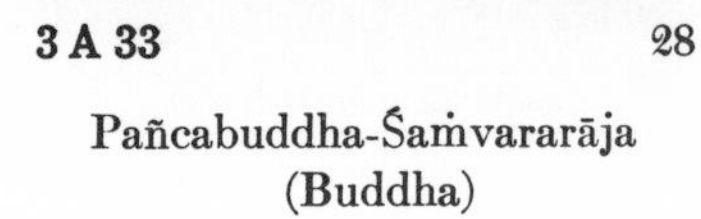

3 A 33 28

Pañcabuddha-Śaṁvararāja
(Buddha)

3 A 34 569

Sita-Śaṁvararāja

3 A 35 4

Śaṁvararāja (Buddha)

大清乾隆年敬造

3 A 36 559

Ghaṇṭāpāda

3 A 37 280

Ratnaḍāka

持香佛母

3 A 40 393

Dhūpā (fo-mu)

補嘎西佛母

3 A 41 696

Pukkasī (fo-mu)

3 A 42 139

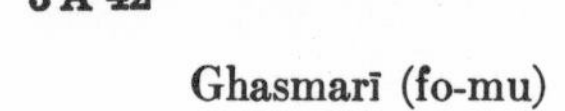

Ghasmarī (fo-mu)

3 A 43 572

Sita-Vetālī (fo-mu)

3 A 44 738

Caurī (fo-mu)

3 A 45 925

Gaurī (fo-mu)

3 A 46 138

Garuḍa-Śaṁvararāja (Buddha)

3 A 47 776

Vajraḍākinī

3 A 48 228

Nṛtyā (fo-mu)

3 A 49 754

Nāro (= Nāḍī)ḍākinī (fo-mu)

3 A 50 470

Gītā (fo-mu)

持花佛母

3 A 53 375

Puṣpā (fo-mu)

3 A 54 380

Aṅkuśī (fo-mu)

持網佛母

3 A 55 372

Jālinīdharā(?) (fo-mu)

3 A 56 373

Pāśī (fo-mu)

3 A 57 382

Ch'ih-ch'ien (fo-mu)

3 A 58 697

Buddhaḍāka (Buddha)

3 A 59 284

Ḍombinī (fo-mu)

3 A 60 612

Caṇḍālī (fo-mu)

3 A 61 487

Śabarī (fo-mu)

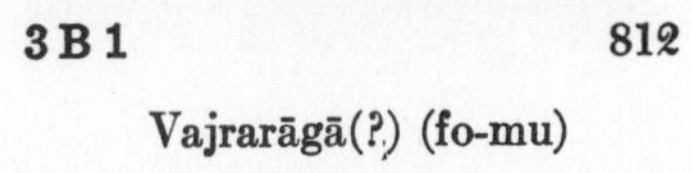

3 B 1 812

Vajrarāgā(?) (fo-mu)

3 B 2 809

Vajraśānti (fo-mu)

金剛地佛母

3 B 3 107

Ḍākinī (fo-mu)

3 B 4 783

Vajrabhūmi (fo-mu)

3 B 5 828

Vajraśabdā (fo-mu)

3 B 6 747

Viṣṇu (deva)

天 火 時

3 B 7 433

Kālāgni (deva)

天 水

3 B 8 479

Varuṇa (deva)

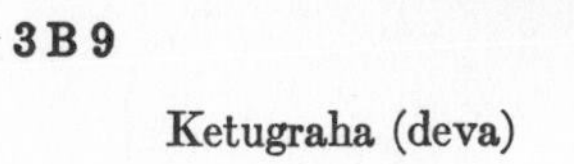

3 B 9 709

Ketugraha (deva)

3 B 10 698

Sita (deva)

3 B 11 98

Ekādaśa (deva)

3 B 12 170

Dvādaśa (deva)

3 B 13 **463**

Brahman (deva)

3 B 15 **139**

Ghasmarī (fo-mu)

3 B 16 **696**

Pukkasī (fo-mu)

沙斡哩佛母

3 B 17 **487**

Śabarī (fo-mu)

3 B 18 212

Mahākāla (deva)

3 B 19 855

Ling-chui t'ien

3 B 20 565

Pi-mu-ko-li-ti t'ien

3 B 21 760

Tula (deva)

3 B 22 681

Yakṣa (deva)

3 B 23 144

Kanyā (deva)

3 B 24 158

Caturbhuja-Vāyu (deva)

3 B 25 295

Shan-sha-ou-lieh t'ien

大清乾隆年敬造

3 B 26 

Birbapa (= Virūpa)

持鬘佛母

3 B 27 396

Mālyā (fo-mu)

3 B 31 42

Buddhakapāla

大清乾隆年敬造
瑜伽虛空佛

3 B 32 556

Yogāmbara (Buddha)

3 B 33 891

Li-shih t'ien

3 B 34 297

Vṛścika (deva)

3 B 35 743

Trayodaśa (deva)

大清乾隆年敬造
樂自在天

3 B 36 466

Nandīśvara(?) (deva)

3 B 39 925

Gaurī (fo-mu)

3 B 40 492

Kurukullā (fo-mu)

3 B 41 39

Jinasāgara-Avalokiteśvara

3 B 42 666

Puṣpa-Garuḍa

大清乾隆年敬造
黑大鵬

3 B 43 936

Kṛṣṇa-Garuḍa

持管佛母

3 B 44 371

Ch'ih-kuan (fo-mu)

3 B 45 137

Māmakī (fo-mu)

白衣佛母

3 B 46 581

Pāṇḍaravāsinī (fo-mu)

3 B 47 402

Tārā (fo-mu)

3 B 49 370

Vīṇādharā (fo-mu)

3 B 50 356

Mukundadharā (fo-mu)

3 B 52 713

Viśva(?)ḍāka (Buddha)

持門鎖佛母

3 B 53 389

Dvāratālakadharā (fo-mu)

持鑰匙佛母

3 B 54 387

Kuñcikādharā (fo-mu)

3 B 55 388

Dvāradharā (fo-mu)

持幔佛母

3 B 56 359

Vitāna(?)dharā (fo-mu)

3 B 57 41

Buddhalocanā (fo-mu)

3 B 58 74

Tsê-la-pa-la-ka fo-mu

3 B 59 612

Caṇḍālī (fo-mu)

3 B 60 799

Vajrabhṛkuṭī (fo-mu)

3 B 61 830

Vajraputtali(?) (fo-mu)

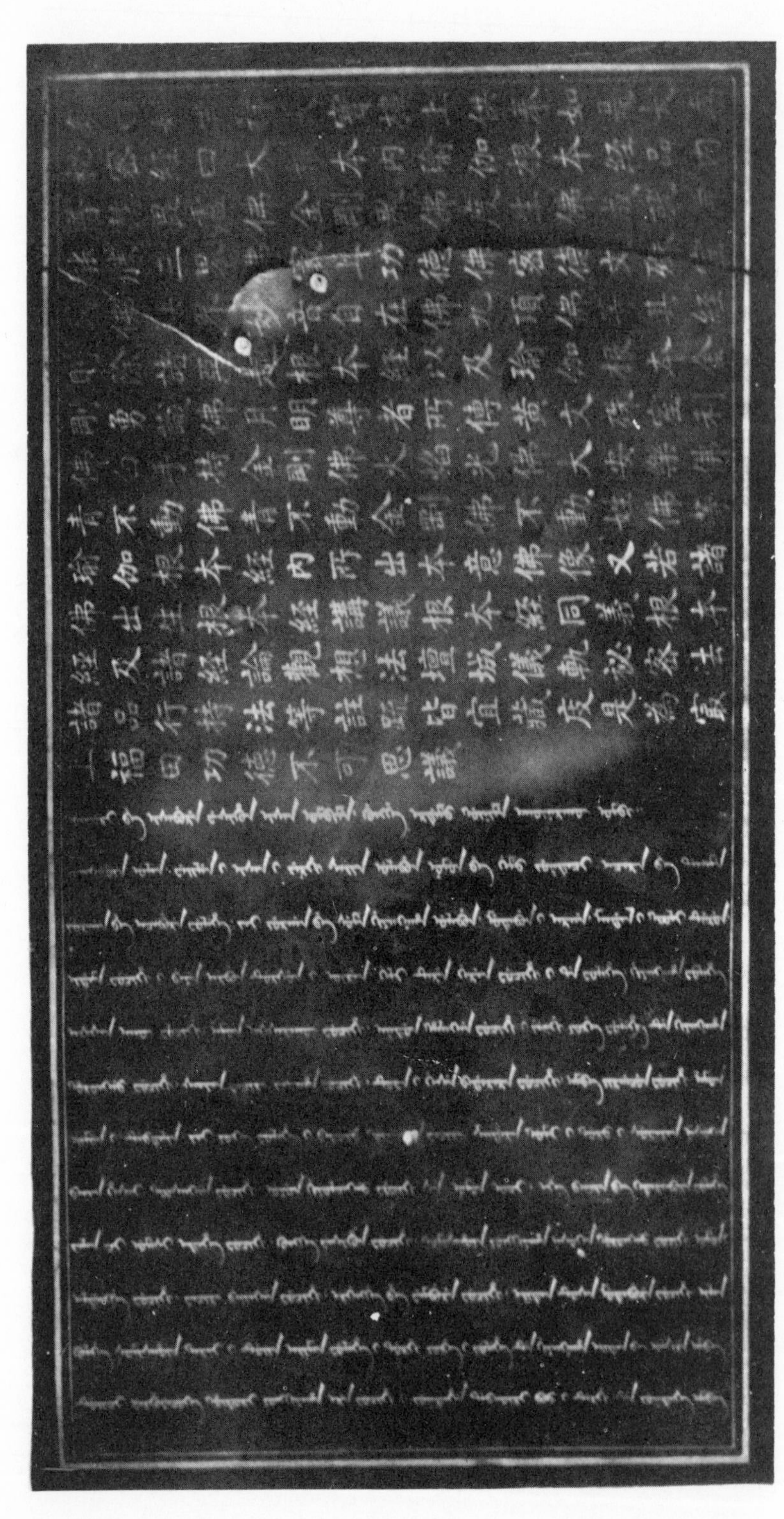

4 A

4 B

大清乾隆年敬造

4 M 5 440

Sarvavid-Vairocana (Buddha)

4 M 1 498

Dharmadhātuvāgīśvara (Buddha)

4 M 2 450

Uttamaśrī (Buddha)

4 M 3 339

Amoghasiddhi (Buddha)

4 M 4 823

Vajradhātu (Buddha)

4 M 6 315

Tu-shêng fo
Tib. ẖgro-ba-ẖdul-ba

4 M 7 641

Trailokyavijayavajra

4 M 8 692

Guhya-Mañjuśrī (Buddha)

4 M 9 16

Navaśikhin(?) (Buddha)
Tib. gc̣ug-dgu

4 A 1 906

Praṇidhāna-Pāramitā

4 A 2 413

Upāyakauśalya-Pāramitā

4 A 3 595

Dhyāna-Pāramitā

4 A 4 615

Vīrya-Pāramitā

普光佛母

4 A 5 437

Samantaprabhā (fo-mu)

法雲佛母

4 A 6 500

Dharmameghā (fo-mu)

善慧佛母

4 A 7 119

Sādhumatī (fo-mu)

不動佛母

4 A 8 9

Acalā (fo-mu)

4 A 9 791

Vajratejas (Bodhisattva)

金剛寶菩薩

4 A 10 794

Vajraratna (Bodhisattva)

寶生佛

4 A 11 276

Ratnasambhava (Buddha)

金剛賢菩薩

4 A 12 838

Vajrasādhu (Bodhisattva)

4 A 13 813

Vajrarāga (Bodhisattva)

4 A 14 327

Kṣānti-Pāramitā

4 A 15 357

Śīla-Pāramitā

4 A 16 334

Dāna-Pāramitā

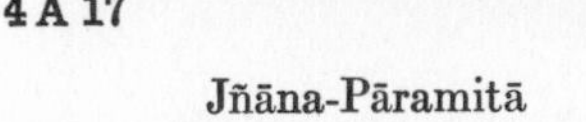

4 A 17 443

Jñāna-Pāramitā

4 A 18 752

Dūraṅgamā (fo-mu)

4 A 19 552

Abhimukhī (fo-mu)

4 A 20 892

Sudurjayā (fo-mu)

光輝佛

4 A 21 58

Dyuti(?) (Buddha)

金剛法佛母

4 A 22 816

Dharmavajrī (fo-mu)

4 A 23 793

Ratnavajrī (fo-mu)

4 A 24 774

Sattvavajrī (fo-mu)

4 A 25 824

Vajradhātu-Vairocana
(Buddha)

4 A 26 567

Prabhākarī (fo-mu)

4 A 27 515

Vimalā (fo-mu)

4 A 28 472

Pramuditā (fo-mu)

4 A 29 568

Cittotpādacaryābhūmi (fo-mu)

4 A 30 315

Tu-shêng fo
Tib. ḫgro-ba-ḫdul-ba

4 A 31 498

Dharmadhātuvāgīśvara (Buddha)

4 A 32 602

Guhya-Mañjuśrī (Buddha)

4 A 33 815

Vajradharma (Buddha)

4 A 34 252

Hung-kuang Vairocana (Buddha)

4 A 35 576

Sita-Vajrapāṇi

4 A 36 440

Sarvavid-Vairocana (Buddha)

4 A 38 **339**

Amoghasiddhi (Buddha)

4 A 39 **276**

Ratnasambhava (Buddha)

不動佛

4 A 40 **8**

Akṣobhya (Buddha)

4 A 41 **306**

Dhvajāgra(?) (Buddha)

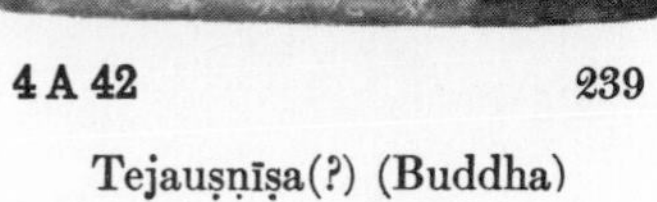

4 A 42 239

Tejauṣṇīṣa(?) (Buddha)

4 A 43 715

Chu-p'in-ting fo

4 A 44 676

Kamaloṣṇīṣa(?) (Buddha)

4 A 45 282

Ratnaśikhin(?) (Buddha)

4 A 46 847

Vajroṣṇīṣa (Buddha)

4 A 47 764

Śākyasiṁha (Buddha)

4 A 48 339

Amoghasiddhi (Buddha)

4 A 49 820

Vajrarāja (Bodhisattva)

4 A 50 775

Vajrasattva (Bodhisattva)

不動佛

4 A 51 8

Akṣobhya (Buddha)

金剛業佛母

4 A 52 810

Karmavajrī (fo-mu)

4 A 53 85

Jayoṣṇīṣa (Buddha)

4 A 54 208

Mahoṣṇīṣa (Buddha)

4 A 55 727

Vikrāntoṣṇīṣa(?) (Buddha)

4 A 56 510

Jvālānaloṣṇīṣa(?) (Buddha)

4 A 57 289

Vijayoṣṇīṣa (Buddha)

4 A 58 239

Tejauṣṇīṣa(?) (Buddha)

4 A 59 208

Mahoṣṇīṣa (Buddha)

4 A 60 575

Sitātapatroṣṇīṣa (Buddha)

4 A 61 407

Tīkṣṇoṣṇīṣa(?) (Buddha)

4 B 1 628

Jālinīprabha (Bodhisattva)

金剛藏菩薩

4 B 2 832

Vajragarbha (Bodhisattva)

無盡智菩薩

4 B 3 526

Akṣayamati (Bodhisattva)

4 B 4 607

Prajñākūṭa (Bodhisattva)

普賢菩薩

4 B 5 442

Samantabhadra (Bodhisattva)

自在生母

4 B 6 657

Upapatti-Vaśitā

4 B 7 653

Ṛddhi-Vaśitā

自在發心母

4 B 8 658

Cittotpāda (= adhimukti?)-Vaśitā

4 B 9 661

Praṇidhāna-Vaśitā

4 B 10 704

Dharma-Pratisaṁvit

4 B 11 705

Nirukti-Pratisaṁvit

4 B 12 707

Artha-Pratisaṁvit

4 B 13 703

Pratibhāna-Pratisaṁvit

4 B 14 502

Śokanirghātanamati (Bodhisattva)

香象菩薩

4 B 15 913

Gandhahastin (Bodhisattva)

勇行菩薩

4 B 16 79

Śūraṅgama (Bodhisattva)

虛空藏菩薩

4 B 17 688

Gaganagañja (Bodhisattva)

自在壽母

4 B 18 652

Āyur-Vaśitā

自在意母

4 B 19 654

Citta-Vaśitā

自在行母

4 B 20 659

Pariṣkāra(?)-Vaśitā

自在行母

4 B 21 659

Karma(?)-Vaśitā

自在智母

4 B 22 655

Jñāna-Vaśitā

自在法母

4 B 23 656

Dharma-Vaśitā

如性母

4 B 24 219

Tathātā(?)

4 B 25 45

Buddhabodhi

大清乾隆年敬造
不動佛

4 B 26 8

Akṣobhya (Buddha)

大清乾隆年敬造

4 B 27 773

Vajrasattva (Buddha)

大清乾隆年敬造

4 B 28 339

Amoghasiddhi (Buddha)

4 B 29 894

Nīla-Acalavajra

4 B 30 639

Trailokyavijaya (Buddha)

4 B 31 450

Uttamaśrī (Buddha)

4 B 32 509

Jvālānala(?) (Buddha)

4 B 33 75

Bala-Pāramitā

母蜜羅波智

4 B 34 446

Prajñā-Pāramitā

母蜜羅波行剛金

4 B 35 835

Vajracaryā-Pāramitā

4 B 36 675

Padmacaryā-Pāramitā

4 B 37 185

Mahāsukha (Buddha)

不動性佛

4 B 38 10

Pu-tung-hsing fo

金剛幢菩薩

4 B 39 796

Vajraketu (Bodhisattva)

金剛笑菩薩

4 B 40 826

Vajrahāsa (Bodhisattva)

無量光佛

4 B 41 532

Amitābha (Buddha)

金剛法菩薩

4 B 42 817

Vajradharma (Bodhisattva)

金剛敏捷菩薩

4 B 43 804

Vajratīkṣṇa (Bodhisattva)

金剛因菩薩

4 B 44 782

Vajrahetu (Bodhissattva)

4 B 45 228

Nṛtyā (fo-mu)

4 B 46 320

Maitreya (Bodhisattva)

4 B 47 555

Amoghadarśin (Bodhisattva)

4 B 48 398

Apāyajaha (Bodhisattva)

金剛語菩薩

4 B 49 837

Vajrabhāṣa (Bodhisattva)

成就佛

4 B 50 339

Amoghasiddhi (Buddha)

金剛業菩薩

4 B 51 811

Vajrakarma (Bodhisattva)

4 B 52 770

Vajrarakṣa (Bodhisattva)

大清乾隆年敬造
金剛藥叉菩薩

4 B 53 834

Vajrayakṣa (Bodhisattva)

大清乾隆年敬造
金剛拳菩薩

4 B 54 803

Vajramuṣṭi (Bodhisattva)

大清乾隆年敬造
嬉戲佛母

4 B 55 749

Lāsyā (fo-mu)

大清乾隆年敬造
持鬘佛母

4 B 56 396

Mālyā (fo-mu)

歌唄佛母

4 B 57 **470**

Gītā (fo-mu)

智慧頂菩薩

4 B 58 **445**

Jñānaketu (Bodhisattva)

4 B 59 *533*

Amitābha (Bodhisattva)

4 B 60 *455*

Candraprabha (Bodhisattva)

4 B 61 129

Bhadrapāla (Bodhisattva)

第五妙吉祥大寶樓上供奉如
是大乘祕密經四大根本內德
行根本品內宏光顯耀菩提佛
伏魔手持金剛佛善行手持金
剛佛黑摧碎金剛佛白馬頭金
剛佛佛眼佛母嘛嘛基佛母白
叉佛母青救度佛母等其經則
大宏光顯耀菩提根本經以及
大宏光顯耀菩提根本伏魔手
持金剛根本等德行根本品內
所出本意佛像皆宜藏度是為
最上福田功德不可思議

5 A

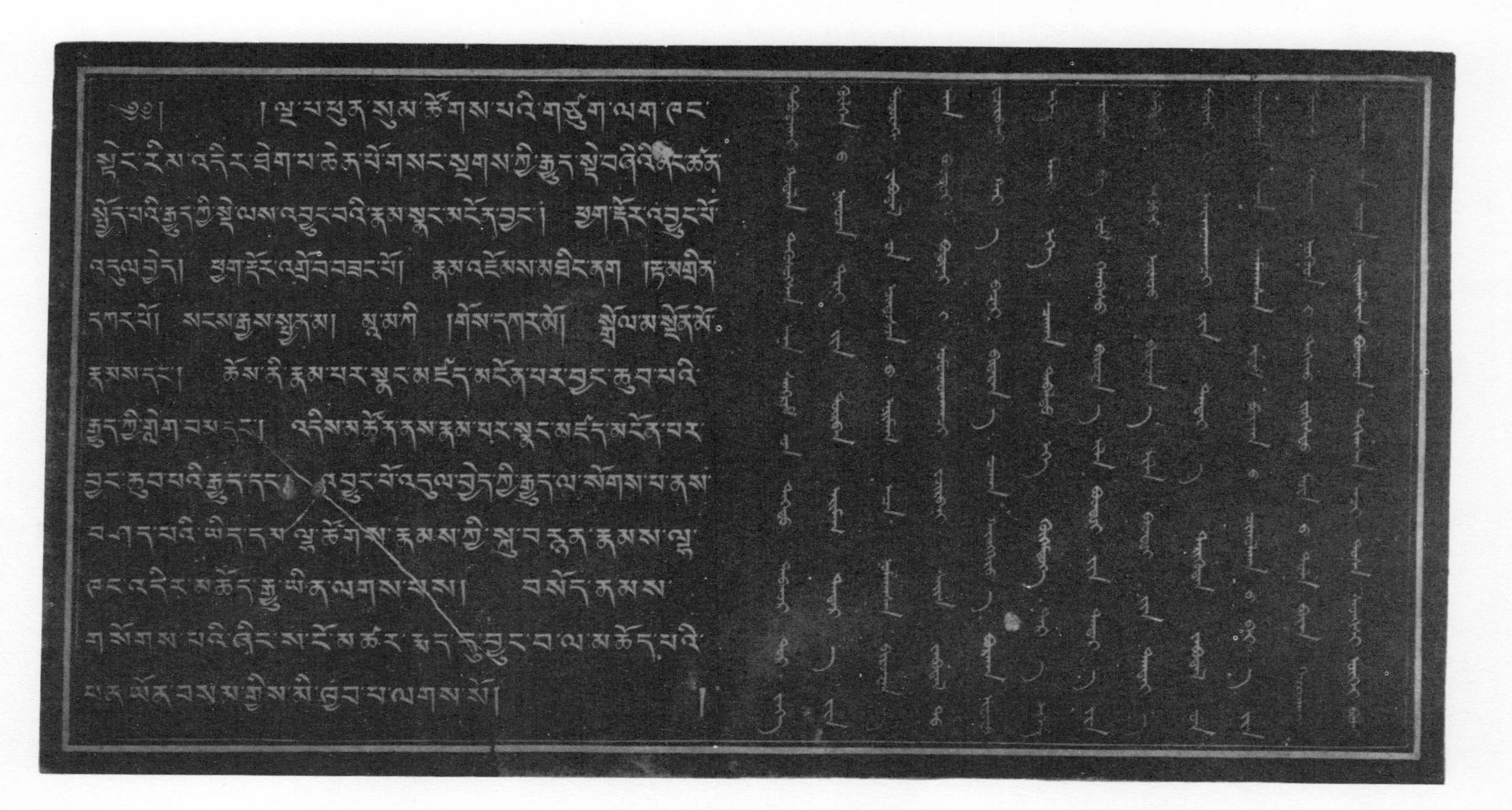
༄༅། །ལྷ་བཙུན་སུམ་ཚོགས་པའི་གཙུག་ལག་ཁང་
སྣེ་ང་རིམ་འདྲེར་ཐེག་པ་ཆེན་པོ་གསང་སྔགས་ཀྱི་རྒྱུད་སྡེ་བཞི་ཞི་ང་ཆེན
སྤྱོད་པའི་རྒྱུད་ཀྱི་སྡེ་ལས་འབྱུང་བའི་རྣམ་སྣང་མངོན་བྱང་། ཕྱག་རྡོར་འབྱུང་པོ
འདུལ་བྱེད། ཕྱག་རྡོར་འགྲོ་བ་བཟང་པོ། རྣམ་འཇོམས་མཐིང་ནག །རྟ་མགྲིན
དཀར་པོ། སངས་རྒྱས་སྤྱན་མ། མཱ་མ་ཀཱི། །གོས་དཀར་མོ། སྒྲོལ་མ་སྔོན་མོ
རྣམས་དང་། ཆོས་ཉིད་རྣམ་པར་སྣང་མཛད་མངོན་པར་བྱང་ཆུབ་པའི
རྒྱུད་ཀྱི་གླེགས་བམ་དང་། འདིས་མཚོན་ནས་རྣམ་པར་སྣང་མཛད་མངོན་བར
བྱང་ཆུབ་པའི་རྒྱུད་དང་། འབྱུང་པོ་འདུལ་བྱེད་ཀྱི་རྒྱུད་ལ་སོགས་པ་ནས
བཤད་པའི་ཡིད་དམ་ལྷ་ཚོགས་རྣམས་ཀྱི་སྐུ་བརྙན་རྣམས་ལྷ
ཁང་འདིར་མཆོད་རྒྱུ་ཡིན་ལུགས་སོ།། བསོད་ནམས
གསོགས་པའི་ཞིང་ས་ངོ་མཚར་རྨད་དུ་བྱུང་བ་ལ་མཆོད་པའི
ཕན་ཡོན་བསམ་གྱིས་མི་ཁྱབ་པ་ལགས་སོ། །

5 B

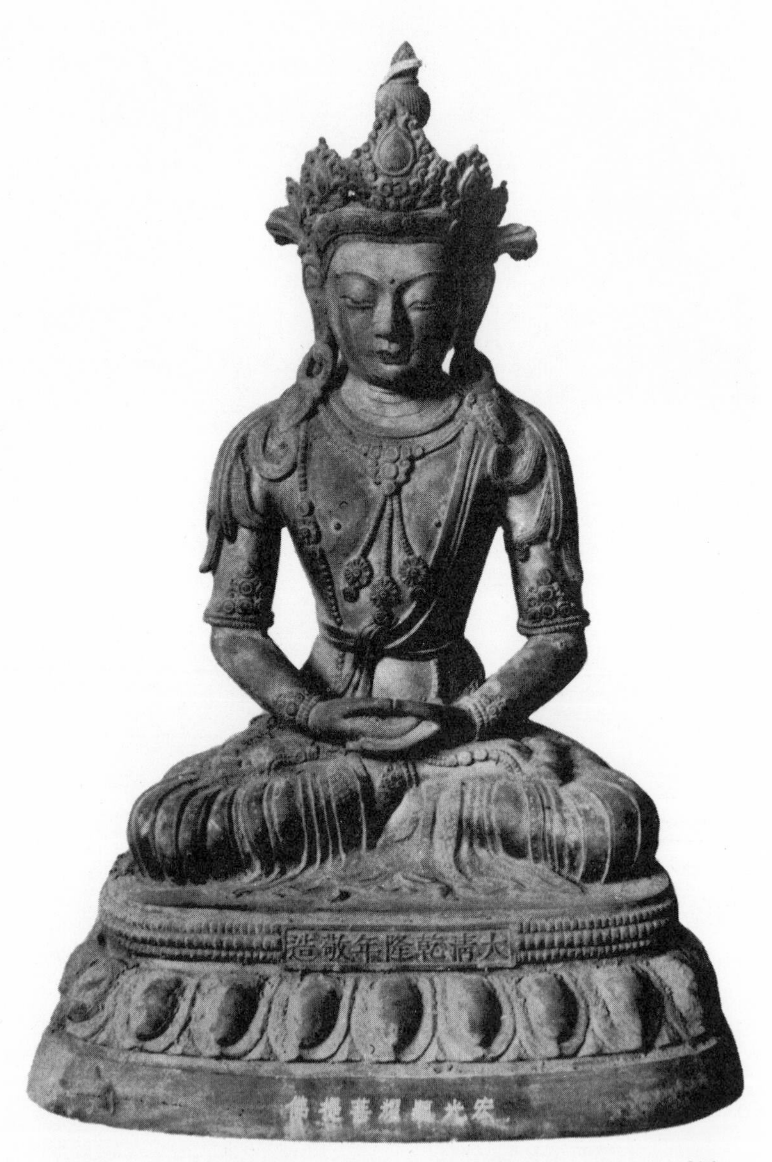
大清乾隆年敬造

5 M 5 — 254

Vairocanābhisambodhi (Buddha)

5 M 1 137

Māmakī (fo-mu)

5 M 2 895

Nīla-Tārā (fo-mu)

5 M 3 583

Sita-Hayagrīvavajra (Buddha)

5 M 4 938

Kṛṣṇa-Vajravidāraṇa (Buddha)

5 M 6 125

Shan-hsing Vajrapāṇi (Buddha)
Tib. ḫgro-ba-bzaṅ-po

5 M 7 35

Bhūtaḍāmara-Vajrapāṇi (Buddha)

5 M 8 581

Pāṇḍaravāsinī (fo-mu)

5 M 9 41

Buddhalocanā (fo-mu)

5 A 1 466

Nandīśvara(?) (deva)

5 A 2 591

Rāhu (deva)

5 A 3 421

Jih-kung t'ien

5 A 4 634

Gaṇapati (deva)

調伏生持手金剛

5 A 5 711

Jagaddama-Vajrapāṇi

調伏毒惡金剛

5 A 6 710

T'iao-fu-tu-wu-chin-kang

勝敵金剛

5 A 7 83

Śatruṁjayavajra

護魔金剛

5 A 8 718

Hu-mo-chin-kang

昂机哩天菩薩

5 A 9 423

Aṅgirodeva (Bodhisattva)

5 A 10 412

Vasiṣṭhadeva (Bodhisattva)

5 A 11 145

Karkaṭa(?)deva (Bodhisattva)

5 A 12 136

Markaṭa(?)deva (Bodhisattva)

5 A 13 **926**

Gautamadeva (Bodhisattva)

5 A 14 **167**

Kārttikeya(?) (deva)

5 A 15 **463**

Brahman (deva)

5 A 16 **747**

Viṣṇu (deva)

大自在天

5 A 17 204

Maheśvara (deva)

5 A 18 643

Nêng-huai-wu-yen-chin-kang

令甚調伏金剛

5 A 19 33

Ling-shên-t'iao-fu-chin-kang

普持金剛

5 A 20 441

Samantadharavajra(?)

令安金剛

5 A 21 32

Śaṅkara(?)vajra

花光鬘天菩薩

5 A 22 665

Hua-kuang-man-t'ien p'u-sa

自在天

5 A 23 651

Īśvara (deva)

威光蘊頂菩薩

5 A 24 237

Tejorāśyuṣṇīṣa (Bodhisattva)

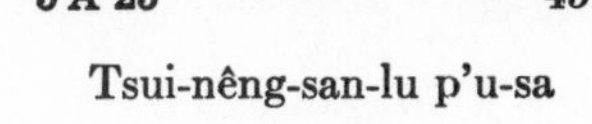

5 A 25 452

Tsui-nêng-san-lu p'u-sa

5 A 26 179

Mahoṣṭhavajra

大勝菩薩

5 A 27 176

Mahājina or Mahājaya (Bodhisattva)

金剛齒菩薩

5 A 28 851

Vajradanta (Bodhisattva)

5 A 29 839

Vajracakra (Bodhisattva)

5 A 30 632

Mei-ming fo-mu

5 A 31 177

Mahāsthāmaprāpta (Bodhisattva)

5 A 32 909

B[illegible]kuṭī (fo-mu)

大清乾隆年敬造
藍救度佛母

5 A 33 679

Nīla-Tārā (fo-mu)

大清乾隆年敬造
觀自在菩薩

5 A 34 702

Avalokiteśvara (Bodhisattva)

大清乾隆年敬造
虛空目菩薩

5 A 35 687

Ākāśanetra (Bodhisattva)

大清乾隆年敬造

5 A 36 254

Vairocanābhisambodhi (Buddha)

尊勝菩薩

5 A 37 288

Vijaya (Bodhisattva)

佛頂菩薩

5 A 38 46

Buddhoṣṇīṣa (Bodhisattva)

白傘蓋菩薩

5 A 39 574

Sitātapatra (Bodhisattva)

無邊聲音菩薩

5 A 40 531

Anantasvaraghoṣa (Bodhisattva)

5 A 41 516

Vimalākāśa (Bodhisattva)

5 A 42 329

Krodhacandravajra

5 A 43 843

Vajrasphoṭī (fo-mu)

5 A 44 795

Vajrāgrā (fo-mu)

5 A 45 137

Māmakī (fo-mu)

5 A 46 678

Nīla-Vajrapāṇi

馬頭金剛

5 A 47 915

Hayagrīvavajra

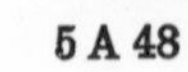

5 A 48 581

Pāṇḍaravāsinī (fo-mu)

5 A 49 912

Kāśyapadeva (Bodhisattva)

5 A 50 508

Agni (deva)

5 A 51 124

Shan-ch'êng-ming-yang-t'ien p'u-sa

5 A 52 740

Su-chi-i-t'ien p'u-sa

5 A 53 84

Abhyudgatoṣṇīṣa(?) (Bodhisattva)

5 A 54 198

Mahodgatoṣṇīṣa(?) (Bodhisattva)

5 A 55 580

Ūrṇā(?) (fo-mu)

5 A 56 590

Locanaprabha (Bodhisattva)

5 A 57 763

Śākyamuni (Buddha)

5 A 58 553

Abhimukha (Bodhisattva)

5 A 59 712

Durdāntadamaka (Bodhisattva)

能勝三界菩薩

5 A 60 640

Trailokyavijaya (Bodhisattva)

不動金剛

5 A 61 11

Akṣobhyavajra

除蓋障天母

5 B 1 879

Sarvanivaraṇaviṣkambhinī (devī)

奇妙菩薩

5 B 2 217

Ch'i-miao p'u-sa

施無畏菩薩

5 B 3 416

Abhayaṁdada (Bodhisattva)

棄諸惡趣菩薩

5 B 4 464

Sarvāpāyajaha (Bodhisattva)

5 B 5 328

Nien-yu p'u-sa

5 B 6 547

Siṁhadhvajā

5 B 7 287

Vijayā

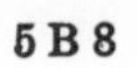

5 B 8 719

Śaṅkhapadmā

救度母

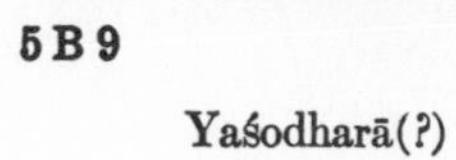

5 B 9 99

Yaśodharā(?)

5 B 10 403

Tārā

妙寶童子

5 B 11 225

Suḍhanakumāra

5 B 12 332

Bhṛkuṭī

馬頭金剛

5 B 13 914

Hayagrīvavajra

5 B 14 627

Jālinīprabhākumāra

5 B 15 269

Ratnamukuṭa (Bodhisattva)

無垢光童子

5 B 16 517

Vimalaprabhākumāra

5 B 17 236

Keśinī (devī)

寶最勝母

5 B 18 271

Ratnavijayā

妙音母

5 B 19 234a

Sarasvatī

5 B 20 216

T'ien-jung-mu

5 B 21 594

Puṇyeśvarī(?)

5 B 22 218

To tsun-mu

5 B 23 277

Ratneśvarī(?)

5 B 24 668

Chuang-yen-mu

5 B 25 885

Lung-chung-shêng-mu

大清乾隆年敬造

5 B 26 941

Kṛṣṇa-Dharmarāja

大清乾隆年敬造
降伏獄鬼菩薩

5 B 27 873

Hsiang-fu-yü-kuei p'u-sa

大清乾隆年敬造
時相天母

5 B 28 434

Kāladhvajā(?) or Kālaketu(?) (devī)

5 B 29 309

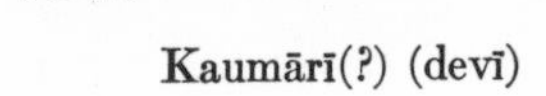

Kaumārī(?) (devī)

5 B 30 758

Nārāyaṇī (devī)

5 B 31 410

Vārāhī (devī)

5 B 32 88

Cāmuṇḍā (devī)

5 B 33 **451**

Vijayā

5 B 34 **432**

Ming-tien tsun-mu

5 B 35 **427**

Ming-yüeh-mu

5 B 36 **511**

Umā

5 B 37 630

Rākṣasa

5 B 38 304

Śakra

5 B 39 479

Varuṇa (deva)

5 B 40 420

Sūrya (deva)

5 B 41 81

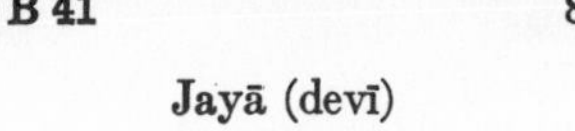

Jayā (devī)

5 B 42 286

Vijayā (devī)

5 B 43 465

Brahman (deva)

5 B 44 164

Pṛthivī (devī)

土地

5 B 45 162

Pṛthivī

5 B 46 585

Sita-Nāgarāja

白龍母

5 B 47 584

Sita-Nāgī

5 B 48 415

Shih-miao-chin-kang

妙音天母

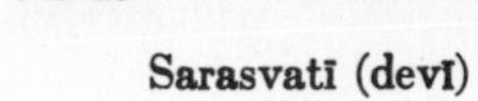

5 B 49 234

Sarasvatī (devī)

那羅延天

5 B 50 757

Nārāyaṇa (deva)

使靁延天

5 B 51 49

Shih-lei-yen t'ien

風天

5 B 52 911

Vāyu (deva)

5 B 53 31

Śaṅkarī(?) (devī)

5 B 54 38

Umā (devī)

5 B 55 456

Candra (deva)

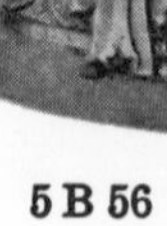

5 B 56 529

Krodhāparājitavajra

無能勝忿怒天母

5 B 57 **528**

Krodhāparājitā (devī)

5 B 58 **106**

Upakeśinī(?) (devī)

諸品天母

5 B 59 714

Citrā(?) (devī)

5 B 60 722

Vasumatī(?) (devī)

5 B 61 644

Ākarṣaṇī(?) (devī)

6 A

6 B

大清乾隆年敬造
無量壽佛

6 M 5 534

Amitāyus (Buddha)

6 M 1 605

Mārīcī (fo-mu)

6 M 2 577

Sita-Tārā (fo-mu)

6 M 3 285

Vijayā (fo-mu)

6 M 4 90

Ekādaśamukha-Avalokiteśvara

6 M 6 155

Caturbhuja-Avalokiteśvara

6 M 7 573

Sitātapatrā (fo-mu)

6 M 8 629

Śyāma-Tārā (fo-mu)

6 M 9 889

Pratisarā (fo-mu)

6 A 1 905

Ê-ni-lo (mahāyakṣasenāpati)

6 A 2 737

Mi-ch'i-lo (mahāyakṣasenāpati)

6 A 3 728

Po-ch'ai-lo (mahāyakṣasenāpati)

6 A 4 260

Kumbhīra (mahāyakṣasenāpati)

6A5 265

Tamodghātamati(?) (Bodhisattva)

6A6 123

Sudarśana (Bodhisattva)

6A7 15

Amoghavikrāmin (Bodhisattva)

6A8 447

Jñānākara (Bodhisattva)

大清乾隆年敬造

6 A 9 673

Padmanarteśvara-Avalokiteśvara
(Bodhisattva)

大清乾隆年敬造

6 A 10 917

Ch'i-hou Avalokiteśvara
(Bodhisattva)

大清乾隆年敬造
大地觀世音菩薩

6 A 11 182

Mahābhūmika-Avalokiteśvara
(Bodhisattva)

大清乾隆年敬造
四面八臂馬頭金剛

6 A 12 159

Caturmukhāṣṭabhuja-
Hayagrīvavajra

6 A 13 7

Trimukhacaturbhuja-Maitreya
(Bodhisattva)

6 A 14 392

Sumeruśikharadhararāja
(Bodhisattva)

6 A 15 321

Dundubhisvara (Bodhisattva)

6 A 16 902

Sumerukūṭa (Bodhisattva)

6 A 17 426

Prabhāmati or Prajñāloka (Bodhisattva)

6 A 18 335

Maitreya (Bodhisattva)

6 A 19 193

Mahāmati (Bodhisattva)

6 A 20 699

Avalokiteśvara (Bodhisattva)

6 A 21 453

Candravairocana (Bodhisattva)

6 A 22 937

Kṛṣṇa-Jambhalavajra

6 A 23 844

Vajraśṛṅkhalā (fo-mu)

6 A 24 821

Vajragāndhārī (fo-mu)

6 A 25 933

Pīta-Aparājitā (fo-mu)

6 A 26 345

Vajrapāṇi (Bodhisattva)

6 A 27 419

Sūryavairocana (Bodhisattva)

6 A 28 404

Chiu-t'o p'u-sa

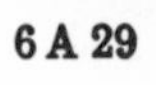

6 A 29 408

Mañjuśrī (Bodhisattva)

6 A 30 571

Sita-Acalavajra

6 A 31 915

Hayagrīvavajra

6 A 32 921

Siṁhavāhana-Mañjuśrī
(Bodhisattva)

6 A 33 408

Mañjuśrī (Bodhisattva)

6 A 34 545

Siṁhanāda-Avalokiteśvara (Bodhisattva)

6 A 35 156

Caturbhuja-Avalokiteśvara (Bodhisattva)

6 A 36 91

Ekādaśamukha-Avalokiteśvara (Bodhisattva)

6 A 37 708

Saṁgrāmatāriṇī (fo-mu)

6 A 38 308

Dhvajāgrakeyūrā (fo-mu)

6 A 39 191

Mahāpratyaṅgirā (fo-mu)

6 A 40 934

Pīta-Mārīcī (fo-mu)

6 A 41 306

Dhvajāgra(?) (Buddha)

6 A 42 406

Tīkṣṇa-Mañjuśrī (Bodhisattva)

6 A 43 605

Mārīcī (fo-mu)

6 A 44 343

Vajrapāṇi

6 A 45 483

Khasarpaṇa-Avalokiteśvara (Bodhisattva)

6 A 46 660

Īśvara (= Lokeśvara)-Avalokiteśvara (Bodhisattva)

6 A 47 573

Sitātapatrā (fo-mu)

6 A 48 609

Maitreya (Buddha) standing statue

6 A 49 932

Pīta-Jambhalavajra

6 A 50 147

Caturbhuja-Acalavajra

6 A 51 618

Rakta-Sarasvatī (fo-mu)

6 A 52 67

Ṣaḍbhuja-Jambhalavajra

6 A 53 876

Jāṅgulī (fo-mu)

6 A 54 582

Sita-Viśvā (fo-mu)

6 A 55 490

Śramaṇā (fo-mu)

6 A 56 338

Sarvārthasādhana-Tārā (fo-mu)

6 A 57 **96**

Sāhasrapramardanī (fo-mu)

6 A 58 **691**

Mantrānudhāraṇī (fo-mu)

6 A 59 264

Śītavatī (fo-mu)

6 A 60 184

Mahāmāyūrī (fo-mu)

6 A 61 663

Prajñāpāramitā (fo-mu)

6 B 1 558

Mārīcī (fo-mu) with jade girdle

6 B 2 92

Dvādaśabhuja-Mārīcī (fo-mu)

6 B 3 69

Ṣaḍbhuja-Parṇaśabarī (fo-mu)

6 B 4 5

Trimukhāṣṭabhuja-rakta-Hayagrīvavajra

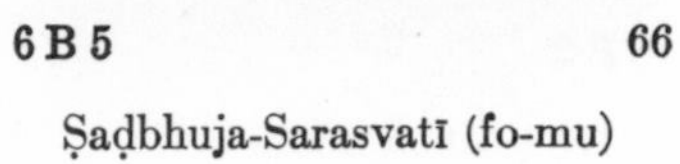

6 B 5 66

Ṣaḍbhuja-Sarasvatī (fo-mu)

6 B 6 192

Ta-chi-fên-mu

6 B 7 530

Aparājitā

6 B 8 859

Śṛṅkhalā(?)

金剛大寶母

6 B 9 786

Ratnavajrī(?)

6 B 10 684

Lan-mu-ta-lieh-ta-na-ma hsi-mu

6 B 11 134

Ma-ha-lieh-tsu-wa-lieh-ma hsi-mu
Mahārājavarā(?)

6 B 12 299

Pa-ta-lieh-ka-lieh-ma hsi-mu
Bhadrākarā(?)

6 B 13 258

Hai-pi-mu

6 B 14 64

Aṣṭabhuja-Vajratārā (fo-mu)

6 B 15 150

Caturbhuja-cintāmaṇicakra-Tārā (fo-mu)

6 B 16 6

Trimukhaṣaḍbhuja-sita-Tārā (fo-mu)

6 B 17 414

Jayadā (fo-mu)

6 B 18 677

Po-hu-lo (mahāyakṣasenāpati)

6 B 19 589

Chên-ta-lo (mahāyakṣasenāpati)

6 B 20 460

Chu-tu-lo (mahāyakṣasenāpati)

6 B 21 476

P'i-chieh-lo (mahāyakṣasenāpati)

母 光 月

6 B 22 454

Candraprabhā

6 B 23 863

A-lieh-ka-ma hsi-mu

6 B 24 135

Ma-lieh-ka-ma hsi-mu

6 B 25 240

Wei-yen-mu

6 B 26 285

Vijayā (fo-mu)

6 B 27 485

Ch'iu-ts'ai fo-mu

6 B 28 399

Vajravidāraṇa (mistake for Vajravidāraṇī?)

6 B 29 330

Fên-nu Wei-chi fo-mu

6 B 30 932

Pīta-Jambhalavajra

大清乾隆年敬造
速勇救度佛母

6 B 31 739

Pravīra(?)-Tārā (fo-mu)

6 B 32 626

Tzŭ-chu-lin Tārā (fo-mu)
Is it khadiravaṇī?

6 B 33 459

Mo-ni-lo (mahāyakṣasenāpati)

6 B 34 247

So-ni-lo (mahāyakṣasenāpati)

6 B 35 161

Indra (mahāyakṣasenāpati)

6 B 36 248

P'o-i-lo (mahāyakṣasenāpati)

6 B 37 577

Sita-Tārā (fo-mu)

6 B 38 534

Amitāyus (Buddha)

6 B 39 889

Pratisarā (fo-mu)

6 B 40 94

Ṣoḍaśabhuja-Avalokiteśvara (Bodhisattva)

6 B 41 876

Jāṅgulī (fo-mu)

6 B 42 578

Sita-Mañjuśrī (Bodhisattva)

6 B 43 174

Mahābalavajra

6 B 44 883

Vighnāntakavajra

6 B 45 750

Rājalīlā-Mañjuśrī (Bodhisattva)

6 B 46 689

Bhramarasvara-Mañjuśrī (Bodhisattva)

6 B 47 588

Nāmasaṅgīti-Mañjuśrī (Bodhisattva)

6 B 48 893

Cīna-Tārā (fo-mu)

6 B 49 916

Ch'i-hou īśvara (= Lokeśvara)-
Avalokiteśvara (Bodhisattva)

6 B 50 468

Trailokyavaśaṁkara-Avalokiteśvara
(Bodhisattva)

6 B 51 617

Caturbhuja-rakta-Avalokiteśvara
(Bodhisattva)

6 B 52 899

Nīlakaṇṭha-īśvara (= Lokeśvara)-
Avalokiteśvara (Bodhisattva)

6 B 53 935

Pañcamukhadvādaśabhuja-kṛṣṇa-Avalokiteśvara (Bodhisattva)

6 B 54 14

Amoghapāśa-īśvara (= Lokeśvara)-Avalokiteśvara (Bodhisattva)

6 B 55 77

Śrīvādirāṭ (Bodhisattva)

6 B 56 523

Anaṅgavajra (Bodhisattva)

6 B 57 21

Dvibhuja-Dharmadhātuvāgīśvara
(Buddha)

6 B 58 875

Durgottāriṇī-Tārā (fo-mu)

二臂一髻佛母

6 B 59 18

Dvibhuja-Ekajaṭā (fo-mu)

四臂準提佛母

6 B 60 152

Caturbhuja-Cundā (fo-mu)

十臂積光佛母

6 B 61 95

Daśabhuja-Mārīcī (fo-mu)

龍樹祖師
1

1 943
Nāgārjuna

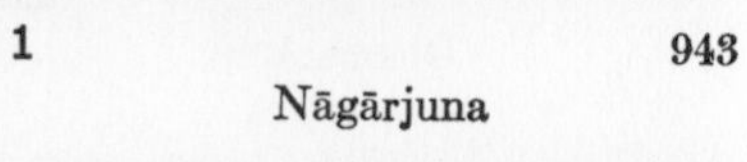

無着祖師
2

2 527
Asaṅga

聖天祖師
3

3 633
Āryadeva

田親祖師
4

4 564
Vasubandhu

明象祖師
5

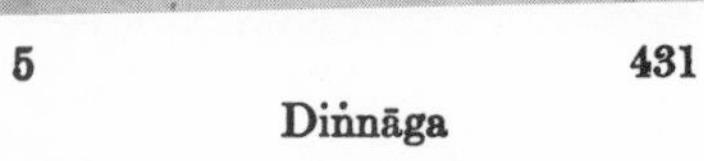

5 431

Diṅnāga

法聲祖師
6

6 499

Dharmakīrti

德光祖師

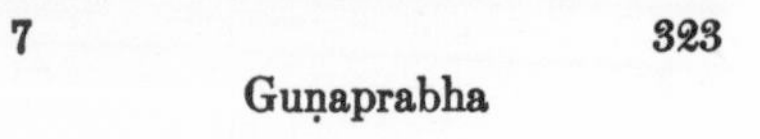

7 323

Guṇaprabha

釋迦光祖師
8

8 762

Śākyaprabha

青目祖師
9

9 **896**

Candrakīrti

善天祖師
10

10 **117**

Śāntideva

喜樂和祖師
11

11 **131**

Saraha

魯兮巴祖師
12

12 **930**

Lūhipāda

甘扎巴祖師
13

13 560
Ghaṇṭāpāda

吉禮斯納巴祖師
14

14 104
Kṛṣṇacārin or Kṛṣṇapāda

拉禮達祖師
15

15 348
Lalita [vajra]

莊秘巴祖師
16

16 669
Ḍombīpāda

德樂巴祖師
17

17 325

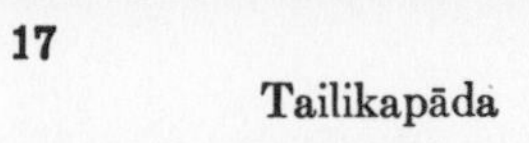

Tailikapāda

那羅巴祖師
18

18 755

Nāḍapāda

阿第沙祖師
19

19 869

Ārya-Atīśa

布倫祖師
20

20 300

ẖBrom-ston

宗喀巴祖師
21

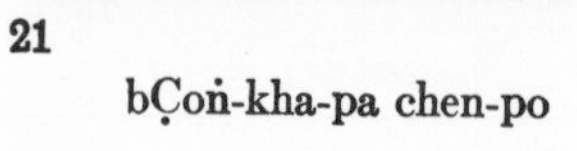

21 257
bÇoṅ-kha-pa chen-po

嘉勒擦布祖師
22

22 133
Yuvarājasvāmin

開主補祖師
23

23 861
Paṇḍitasiddhasvāmin

頭華達賴喇嘛
24

24 904
Siddhasaṅgha

25

25 550
Svāmimahāpaṇḍita-
Sumatidharmadhvaja

五輩達賴喇嘛
26

26 29
Svāmi-Vāgīśvarasumatisāgara

班臣羅卜藏葉施
27

27 551
Mahāpaṇḍita-Sumatijñāna

達賴喇嘛噶勒藏佳穆磋
28

28 746
Dalai Lama Kalpabhadrasamudra

大持金剛
29

29 196
Jina Vajradhara

金剛文殊秘密佛
30

30 805
Guhyasamāja-Mañjuvajra

精明文殊
31

31 613
Antarasādhana-Mañjughoṣa

不動金剛秘密佛
32

32 12
Guhyasamāja-Akṣobhyavajra

觀自在秘密佛
33
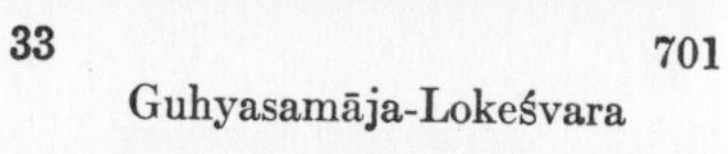

33 701
Guhyasamāja-Lokeśvara

佛海觀世音
34

34 39
Jinasāgara-Avalokiteśvara

時輪王佛
35

35 436
Kālacakra

上樂王佛
36

36 4
Śrī-Cakrasaṁvara

白上樂王佛
37

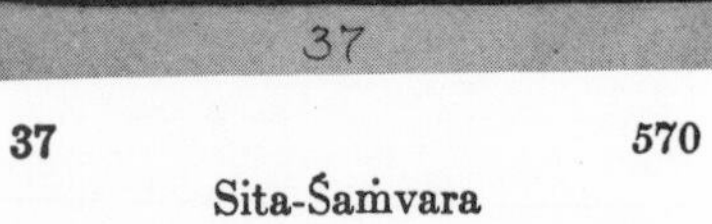

37 570
Sita-Śaṁvara

金剛勇識上樂王佛
38

38 772
Vajrasattva-Śaṁvara

本生上樂王佛
39

39 458
Sahaja-Śaṁvara

大鵬上樂王佛
40

40 209
Garuḍa-Śaṁvara

大鵬金剛佛
41

41 210
Vajragaruḍa (śabala)

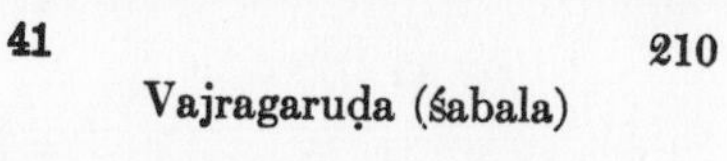

威羅瓦金剛
42

42 245
Bhairava

黑敵威羅瓦金剛
43

43 939
Kṛṣṇāri

六面威羅瓦金剛
44

44 71
Ṣaṇmukha

紅威羅瓦金剛
45

45 **619**
Rakta-Yamāri

一勇威羅瓦金剛
46

46 **3**
Ekavīra-Bhairava

喜金剛
47

47 **132**
Hevajra

喜心金剛
48

48 **130**
Garbha(?)-Hevajra

甘露金剛
49

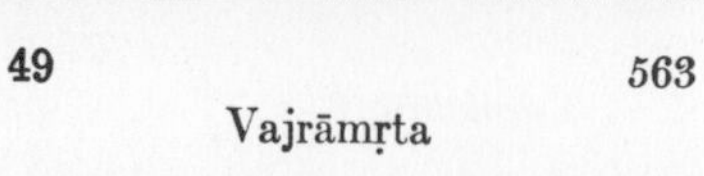

49 563
Vajrāmṛta

大幻金剛
50

50 189
Mahāmāyā

佛陀嘎巴拉金剛
51

51 44
Buddhakapāla

智慧空行佛母
52

52 444
Jñānaḍākinī

無我佛母
53

53 522
Nairātmā

金剛亥母
54

54 769
Vajravārāhī

空行佛母
55

55 608
Ḍākinī

大威吽聲金剛
56

56 183
Vajrahūṁkāra

四座金剛
57

57 **146**
Vajracatuḥpīṭha

瑜迦虛空佛
58

58 **557**
Yogāmbara

大輪手持金剛
59

59 **205**
Mahācakra-Vajrapāṇi

智行佛母
60

60 **448**
Kurukullā

秘密馬頭金剛
61

61 599
Guhyasādhana-Hayagrīva

蓮花妙舞自在馬頭金剛
62

62 674
Padmanarteśvara-Hayagrīva

四臂陰陽無量壽佛
63

63 157
Caturbhuja-Amitāyus

無量壽佛
64

64 534
Amitāyus

金剛性佛
65

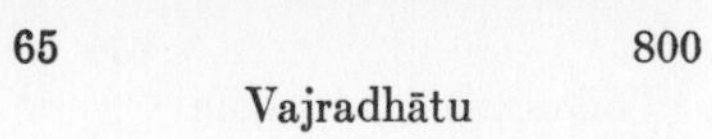

65 800
Vajradhātu

宏光釋迦獅子佛
66

66 253
Vairocana-Śākyasiṁha

法性妙音自在佛
67

67 495
Dharmadhātuvāgīśvara

普慧宏光佛
68

68 439
Sarvavid-Vairocana

金剛勇識佛
69

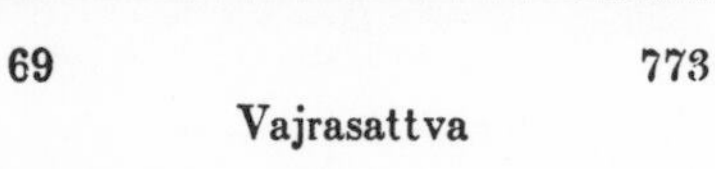

69 773
Vajrasattva

宏光顯耀菩提佛
70

70 254
Vairocanābhisambodhi

伏魔手持金剛
71

71 34
Bhūtaḍāmara-Vajrapāṇi

青衣手持金剛
72

72 897
Nīlāmbaradhara-Vajrapāṇi

威烈手持金剛
73
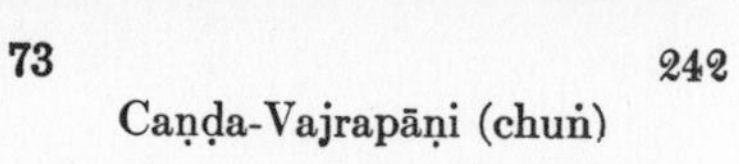

73 242
Caṇḍa-Vajrapāṇi (chuṅ)

顯行手持金剛
74

74 908
Ācārya-Vajrapāṇi

威烈三頭六臂手持金剛
75

75 241
Trimukha-ṣaḍbhuja-Caṇḍa

鐵劍馬頭金剛
76

76 857
Lohakhaḍga-Hayagrīva

毘盧佛
77

77 475
Vairocana

不動佛
78

78 8
Akṣobhya

79 270
Ratnasambhava

阿彌陀佛
80

80 864
Amitābha

成就佛
81

81 339
Amoghasiddhi

釋迦牟尼佛
82

82 763
Śākyamuni

83 767
Vajragarbhapramardin

寳光佛
84

84 268
Ratnārcis

龍尊王佛
85

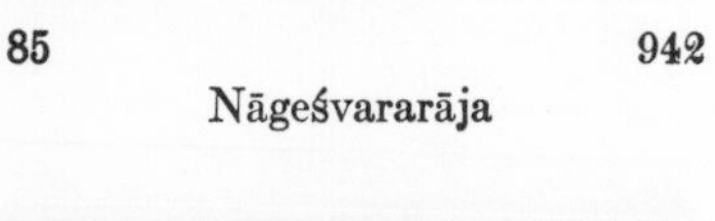

85 942
Nāgeśvararāja

精進軍佛
86

86 616
Vīrasena

精進喜佛
87

87 614
Vīranandin

寶火佛
88

88 275
Ratnāgni

寶月光佛
89

89 273
Ratnacandraprabha

現無愚佛
90

90 554
Amoghadarśin

寶月佛
91

91 272
Ratnacandra

無垢佛
92

92 514
Vimala

勇施佛
93

93 78
Śūradatta

清淨佛
94

94 503
Brahman

清淨施佛
95

95 505
Brahmadatta

水天佛
96

96 480
Varuṇa

水天中天佛
97

97 481
Varuṇadeva

賢德佛
98

98 726
Bhadraśrī

栴檀功德佛
99

99 461
Candanaśrī

無量掬光佛
100

100 535
Anantaujas

光德佛
101

101 56
Prabhāsaśrī

無憂德佛
102

102 521
Aśokaśrī

那羅延佛
103

103 756
Nārāyaṇa

功德華佛
104

104 76
Kusumaśrī

清淨光遊戲神通佛
105

105 504
Brahmajyotirvikrīḍitābhijña

蓮花光遊戲神通佛
106

106 671
Padmajyotirvikrīḍitābhijña

財功德佛
107

107 720
Dhanaśrī

德念佛
108

108 324
Smṛtiśrī

善名稱功德佛
109

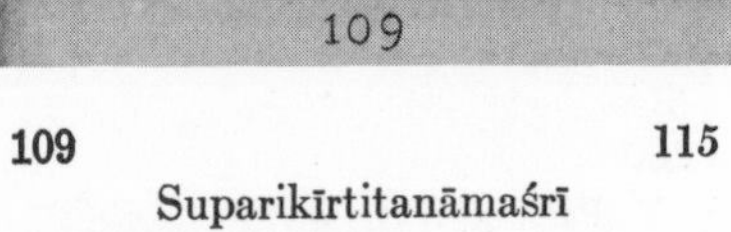

109 115

Suparikīrtitanāmaśrī

紅燄帝幢王佛
110

110 622

Indraketudhvajarāja

善遊步功德佛
111

111 128

Suvikrāntaśrī

鬬戰勝佛
112

112 928

Yuddhajaya

善遊步佛
113

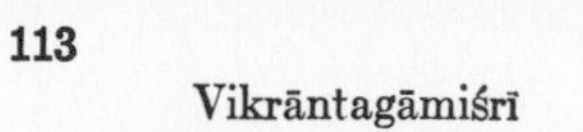

113 127
Vikrāntagāmiśrī

周匝莊嚴功德佛
114

114 109
Samantāvabhāsavyūhaśrī

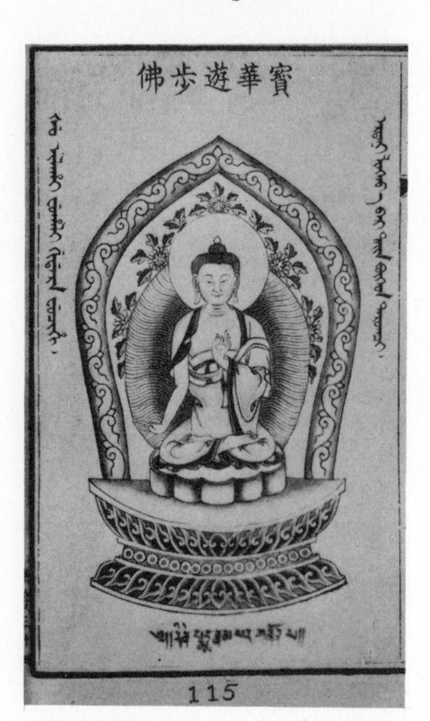
寳華遊步佛
115

115 278
Ratnapadmavikrāmin

寳蓮花善住須彌山王佛
116

116 279
Śailendrarāja (Buddha)

隨應佛
117

117 888
Anucārin(?) (Buddha)

顯聖王佛
118

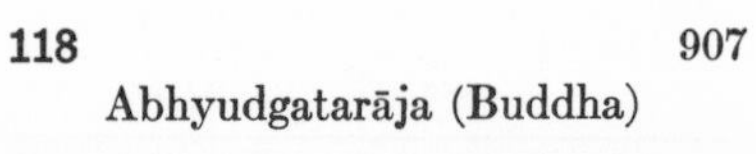

118 907
Abhyudgatarāja (Buddha)

119

119 121
ẖKhon-daṅ(?)-rgyags-pa-rnam-gnon

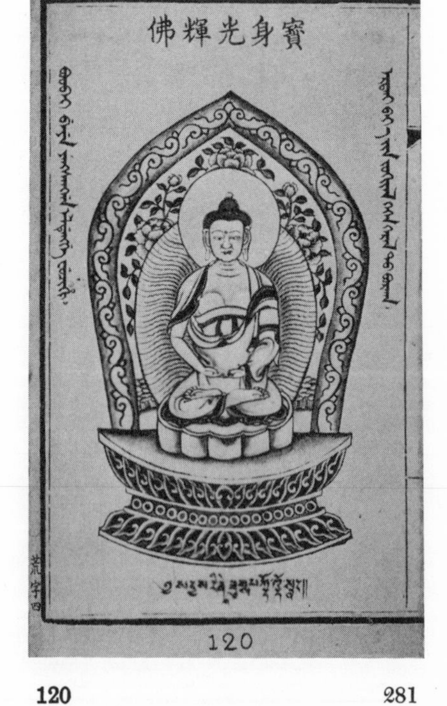
寶身光輝佛
120

120 281
Ratnāṅgavyūhadyuti (Buddha)

善滅魔障佛
荒字五
121

121 122
Saṅs-rgyas bdud-daṅ-yid-gñis-kun-ẖjoms(?)

不廻吉祥輪佛
荒字六
122

122 13
Avaivartikacakrasambhavaśrī(?)

寶傘勝佛
荒字七
123

123 266
Ratnacchattrodgata (Buddha)

隨引菩提佛
荒字八
124

124 886
Saṅs-rgyas byaṅ-sems-ẖdul-ba

無畏滅冥佛
125

125 *525*

Nirbhayavigatatamorāja(?)

初慈决疑佛
126

126 73

Prathamacittotpādasaṁśayacchedika(?)

毘婆尸佛
127

127 474

Vipaśyin (Buddha)

尸棄佛
128

128 294

Śikhin

毘舍浮佛
129

129 477
Viśvabhū

拘留孫佛
130

130 346
Krakucchanda

拘那舍牟尼佛
131

131 347
Kanakamuni

迦葉佛
132

132 733
Kāśyapa

善名稱吉祥王如來
133

133 116

Suparikīrtitanāmaśrīrāja

寶月智嚴光音自在王如來
134

134 274

Ratnacandrapadmapratimaṇḍita-paṇḍita(?) tejaḥsvaraghoṣarāja (Buddha)

金色寶光妙行成就如來
135

135 853

Suvarṇabhadravimalaratnaprabhā-savrata

無憂勝吉祥如來
136

136 519

Aśokottamaśrī

法海審音如來
137

137 497
Dharmakīrtisāgaraghoṣa

法海勝慧遊戲神通如來
138

138 496
Dharmasāgarāgra(?)mativikrī-
ḍitābhijñārāja

藥師琉璃光王如來
139

139 683
Bhaiaṣjyaguru-Vaiḍūryaprabhārāja

獅吼佛
140

140 542
Siṁhanāda (Jina)

金剛不動佛
141

141 766
Vajrākṣobhya

積光吉祥王佛
142

142 606
Raśmisamudgataśrīkūṭarāja

普慧佛
143

143 438
Samantadarśin (Jina)

寶頂佛
144

144 282
Ratnaśikhin

大白文殊
145

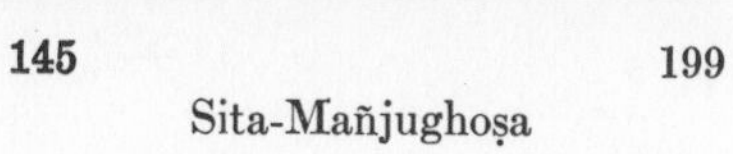

145 199
Sita-Mañjughoṣa

童子文殊
146

146 610
Kumārabhūta-Mañjuśrī

永輪文殊
147

147 484
Sthiracakra-Mañjughoṣa

秘密文殊
148

148 597
Guhyasādhana-Mañjughoṣa

獅吼文殊
149

149 543
Siṁhanāda-Mañjughoṣa

妙語尊帝文殊
150

150 232
Vādirāḍ-Mañjughoṣa

八臂法性妙語自在文殊
151

151 62
Aṣṭabhuja-Dharmadhātuvāgīśvara-Mañjughoṣa

妙音自在文殊
152

152 235
Bhadrasvareśvara(?)rāja-Mañjughoṣa

遊戲自在文殊
153

153 751
Rājalīlā-Mañjuśrī

大勝三界自在文殊
154

154 175
Trailokyavaśyādhikāra-Mañjughoṣa

真實名尊四臂文殊
155

155 587
Caturbhuja-Nāmasaṁgīti-Mañjughoṣa

慧輪文殊
156

156 337
Prajñācakra-Mañjughoṣa (daṅ-po?)

敏捷文殊
157

157 405
'Tīkṣṇa–Mañjuśrī

四臂觀世音
158

158 155
Caturbhuja-Avalokiteśvara

開花觀世音
159

159 862
Padmavikāsana-Avalokiteśvara

水月觀世音
160

160 482
Khasarpaṇa-Avalokiteśvara

獅吼觀世音
161

161 544
Siṁhanāda-Avalokiteśvara

騎犼觀世音
162

162 919
Hālāhala-Lokeśvara

金剛妙法觀世音
163

163 790
Vajradharma-Avalokiteśvara

二臂蓮花妙舞自在觀世音
164

164 25
Dvibhuja-Padmanarteśvara-Avalokiteśvara

十八臂蓮花妙舞自在觀世音
165

165 93
Aṣṭadaśabhuja-Padmanarteśvara

騎犼自在觀世音
166

166 918
Harihariváhana-Lokeśvara

權衡三界觀世音
167

167 467
Trailokyavaśaṁkara-Avalokiteśvara

四臂紅自在觀世音
168

168 153
Caturbhuja-rakta-Lokeśvara

青項自在觀世音
169

169 898
Nīlakaṇṭha-Lokeśvara

重疊廣幻觀世音
170

170 765
Māyājālakrama-Avalokiteśvara

成鎖觀世音
171

171 341
Amoghapāśa

大地紅色觀世音
172

172 181
Mahābhūmika(?)-rakta-Avalokiteśvara

十一面大悲觀世音
173

虛空王菩薩
174

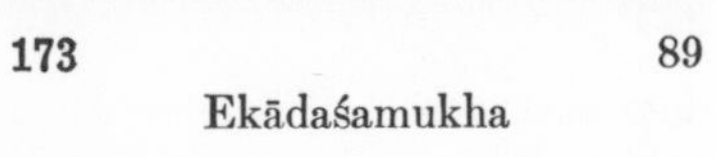
173 89
Ekādaśamukha

174 686
Gaganarāja

如意觀世音
175

175 222
Cittaviśrāmaṇa-Avalokiteśvara

大寶如意觀世音
176

176 187
Cintāmaṇi-Avalokiteśvara

金剛不壞觀世音
177

177 768
Vajragarbhapramardin-Avalokiteśvara

金剛拳印菩薩
178

178 802
Vajramuṣṭi

金剛夜义菩薩
179

179 785
Vajrayakṣa

金剛保護菩薩
180

180 771
Vajrarakṣa

金剛智行菩薩
181

181 808
Vajrakarma

金剛說法菩薩
182

182 836
Vajrabhāṣa

金剛因緣菩薩
183

183 781
Vajrahetu

金剛敏捷菩薩
184

184 804
Vajratīkṣṇa

金剛妙法菩薩
185

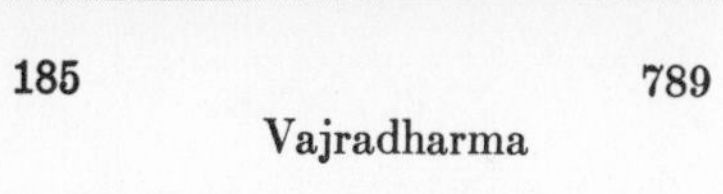

185 789
Vajradharma

金剛喜笑菩薩
186

186 779
Vajrahāsa

金剛幢蓋菩薩
187

187 797
Vajraketu

金剛威德菩薩
188

188 798
Vajratejas

金剛大寶菩薩
189

189 787
Vajraratna

金剛善賢菩薩
190

190 780
Vajrasādhu

金剛喜慕菩薩
191

191 778
Vajrarāga

金剛大帝菩薩
192

192 788
Vajrarāja

金剛勇識菩薩
193

193 775
Vajrasattva (Bodhisattva)

四臂彌勒
194

194 151
Caturbhuja-Maitreya

二臂彌勒
195

195 20
Dvibhuja-Maitreya

虛空藏菩薩
196

196 688
Ākāśagarbha

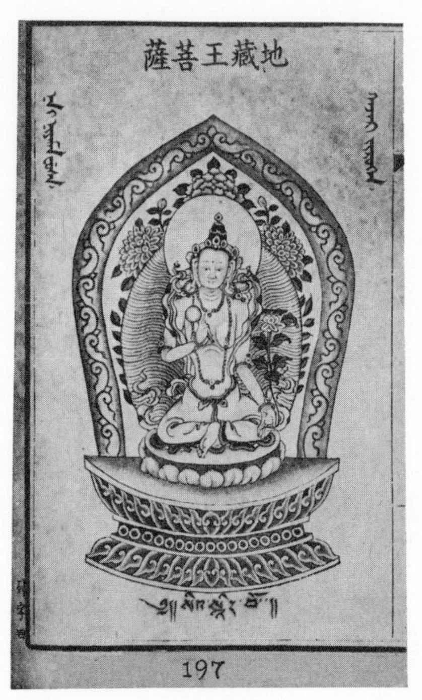
地藏王菩薩
197

197 166
Kṣitigarbha

普賢菩薩
列字五
198

198 442
Samantabhadra

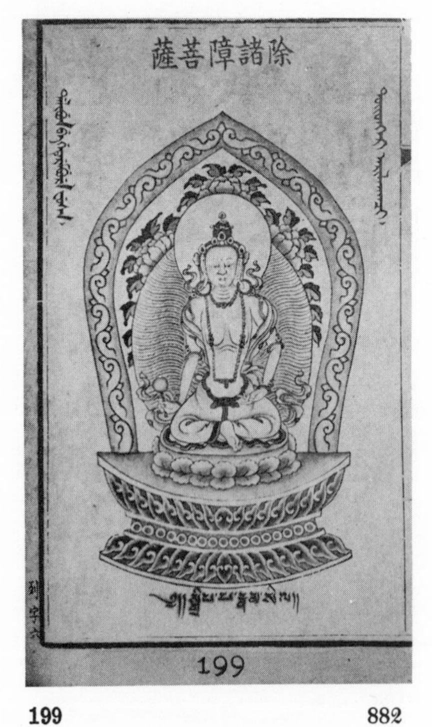
除諸障菩薩
列字六
199

199 882
Sarvanivaraṇaviṣkambhin

騎象普賢菩薩
列字七
200

200 923
Hastivāhana-Samantabhadra

大千摧碎佛母
201

201 178
Mahāsāhasrapramardanī

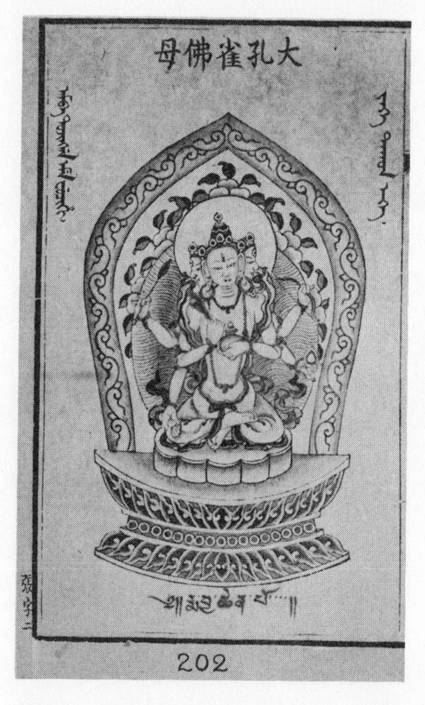
大孔雀佛母
202

202 184
Mahāmāyūrī

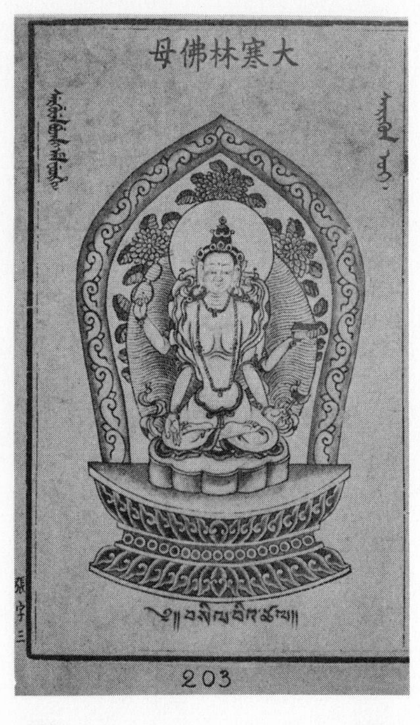
大寒林佛母
203

203 186
Śītavatī

密咒隨持佛母
204

204 261
Mantrānudhāraṇī

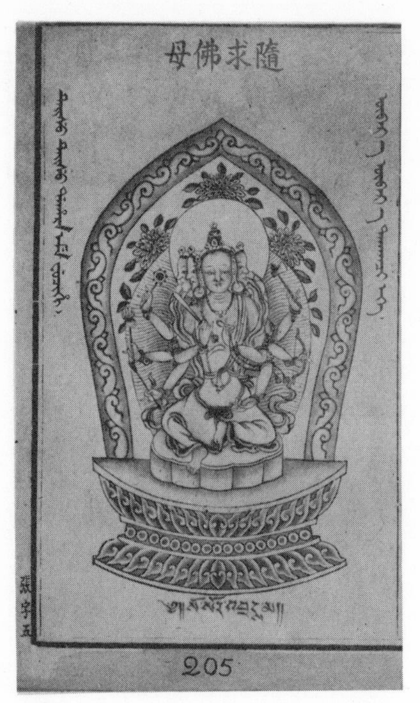
隨求佛母
205

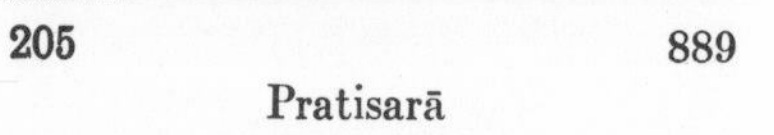

205 889
Pratisarā

除諸惡難救度佛母
206

206 881
Khadiravaṇī-Tārā

尊者速勇救度佛母
207

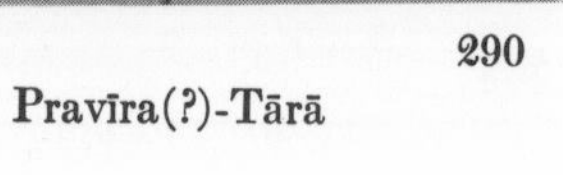

207 290
Pravīra(?)-Tārā

大善秋月救度佛母
208

208 180
Candrakānti(?) -Tārā

大慧金色救度佛母
209

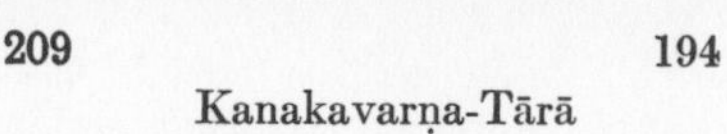

209 194
Kanakavarṇa-Tārā

灌頂遵勝救度佛母
210

210 507
Uṣṇīṣa-Tārā

虛空吽音救度佛母
211

211 685
Hūṁsvaranādinī-Tārā

能勝三界救度佛母
212

212 638
Vijaya-Tārā

能摧惡敵救度佛母
213

213 646
Aparājita-Tārā

能摧怨魔救度佛母
214

214 645
Mārasūdana-Tārā

涅槃寂滅救度佛母
215

215 506
Śokavinodana-Tārā

攝伏世間救度佛母
216

216 401
Jagadvaśī(?)-Tārā

能生吉祥救度佛母
217

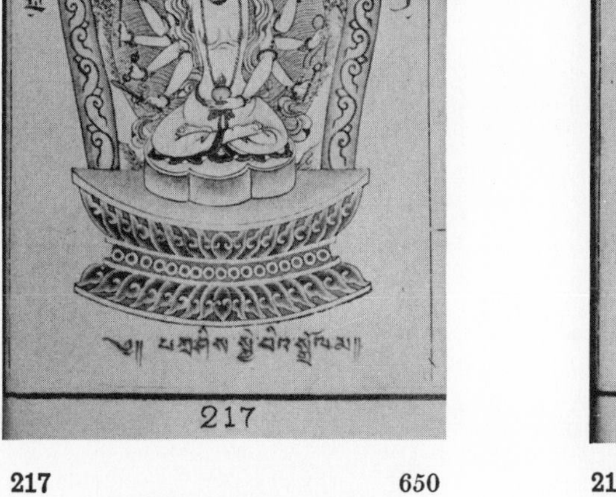

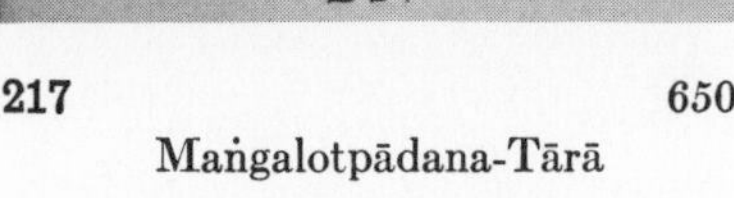

217 650
Maṅgalotpādana-Tārā

如火熾盛救度佛母
218

218 223
Pācaka-Tārā

顰眉威相救度佛母
219

219 910
Kruddha-kālī-Tārā

大柔善救度佛母
220

220 197
Mahāśānti-Tārā

明咒吽聲救度佛母
221

221 **425**
Rāganisūdana-Tārā

度脫衰敗救度佛母
222

222 **316**
Sukhada-Tārā

能動三界救度佛母
223

223 **637**
Sita-Vijaya-Tārā

能滅諸苦救度佛母
224

224 **647**
Duḥkhadahana-Tārā

成就一切救度佛母
225

225 338
Siddhida-Tārā

吉祥圓滿救度佛母
226

226 102
Paripūrṇa (or Parinişpanna)-Tārā

除諸惡毒救度佛母
227

227 880
Jāṅgulī-Tārā

金剛宮室救度佛母
228

228 792
[Vajra] pañjarabhāṣita-Vajratārā

震旦救度佛母
229
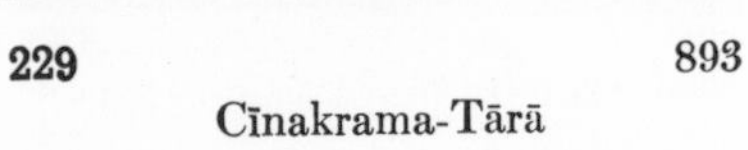

229 893
Cīnakrama-Tārā

如意寶輪白救度佛母
230

230 221
Cintāmaṇicakra-sita-Tārā

四臂如意自在救度佛母
231

231 149
Caturbhuja-Cintāmaṇirājñī

六臂白衣救度佛母
232

232 68
Ṣaḍbhuja-sita-Tārā

布田救度佛母
233

233 301
Dhanada-Tārā

除惡趣救度佛母
234

234 875
Durgottāriṇī-Tārā

一切成就救度佛母
235

235 1
Sarvārthasādhana-Tārā

大聖除毒佛母
236

236 203
Ārya-Jāṅgulī

二十四臂一髻佛母
237

237 17
Caturviṁśatibhuja-Ekajaṭā (devī)

諸相佛母
238

238 716
Viśvamātṛ

二臂一髻佛母
239

239 18
Ekajaṭā (devī)

四臂準提佛母
240

240 152
Caturbhuja-Cundā (devī)

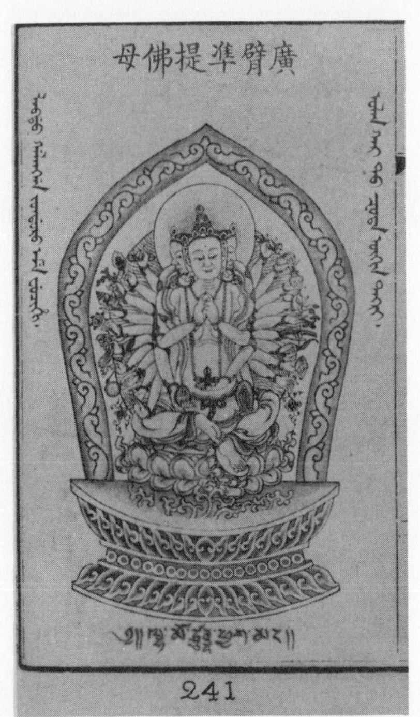

廣臂準提佛母
241

241 318
Bahubhuja-Cundā (devī)

十臂積光佛母
242

242 95
Daśabhuja-Mārīcī

八臂積光佛母
243

243 63
Aṣṭabhuja-Mārīcī

二臂積光佛母
244

244 22
Dvibhuja-Mārīcī

壁組積光佛母
245

245 *558*

Mārīcī (with jade girdle)

金剛性王積光佛母
246

246 801

Vajradhātvīśvarī-Mārīcī

尊勝佛母
247

247 285

Uṣṇīṣavijayā

大聖白傘蓋佛母
248

248 202

Ārya-Sitātapatrā

六臂葉衣佛母
249

249 69
Ṣaḍbhuja-Parṇaśabarī

二臂葉衣佛母
250

250 24
Dvibhuja-Parṇaśabarī

二臂般若佛母
251

251 23
Dvibhuja-Prajñāpāramitā

四臂般若佛母
252

252 154
Caturbhuja-Prajñāpāramitā

六臂金剛妙音佛母
253

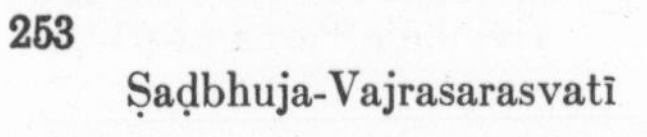

253 70
Ṣaḍbhuja-Vajrasarasvatī

二臂金剛妙音佛母
254

254 26
Dvibhuja-Vajrasarasvatī

持琶妙音佛母
255

255 369
Vīṇā-Sarasvatī

顰眉佛母
256

256 909
Bhṛkuṭī (devī)

匝呼呰嘎佛母
257

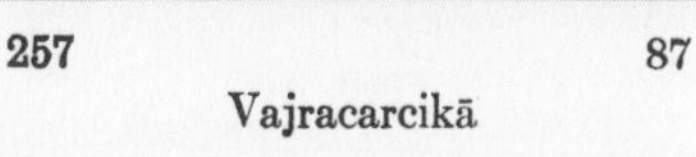

257 87
Vajracarcikā

二臂隨求佛母
258

258 27
Dvibhuja-Pratisarā

大迴佛母
259

259 191
Mahāpratyaṅgirā

幢頂膊嚴佛母
260

260 307
Dhvajāgrakeyūrā

無敵佛母
261

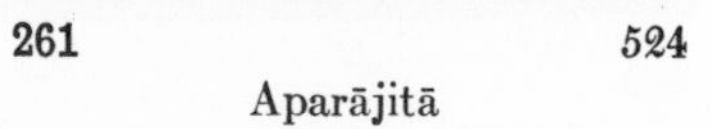

261 524
Aparājitā

金剛甘陀羅佛母
262

262 822
Vajragāndhārī

妙法金剛佛母
263

263 226
Dharmavajrī

智行金剛佛母
264

264 449
Karmavajrī

勇識金剛佛母
265

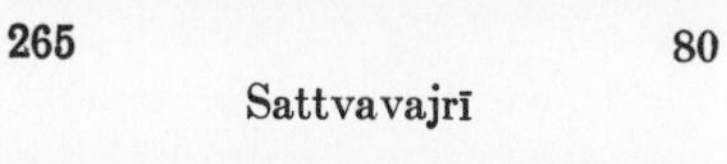

265 80
Sattvavajrī

大寶金剛佛母
266

266 188
Ratnavajrī

沙羅門佛母
267

267 489
Śramaṇā (devī)

長祿佛母
268

268 860
Dhanadā

斗母
269

269 **409**
Grahamātṛkā

白明慧金剛亥母
270

270 **579**
Prajñālokakṛtya-sita-Vajravārāhī

一切成就金剛亥母
271

271 **2**
Sarvārthasādhana-Vārāhī

因竭陀尊者
272

272 **160**
Aṅgaja

阿氏多尊者
273

273 866
Ajita

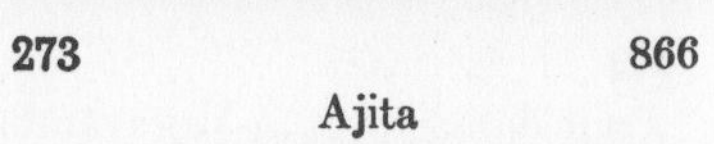

伐那婆斯尊者
274

274 36
Vaṇavāsin

迦裏迦尊者
275

275 734
Kālika

伐闍羅佛多尊者
276

276 37
Vajrīputra

跋陀羅尊者
277

277 Bhadra **729**

迦諾迦伐蹉尊者
278

278 Kaṇakavatsa **735**

迦諾迦跋黎墮闍尊者
279

279 Kanakabharadvāja **736**

巴沽拉尊者
280

280 Bakula **298**

羅沽羅尊者
281

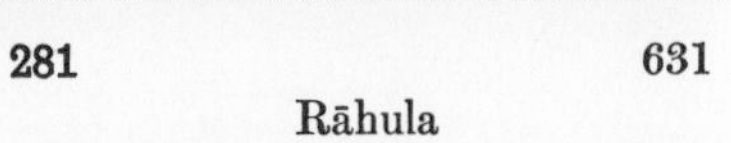
281 631
Rāhula

注茶半托尊者
282

282 491
Cūḍapanthaka

賓度羅跋羅墮尊者
283

283 724
Piṇḍolabharadvāja

半托迦尊者
284

284 97
Panthaka

那迦犀尊者
285

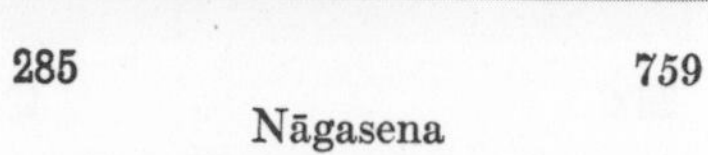

285 759
Nāgasena

戒博迦尊者
286

286 342
Gopaka

阿秘特尊者
287

287 868
Abheda

達摩多羅
288

288 744
Upāsaka-Dharmatala

布袋和尚
289

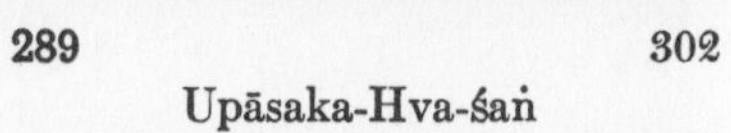

289 302
Upāsaka-Hva-śaṅ

大迦葉
290

290 207
Mahākāśyapa

阿難
291

291 872
Ānanda

沙納衣
292

292 488
Śāṇakavāsin

優婆俱多
293

293 55

Upagupta

氏氏迦
294

294 478

Dhītika

吉利納
295

295 101

Kāla

善觀
296

296 126

Sudarśana

六臂勇保護法
297

297 65
Ṣaḍbhuja-Mahākāla

牛首勇保護法
298

298 540
ẖBroṅ-zhal-can

騎獅勇保護法
299

299 920
Siṁhavāhana-Ṭakṣad
(= Raudrāntaka = Mahākāla)

雄威勇保護法
300

300 890
Mahākāla-Ṭakṣad
(= Raudrāntaka = Mahākāla)

騎虎勇保護法
301

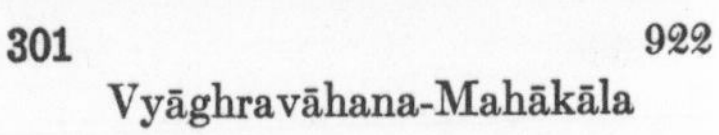

301 922
Vyāghravāhana-Mahākāla

善德勇保護法
302

302 118
Bhagavad-Mahākāla

持棒勇保護法
303

303 361
Daṇḍa [dhara]-Mahākāla

慈烏面勇保護法
304

304 336
Kākāsya-Karmanātha

宮室勇保護法
305

305 259
Mahākāla-gur (= pañjara?)

四臂勇保護法
306

306 148
Caturbhuja-Mahākāla

頗羅門勇保護法
307

307 903
Brāhmaṇarūpa-[Mahākāla]

大黑雄威護法
308

308 214
Kṛṣṇa-Ṭakṣad
(= Raudrāntaka = Mahākāla)

頂螺天母護法
309

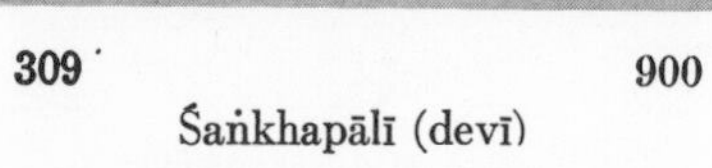

309 900
Śaṅkhapālī (devī)

能烘諸敵天母護法
310

310 648
Dhūmāvatī (devī)

二臂天母護法
311

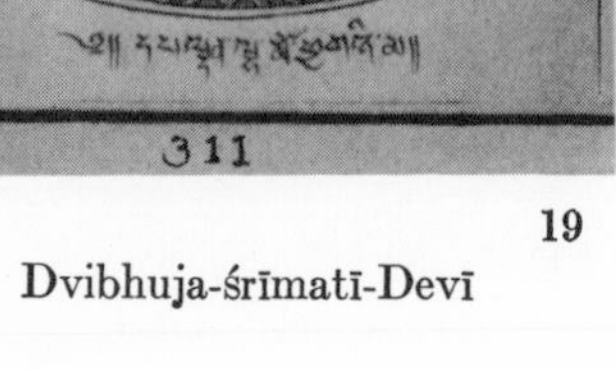

311 19
Dvibhuja-śrīmatī-Devī

法帝護法
312

312 494
Dharmarāja

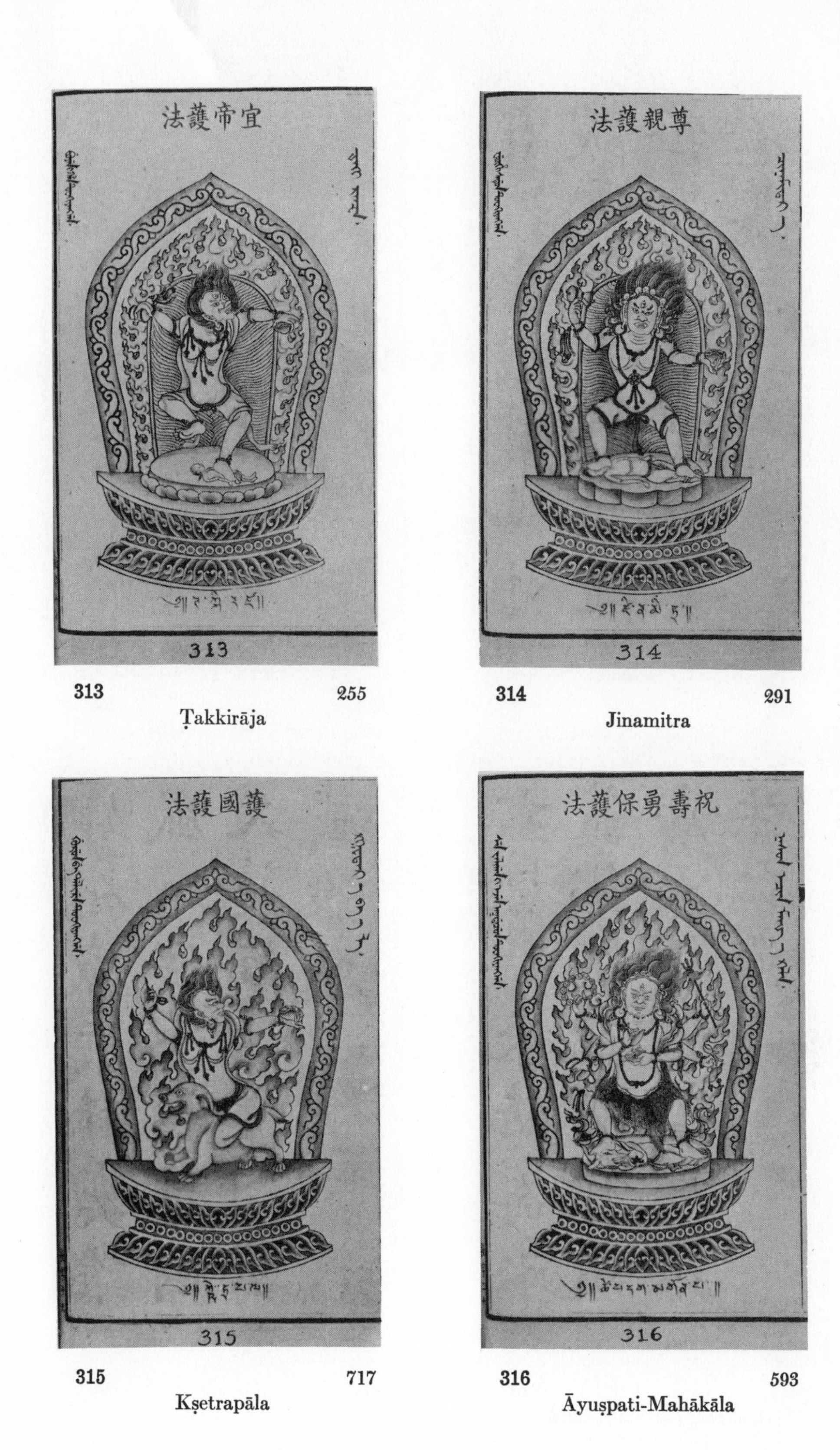

法護帝宜
313
法護親尊
314
法護國護
315
法護保勇壽祝
316

313 Ṭakkirāja 255

314 Jinamitra 291

315 Kṣetrapāla 717

316 Āyuṣpati-Mahākāla 593

如意大白勇保護法
317

317 **220**
Sita-Cintāmaṇi-Mahākāla

大白祝壽財寶護法
318

318 **200**
Sita-Āyurvardhana-Vaiśravaṇa

大黑雄威財寶護法
319

319 **215**
Raudra-kṛṣṇa-Vaiśravaṇa

財寶天王
320

320 **721**
Mahārāja-Vaiśravaṇa

紅戟財寶護法
321

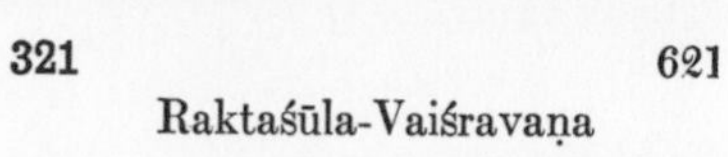

321 621

Raktaśūla-Vaiśravaṇa

大黃財寶護法
322

322 211

Mahāpīta-Vaiśravaṇa

地主永寧天母
323

323 163

Dṛḍhā-Pṛthivī (devī)

妙舞財寶護法
324

324 230

Nartakavara-Vaiśravaṇa

增長天王
325

325 168
Virūḍhaka

廣目天王
326

326 317
Virūpākṣa

持國天王
327

327 355
Dhṛtarāṣṭra

帝釋
328

328 304
Śatakratu

梵王
329

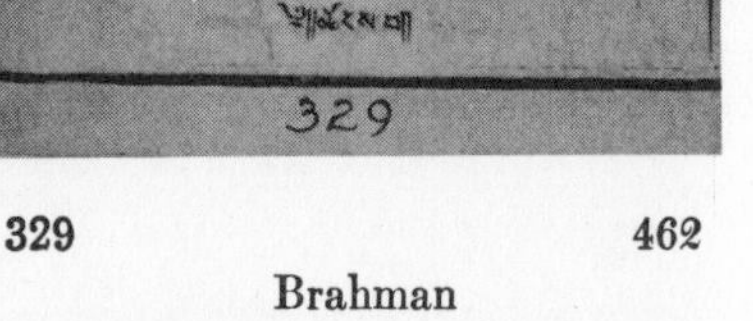

329 462
Brahman

簪芝噶天母護法
330

330 611
Caṇḍikā (devī)

值春天母護法
331

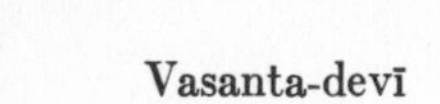

331 52
Vasanta-devī

值夏天母護法
332

332 51
Varṣā-devī

值秋天母護法
333

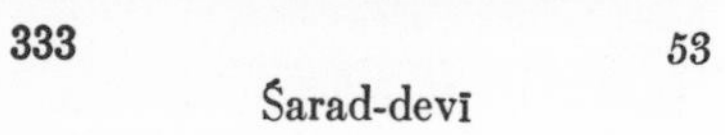

333 *53*
Śarad-devī

值冬天母護法
334

334 50
Hemanta-devī

吉祥長壽天母護法
335

335 103
Maṅgaladīrghāyus

大紅勇保護法
336

336 201
Beg-çe
Ch. Mahārakta-Mahākāla

墳主護法
337

337 169
Citipati

青不動金剛
338

338 894
Nīla-Acala

黃布祿金剛
339

339 932
Pīta-Jambhala

白不動金剛
340

340 571
Sita-Acala

六臂布禄金剛
341

341 67
Ṣaḍbhuja-Jambhala

大力金剛
342

342 174
Krodhamahābala

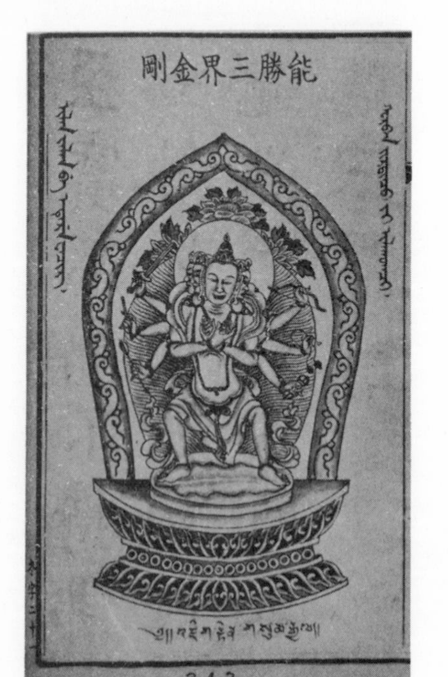
能勝三界金剛
343

343 641
Trailokyarāja

344 937
Kṛṣṇa-Jambhala

除魔金剛
345

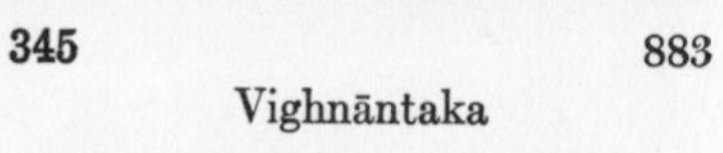

345 883
Vighnāntaka

甘露潭金剛
346

346 562
Amṛtakuṇḍalin

金鐲金剛
347

347 854
Vajraśṛṅkhalā

八猴不動金剛
348

348 61
Aṣṭakapi-Acala

烈焰金剛
349

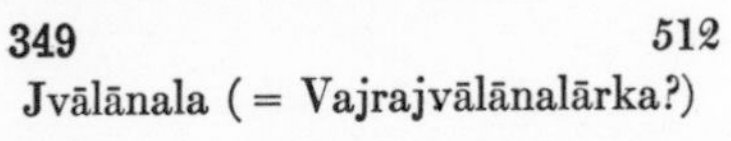

349 512
Jvālānala (= Vajrajvālānalārka?)

四臂不動金剛
350

350 147
Caturbhuja-Acala

威積佛母
351

351 243
Khro-mo-sme-brçegs

摧碎金剛佛母
352

352 400
Vajravidāraṇī

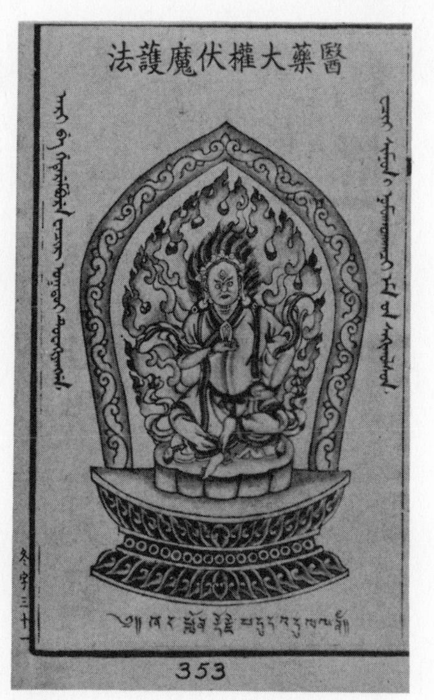
醫藥大權伏魔護法
353

353 **761**
Zhaṅ-blon-rdo-rje-bdud-ḫdul

夜义賢滿護法
354

354 **171**
Yakṣa-Pūrṇabhadra

騎龍白布祿金剛
355

355 **924**
Sita-nāgavāhana-Jambhala

威積金剛
356

356 **244**
Khro-bo-me-brçegs

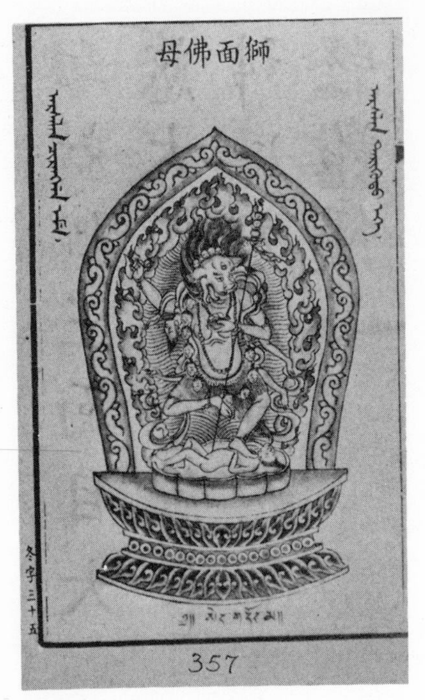
獅面佛母
冬字三十五
357

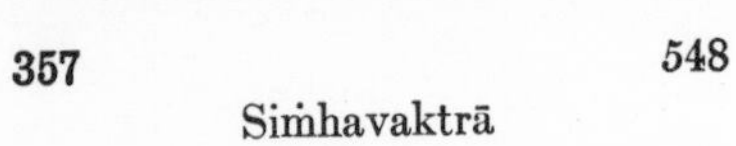

357 548
Simhavaktrā

能烘諸障金剛
冬字三十六
358

358 649
Bhagavad-Bhayanāśana

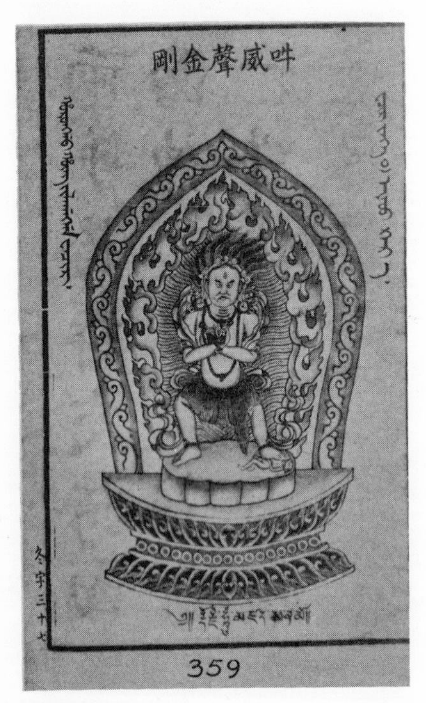
吽威聲金剛
冬字三十七
359

359 108
Vajrahūṁkāra

紅部落王金剛
冬字三十八
360

360 625
Mahārakta-Gaṇapati